Other Books by Joey Green

Joey Green's Amazing Pet Cures

1,138 Quick and Simple Pet Remedies
Using Everyday Brand-Name Products

by Joey Green

RODALE.

The author has compiled the information contained herein from a variety of sources, and neither the author, publisher, manufacturers, nor distributors can assume responsibility for the effectiveness of the suggestions. Caution is urged in the use of the cleaning solutions, folk medicine remedies, and pest control substances.

The brand-name products mentioned in this book are registered trademarks. The companies that own these trademarks and make these products do not endorse, recommend, or accept liability for any use of their products other than those uses indicated on the package label or in current company brochures. This book should not be regarded as a substitute for professional medical treatment, and neither the author, publisher, manufacturers, nor distributors can accept legal responsibility for any problem arising out of the use of or experimentation with the methods described. For a full listing of trademarks, please see page 319.

Direct and trade editions are both being published in 2011.

Rodale books may be purchased for business or promotional use or for special sales. For information, please write to: Special Markets Department, Rodale Inc., 733 Third Avenue, New York, NY 10017

Printed in the United States of America
Rodale Inc. makes every effort to use acid-free ∞, recycled paper ♻.

Book design by Christopher Rhoads
Illustrations © Glen Mullaly

Library of Congress Cataloging-in-Publication Data
Green, Joey.
    Joey Green's amazing pet cures : 1,138 simple pet remedies using everyday brand-name products / Joey Green.
        p.   cm.
    Includes index.
    ISBN 978–1–60529–129–1 hardcover
    ISBN 978–1–60529–128–4 paperback
    1. Pets—Diseases—Alternative treatment.   2. Pets—Health.   3. Pets—Nutrition.
    4. Brand name products—United States.   I. Title.
    SF413.G68   2010
    636.088'7—dc22   2011000140
Distributed to the trade by Macmillan
2   4   6   8   10 9 7 5 3 1   hardcover
2   4   6   8   10 9 7 5 3 1   paperback

For more of our products visit **rodalestore.com** or call 800-848-4735

For Doug and Suzy

Contents

But First, a Word from Our Sponsor

One beautiful morning, I walked out the front door of our house to discover that a neighbor's dog had left an unwanted present on our grassy swale, right next to our mailbox. So I took a Ziploc Storage Bag from the kitchen, turned it inside out, and put in on my hand like a glove. After picking up the bothersome mess on the lawn, I turned the plastic bag right-side out, sealed it shut, and put it in the trash—pleased with my ingenuity.

The next day, I walked outside to check the mail only to discover not one but two unwanted presents sitting in the exact same spot as the day before. This time I left the evidence untouched and put up a sign that read, "Please clean up after your dog." Three days later, the sign and the proof remained on the lawn. So I grabbed a large Ziploc Storage Bag, cleaned up the mess, and removed my ineffective sign—much less pleased with my ingenuity.

Realizing that I couldn't retrain this inconsiderate neighbor, I decided to retrain the dog. I took a canister of McCormick Ground (Cayenne) Red Pepper and peppered the swale where the dog had done his business. In fact, every other day for the next two weeks, I went out and peppered the grass to make sure the dog, with his acute sense of smell, got the message loud and clear. The dog never soiled in front of our house again. He had instinctively sought greener pastures.

Meanwhile, our family cat Einstein (named after someone famous, I can't remember who) started unrolling the toilet paper in our bathroom. At first we simply kept the bathroom doors shut, but Einstein (inspired by his namesake) figured out how to open the doors by leaping up at the handles. When I hung the toilet paper roll in the opposite direction so that the paper unwound from underneath, Einstein changed his strategy and began shredding the entire roll of toilet paper.

I refused to be outsmarted by a cat. Instead, I mischievously filled a Dixie Cup halfway with water and balanced it on the top of a full roll of toilet paper.

When Einstein tried to use the new roll as a scratching post, an unexpected splash of water and the crash of a paper cup sent him darting across the house. He quickly ceased clawing our toilet paper and shifted his attention to our furniture. Not to be outdone, I filled a spray bottle with rubbing alcohol, added one-half teaspoon Country Time Lemonade drink mix, shook it up, and gently misted the sofas. Like all felines, Einstein hates the smell of lemon, and he has learned to keep his claws off the furniture. The side-benefit? Our house now smells lemon fresh.

When I told family and friends about my animal misadventures, they all suggested that I stop hoarding my knowledge and write a book to reveal all the miraculous ways to use the brand-name products you already have around the house to cope with your pets.

"But I know nothing about animals," I insisted, until I realized that I've spent my life surrounded by animals. Growing up, we had two aquariums filled with tropical fish—until my father decided model trains were a less demanding hobby. We had a dog named Ruff (who was petrified of thunder) and a second dog named Smokey (who was petrified of Ruff). My grandmother had a parakeet that she taught to say, "Gimme gelt, Harry"—the world *gelt* being Yiddish for "money" and Harry being the name of my grandfather. When I got married, my wife came with a cat named Lionel, who once survived a fall from a five-story window, accumulated more frequent flier mileage than most people I know, and lived for twenty-one years. When we bought our house, the previous owners bestowed their rabbit upon us, and over the years we've taken care of bunnies named Bugs, Bugsly, Hopscotch, and Ernest. Our kids won a goldfish at a carnival, and, while carnival fish tend to die within a month, my wife managed to keep Rainbow alive for five years. I also happen to be related to a horse. My cousins owned the Triple Crown winner Affirmed, which I consider my greatest claim to fame.

And so, to help pet lovers everywhere, I decided to unearth and divulge all the incredible alternative uses for brand-name products kept secret from the American public. During my quest I made some remarkable discoveries. Downy Fabric Softener softens your pet's fur coat. Arm & Hammer Baking Soda deodorizes a cat litter box. Tabasco Pepper Sauce prevents cats from scratching furniture. L'eggs Sheer Energy Panty Hose double as a muzzle. Maxwell House Coffee stops cats from digging up houseplants. Huggies Baby Wipes clean a dog's dirty paws. Morton Salt kills fleas. Pam Cooking Spray silences a squeaky hamster wheel. But I had to know more. Who invented Milk-Bone dog biscuits? Where is Hartz Mountain? What the heck is catnip? And where can I buy Purina Loch Ness Monster Chow?

The result of my obsessive journey into the animal kingdom is a book that— I'm proud to say—contains hundreds of unusual yet practical ways to take care of your dog, cat, bird, fish, gerbil, horse, or rabbit using brand-name products you'd never expect, like Bounce, Dannon Yogurt, Listerine, Miracle Whip, Quaker Oats, and Vicks VapoRub. Sure, these tips might sound outlandish and absurd, but they really do work, and your pets will love you for your uncanny ingenuity. I hope these quirky hints help you shower your pets with love and care, so in return, you'll be greeted with loyalty and affection—rather than the unwelcome gifts I found on my front lawn.

Allergies

For Dogs and Cats

- **Benadryl.** To ease itchy skin, you can give your pet one to three milligrams of Benadryl daily for every pound your pet weighs. Consult your veterinarian for the precise dosage for your particular pet. Benadryl contains the antihistamine diphenhydramine, which thwarts the effects of histamine, a compound released by the body that causes itching. Your veterinarian may suggest trying a variety of antihistamines to determine which one works best for your pet.

- **Cheerios and L'eggs Sheer Energy Panty Hose.** Using a blender, grind one cup Cheerios into a fine powder. Cut off the foot from a clean, used pair of L'eggs Sheer Energy Panty Hose, fill with the powdered oats, and tie a knot in the nylon. Tie the oatmeal sachet to the spigot, letting it dangle in the flow of water as the tub fills with cool water. Bathe your pet for five to ten minutes in this inexpensive and soothing oatmeal bath.

- **Dannon Yogurt.** According to the *International Journal of Immunotherapy*, eating yogurt with active cultures enhances the body's immune system by increasing the production of gamma interferons, which play a key role in fighting certain allergies and viral infections. Give one-half teaspoon of plain Dannon Yogurt to cats at each feeding, and one tablespoons of plain Dannon Yogurt to dogs. Cats and dogs generally enjoy yogurt, so there's no need to mix it into their food. Even lactose-intolerant pets can digest yogurt without any ill effects.

- **Endust.** Static electricity attracts dust to the edges of fan blades as they turn. The fan blades then disperse the dust throughout the room. Spraying Endust on the blades of overhead ceiling fans and oscillating fans and wiping them clean lubricates the blades, preventing dust from settling on them.

- **Quaker Oats** and **L'eggs Sheer Energy Panty Hose.** Using a blender, grind one cup Quaker Oats into a fine powder. Cut off the foot from a clean, used pair of L'eggs Sheer Energy Panty Hose, fill with the powdered oats, and tie a knot in the nylon. Tie the oatmeal sachet to the spigot, letting it dangle in the flow of water as the tub fills with cool water. Bathe your pet for five to ten minutes in this inexpensive and soothing oatmeal bath.

- **Uncle Ben's Converted Brand Rice** and **Gerber Baby Food.** To determine which foods are causing an allergic reaction in your dog or cat, put your pet on an elimination diet. Stop feeding your pet her regular food, treats, rawhide chews, and vitamins, and switch to a completely new food with which she has no previous exposure, such as a hypoallergenic diet consisting of cooked Uncle Ben's Converted Brand Rice mixed with Gerber 2nd Foods Meats Turkey and Turkey Gravy (unless you're already feeding your pet rice or turkey). While grocery stores do sell pet foods in this flavor, pet foods also contain other ingredients, such as wheat, soy, or corn. Since cats don't eat rice,

GET YOUR PET TO THE VET

Start from scratch! If your pet scratches feverishly, stripping off hair, damaging skin, and causing infection, take her to your veterinarian to determine if she needs allergy shots or if something else is causing the skin irritation.

Pet Tricks
If You're Allergic to Your Pet

- **Huggies Baby Wipes.** Wipe down your pet daily with some hypoallergenic, fragrance free Huggies Baby Wipes to lessen dander and shedding.

- **Johnson's Baby Shampoo.** Have a family member or friend bathe your pet with Johnson's Baby Shampoo on a weekly basis to reduce shedding and decrease the amount of dander.

- **Mr. Coffee Filters.** If you're experiencing a strong allergic reaction, hold a Mr. Coffee Filter over your nose and mouth as a dust mask and breathe normally.

- **Purell Instant Hand Sanitizer.** After touching your pet, wash your hands with Purell Instant Hand Sanitizer.

- **Scotch Packaging Tape.** Remove pet hair and dander from clothing and upholstery by wrapping a strip of Scotch Packaging Tape around your hand, adhesive side out, and patting your clothes and furniture.

feed your feline only the baby food. When your pet's symptoms disappear, start introducing her old foods one at a time, until her symptoms reoccur so you can identify which food triggers the allergic reaction.

For Dogs Only

- **Epsom Salt.** If an allergy gives your dog itchy feet, fill the bathtub with one or two inches of water (enough to cover your dog's paws) and dissolve three cups Epsom Salt in the water. Stand your dog in the tub for five to ten minutes, allowing the Epsom Salt to relieve the itch. Do not let your dog drink the water, since Epsom Salt can have a laxative effect. Remove the dog from the tub and gently pat her feet dry.

- Instead of getting red eyes, a runny nose, and sneezing attacks, pets with allergies or hay fever get unbearably itchy.

- Bathing your pet in cool water for five to ten minutes helps soothe itchy skin. Never use warm water, which exacerbates the itch.

- To help your pet combat allergies, keep him indoors when the pollen count rises during the spring and summer, particularly in early morning and in the evening.

- Vacuum and dust your home often to remove as much pollen and dust as possible, and change the air-conditioning filters once a month. You can also try to restrict your pet to rooms in your house with tile or wood floors and blinds, rather than rooms with carpeting and drapes, which retain dust and pollen.

- To reduce dust mites that may be causing your pet's allergies, launder your pet's bedding once a week.

- The fragrance and dust from a particular brand of cat box litter may be causing your dog or cat to experience an allergic reaction. Consider switching brands.

- A wide variety of environmental factors can trigger allergies in pets, including chlorine levels in water, household cleansers, flea bites, chemicals in furniture and carpet, and medications.

- Just as people can be allergic to pets, pets can be allergic to people.

- In people, allergies are caused by house dust, mold spores, pollen, and the dandruff or hair of household pets. If you suspect that you're suffering an allergic reaction to your pet, before giving him away, have yourself tested to determine the real source of the allergy.

- Contrary to popular belief, people who are allergic to cats are not allergic to the fur. They're allergic to Fel D1, an element found in cat saliva and deposited on the skin and fur when the cat grooms itself. The Fel D1 becomes airborne through dander, the dried flakes of skin, saliva, and secretions that fall from the cat through petting, jumping, or shaking.

- If you live with both a pet and an allergy, keep your bedroom off-limits to the animal. Have a nonallergic member of the family do the dusting and vacuuming and clean the litter box. Have that same person groom the animal outdoors and bathe the animal weekly.

Aquariums

Aeration

- **Maxwell House Coffee.** To make a temporary aerator during a power blackout, use a hammer and a nail to punch a small hole in the bottom of a clean, empty Maxwell House Coffee can. Dip the can into the fish tank to fill it with water, and sit the can on top of the corner edges of the aquarium, positioned so the water drips from the can and back into the tank. The dripping water breaks the surface tension of the aquarium water, allowing sufficient gas exchange between the water and the air; more carbon dioxide is released into the atmosphere and more dissolved oxygen is taken by the water. When the water empties from the can, refill it—until the electricity comes back on.

Backdrop

- **Scotch Tape.** Rather than buying an expensive plastic backdrop at a pet shop, use Scotch Tape to adhere a sheet of decorative wrapping paper to the back of the aquarium.

Cleaning

- **Arm & Hammer Baking Soda.** To clean and deodorize an aquarium, remove the fish, plants, and toys from the tank, sprinkle Arm & Hammer Baking Soda on a damp sponge and scrub. Rinse thoroughly and dry.

- **Clorox Bleach.** To thoroughly clean an aquarium and kill any algae, remove all the contents from the enclosure and immerse them in a bin filled with one part Clorox Bleach and nineteen parts water. Let sit for one hour, and then rinse clean and sun dry. Discard all used gravel. To disinfect the enclosure, fill a sixteen-ounce trigger-spray bottle with two cups water and add two tablespoons Clorox Bleach. Spray the entire enclosure, let stand for fifteen minutes, and rinse thoroughly with water and dry with a clean towel.

- **Heinz White Vinegar.** To clean mineral deposits and water lines from inside an aquarium or fish bowl, wipe the stains with a sponge (or clean, used pair of L'eggs Sheer Energy Panty Hose) saturated with Heinz White Vinegar. Rinse well. To remove stubborn stains, saturate a Bounty Paper Towel with Heinz White Vinegar and place it against the stain so the damp paper towel adheres to the glass. Let it sit overnight. In the morning, rinse clean.

- **Ziploc Freezer Bags.** Before cleaning an aquarium or anytime you need to move fish, place the fish from the tank in Ziploc Freezer Bags filled with water from the tank. Once you've cleaned the tank and refilled it with water, reintroduce the fish to your aquarium by floating the Ziploc Freezer Bags in your aquarium for an hour so the water in the bag gradually reaches the same temperature as the water in the tank. Once the fish have grown accustomed to the water temperature, open the bag, releasing the fish into the tank.

Decorations

- **Clorox Bleach.** Before adding decorations to an aquarium, soak them in one part plain Clorox Bleach to sixteen parts water for one week. Rinse thoroughly and let air-dry.

PET PEEVES

A FINE KETTLE OF FISH

- To avoid contaminating the water in an aquarium with your hands, use plastic salad tongs or a plastic spaghetti grabber to move decorations, plants, rocks, and forts in the tank.

- To keep fish healthy, change approximately 20 percent of the water in a freshwater aquarium every three to four weeks, and 25 percent of the water in a saltwater aquarium every two to three weeks. Use a length of plastic tubing as a siphon. Pinch one end of the tube closed with your fingers from one hand, fill the open end of the tube with water from the tap, and pinch the open end of the tube closed with your fingers from your free hand. Carry the tube to the aquarium, place one end in the water at the bottom of the tank (where the debris settles), place the other end in a bucket sitting a few feet below the tank, and stop pinching the ends of the tubes. Water will flow from the tank to the bucket. When you've drained the proper amount of the water from the aquarium, refill the tank with water that has been sitting in a bucket at room temperature for several hours. (In a saltwater aquarium, use "sea-mix" to maintain the proper water density.) Hold a plate at an angle at the surface and pour the water onto the plate to avoid disturbing the fish.

- Never use soap to clean a fish bowl. The residue from the soap will kill the fish. And never use sponges, rags, brushes, or buckets that have been used with soap.

- When you add fresh water to an aquarium filled with fish, the fish typically cluster in one corner of the tank, enabling you to pour the water where no fish are swimming.

- Place your aquarium on a firm, level base positioned away from direct sunlight or any cold drafts. Keep the tank away from windows. Too much sunlight can overheat the water, causing algae to overgrow in the tank.

- Do not line the tank hood with Reynolds Wrap to reflect light back into the tank. The aluminum foil obstructs the ventilation holes, preventing unwanted carbon dioxide and heat from escaping.

- When changing aquarium water, use water with the same composition and temperature.

- Replace the evaporated water from a salt water tank with fresh water. Only the water—not the salt—evaporates from saltwater tanks. Adding more salt water would over saturate the tank with salt, killing the fish.

- When moving fish from one tank to another, make certain the water conditions in both tanks are identical.

- **L'eggs Sheer Energy Panty Hose** and **Oral-B Dental Floss.** To secure a plastic plant in position at the bottom of an aquarium, use a pair of scissors to cut the foot from a pair of clean, used L'eggs Sheer Energy Panty Hose. Fill the panty hose foot with six marbles, place the roots of the plastic plant inside the nylon sack, and tie the open end of the panty hose closed with a piece of Oral-B Dental Floss. Place the weighted bag at the bottom of the tank and cover it with gravel.

- **Waterpik.** Use a Waterpik as a miniature high-pressure sprayer to clean algae, grime, and debris from the small leaves of plastic plants and other decorations, the same way that you might use a high-pressure sprayer to clean your house or car.

Protecting

- **L'eggs Sheer Energy Panty Hose.** Stretching a clean, used pair of L'eggs Sheer Energy Panty Hose over the top of a fishbowl prevents fish from jumping out or a cat from getting in.

Siphoning

- **L'eggs Sheer Energy Panty Hose.** To prevent a siphon from sucking up small fish or gravel, cut the toe from a clean, used pair of L'eggs Sheer Energy Panty Hose, insert the end of the siphon tube into the nylon toe, and secure it in place with a rubber band (making sure not to squeeze the end of the tube shut).

Water Changes

- **Cool Whip.** To add fresh water to the tank, use a clean, empty Cool Whip tub to scoop the fresh water.

- **Glad Trash Bags.** Before using a large plastic wastebasket to mix up salt water or dechlorinate water for your aquarium, line the wastebasket or garbage can with a clean, new Glad Trash Bag to avoid the possibility of transferring any hazardous substances into the tank. When you're finished filling the tank, reuse the trash bag for its original purpose.

Bad Breath

For Dogs and Cats

- **Oral-B Toothbrush.** To prevent bad breath, brush your pet's teeth twice a day, if possible, or at least twice a week. Brushing your pet's teeth greatly reduces bad breath and prevents plaque buildup, which make bad breath worse. For ways to brush your pet's teeth, see page 284.

For Dogs Only

- **Arm & Hammer Baking Soda.** A puppy shedding his baby teeth frequently drools and has bad breath. Dampen a toothbrush (see Oral-B Toothbrush above), dip it in Arm & Hammer Baking Soda, and brush the puppy's teeth. The baking soda soothes the gums and minimizes the odor.

- **Listerine Cool Mint.** Mix a capful of Listerine Cool Mint in a cup of water, pour the solution in a spray bottle, and spray your dog's mouth (and entire coat while you're at it). The minty mouthwash will freshen the dog's breath and coat.

- **McCormick Pure Peppermint Extract.** To freshen your dog's breath, add a few drops of McCormick Pure Peppermint Extract to her drinking water every time you refill her drinking bowl.

- **Uncle Ben's Whole Grain Brown Rice.** Cook up a cup of Uncle Ben's Whole Grain Brown Rice according to the directions on the box, let cool, and replace a small portion of your pet's regular food with the rice at every mealtime. Whole grains aid the digestive process, and better digestion means better breath.

PET PEEVES
SAVING YOUR BREATH

- Bad breath usually indicates tooth or gum disease, or possibly more serious problems.

- To prevent bad breath, give your dog hard biscuits and rawhide toys or sticks to chew on and brush your dog's teeth and gums. Rawhide bones scrape away plaque buildup.

- If, after brushing your dog or cat's teeth, you find that your pet still has bad breath, take her to your veterinarian for a dental cleaning and to check for signs of gingivitis, periodontal disease, or plaque buildup.

- Bad breath in dogs and cats may also be a symptom of a liver disorder, diabetes, or kidney disease.

- Switching to dry food, rather than canned food, can help eliminate bad breath. The dry food grazes the teeth, scraping off plaque.

- To reduce bad breath, feed your pet once or twice a day and then remove the food if she doesn't finish her meal within thirty minutes. Allowing your pet to nibble from her food dish all day long merely feeds the bacteria in her mouth all day long.

- Cease feeding your pet table scraps flavored with garlic.

Barking

For Dogs Only

- **Campbell's Beef Broth.** To train your dog to chew on a toy rather than bark incessantly, cook up a can of Campbell's Beef Broth according to the directions on the label. Soak a rawhide bone or any other toy in the broth for five minutes, and let it dry. Attach a string to the chew toy and drag it past your pet to arouse his attention. When your pet starts chewing on the toy, warmly shower him with praise and enthusiastically repeat the word "Chew!" After repeating this tactic on several occasions, your pet will soon learn to chew his toy whenever you say "Chew!" Should your dog start barking uncontrollably, command him to "Chew!"—to quickly divert his attention from barking.

- **Coca-Cola.** To stop your dog from barking, put a few pennies in a clean, empty Coca-Cola can, tape the opening shut, and simply shake the can a few times. Dogs find the sound of coins jangling in a can disconcerting and will likely stop barking.

- **Orville Redenbacher Gourmet Popping Corn.** To make a shaker, place a dozen unpopped kernels of Orville Redenbacher Gourmet Popping Corn in a clean, empty plastic water bottle and seal the cap on tightly. Whenever your dog barks, rattle the homemade maraca. The jarring noise will prompt your dog to stop barking.

- **ReaLemon.** To train a dog to stop barking, when your dog starts barking, squirt some ReaLemon lemon juice in the dog's mouth (not eyes) and say "Quiet!" The lemon juice is nontoxic and harmless, providing simple and effective negative reinforcement for behavior modification.

PET PEEVES
BARKING UP THE WRONG TREE

- A confusing environment makes dogs aggressive or anxious, prompting constant barking.

- If your dog barks out of control, the typical response is to yell for the dog to stop. Unfortunately, a dog interprets yelling as encouragement. Instead, shower your dog with praise to thank him for barking. Once he understands that you've received his message, he's more likely to stop. If he keeps barking, say "Quiet!" firmly, and when he does, praise him and reward him with a treat as positive reinforcement.

- Dogs frequently bark as a response to outside noises. To subdue the barking, block those outside noises with a white noise machine, by playing music at a standard volume in your home, or by running the vacuum cleaner, washing machine, or dishwasher.

- Another technique to get your dog to bark less: Give your pet more exercise to calm his nerves and tire him out. Frequent walks and more playtime relaxes dogs.

- Barking can be caused by stress and boredom. To reduce stress and relieve boredom, give your dog a chew toy.

- To get your dog to stop barking relentlessly, say "No!" and squirt water from a squirt gun or spray bottle at his body (not face).

- If you're the victim of a barking dog owned by an inconsiderate neighbor, purchase an electronic device that, triggered by the sound of a dog barking, emits a loud ultrasonic sound, inaudible to humans, that the offending dog will find displeasing. You can attach the device to an outside wall of your home or a fence post, point it in the direction of the barking dog, and set it to go off only after a certain number of barks.

BATHING

For Dogs and Cats

- **Arm & Hammer Baking Soda.** To soften and deodorize your pet's coat and make the fur glimmer, add one tablespoon Arm & Hammer Baking Soda per gallon of water for the final rinse.

- **Castor Oil.** Before giving your dog or cat a bath, put a drop of castor oil in each eye to prevent soap irritation.

- **Downy Fabric Softener.** When bathing your dog or cat, mix one capful Downy Fabric Softener in one-half gallon water and use as final rinse. After applying the Downy, rinse your pet again. This treatment leaves your pet's coat feeling soft and smelling April fresh.

- **Glad Trash Bags.** To avoid getting soaked when giving your dog or cat a bath, cut holes in a Glad Trash Bag for your head and arms and wear the impromptu raincoat to keep yourself dry during the ordeal.

- **Heinz White Vinegar.** Adding one tablespoon Heinz White Vinegar per gallon of water for the final rinse will soften and deodorize your pet's coat, giving the fur a healthy sheen.

- **Huggies Baby Wipes.** Before giving your dog or cat a bath, wipe around the pet's anus with a Huggies Baby Wipe and use a pair of scissors to carefully trim any long fur near the anus that might get soiled.

- **Johnson's Baby Oil.** Before giving your dog or cat a bath, place a cotton ball moistened with Johnson's Baby Oil in each of your pet's ears to keep out water. Just be sure the remove the cotton balls afterward.

- **Johnson's Baby Shampoo.** When bathing your dog or cat, use Johnson's Baby Shampoo. It's gentle enough for pets, won't hurt their eyes, and leaves a pleasant smell.

- **L'eggs Sheer Energy Panty Hose.** If your dog or cat tends to bite when confronted with a bath, improvise a muzzle by cutting off a leg from a clean, used pair of L'eggs Sheer Energy Panty Hose, wrapping it several times around your pet's mouth, and tying the ends back behind the animal's ears. Do not cover the animal's nostrils, and remove the impromptu muzzle if the pet experiences difficulty breathing, starts vomiting, or bleeds from the mouth.

- **Murphy Oil Soap.** To give a dog or cat a bath, add a few drops of Murphy Oil Soap in your pet's bath water to moisturize and soften the skin and coat. Murphy Oil Soap is pure vegetable oil soap that will not harm a dog or cat's sensitive skin.

- **ReaLemon.** When bathing your dog or cat, add one tablespoon ReaLemon lemon juice per gallon of water for the final rinse to give your pet a softer, shinier coat that smells lemon-fresh.

- **Star Olive Oil.** Before giving your dog or cat a bath, apply a drop of Star Olive Oil to your dog or cat's eyes to prevent irritation from the shampoo.

- **Vaseline Petroleum Jelly.** To protect your dog or cat's eyes from bath water and soap, apply some Vaseline Petroleum Jelly around the eyes.

IT'S A DOG'S LIFE
HOW TO GIVE A DOG A BATH

- Consider putting on a bathing suit before you begin.

- Place a rubber mat on the floor of the bathtub to prevent the dog from slipping and sliding.

- Fill the tub with several inches of lukewarm water.

- Put your dog on a leash, bring your dog into the room, close the door, and lift your dog into the tub.

- Place a cotton ball in each of the dog's ears to protect them from water.

- Using a plastic water pitcher, watering can, or hand-held shower attachment, gently saturate the dog with water, from the neck to this tail.

- Shampoo the dog, working up a good lather and pressing your fingers down to his skin.

- Wash the face last, using a soapy sponge or washcloth.

- Rinse thoroughly to remove all of the shampoo or soap.

- Add a little baking soda, lemon juice, or vinegar to the final rinse.

- Let the dog shake himself off a few times (behind a shower curtain), and then use a couple of big clean towels to dry your pet.

- Remove the cotton from your pet's ears.

- Keep your dog in a warm place until he dries completely.

- Once your pet is dry, brush him well.

For Dogs Only

- **Arm & Hammer Clean Shower.** To give your dog a bath, spray the pet with Clean Shower, and then rinse thoroughly with water.

- **Bounce.** To get rid of the smell of a wet dog, wipe down the animal with Bounce dryer sheets, making the dog springtime fresh.

- **Glycerin, Lemon Joy, and Heinz White Vinegar.** To make a gentle homemade shampoo for puppies and dogs with extra dry skin, mix one-third cup glycerin, one cup Lemon Joy, one cup Heinz White Vinegar, and one quart water in a sealable airtight container (or a clean, empty, one-liter bottle). Shake well before each use.

- **Heinz Apple Cider Vinegar.** To tame your dog's skin infections, mix one cup Heinz Apple Cider Vinegar and three cups water. After your dog's bath, rinse your pet with the solution.

- **Huggies Baby Wipes.** To bathe your dog less frequently, wipe down your dog's coat with hypoallergenic, fragrance-free Huggies Baby Wipes.

- **Johnson's Baby Oil.** To give your dog a shiny coat, add one tablespoon Johnson's Baby Oil to the final rinse water.

- **Nestlé Carnation NonFat Dry Milk.** Wash your dog with powdered milk. Add two cups Nestlé Carnation NonFat Dry Milk to the bath water to neutralize bad smells and soften the dog's coat.

- **Palmolive Dishwashing Liquid.** This mild dishwashing detergent makes an excellent shampoo for dogs.

Drains

- **L'eggs Sheer Energy Panty Hose.** To keep the bathtub or sink drain clog-free when bathing your dog or cat, stuff a balled-up pair of L'eggs Sheer Energy Panty Hose into the drain to catch the loose hairs.

- **S.O.S Steel Wool Soap Pads.** To prevent a clogged drain when bathing a dog, place a ball made from an S.O.S Steel Wool Soap Pad in the drain opening to catch stray hairs.

- **Wilson Tennis Ball.** If you're determined to give your pet a bath but can't find the plug for your bathtub, use a Wilson Tennis Ball to block the drain. The suction from the drain will hold the ball in place. Just face your pet in the opposite direction, so he doesn't notice the ball and pluck it free.

- **Ziploc Storage Bag.** If you've lost the stopper for the drain in the bathtub, fill a Ziploc Storage Bag with water, seal it shut, and place it over the drain hole. The suction from the drain will hold the plastic bag in place, corking the drain.

Dry Shampoos
For Dogs and Cats

- **Arm & Hammer Baking Soda.** Too cold to give your dog or cat a bath? How about a dry shampoo? Make sure your pet is dry, and then sprinkle your pet with Arm & Hammer Baking Soda, rub the white powder into her coat, and then brush clean. The baking soda absorbs dirt and grime and leaves your pet smelling clean and fresh. (Do not use on pets restricted to a low-sodium diet, in case your pet licks the sodium bicarbonate from her fur.)

- **Gold Medal Flour.** To give your pet a dry shampoo, sprinkle Gold Medal Flour in the animal's coat, work it in with your fingertips, and brush it out. When American pioneers crossed the country in covered wagons, the women used handfuls of flour in their hair as a dry shampoo to absorb the oils from their hair.

- **Kingsford's Corn Starch.** To give a dog or cat a dry shampoo, sprinkle Kingsford's Corn Starch into your dog or cat's fur, work into the coat, and then comb and brush clean. The cornstarch absorbs grease, dirt, and odors.

THE CAT'S MEOW
HOW TO GIVE A CAT A BATH

- Clip your cat's claws a day or two before the bath.

- Place a rubber mat (or a folded terry cloth towel) at the bottom of a sink or bathtub to give your cat something to grip.

- If you're going to be using a plastic pitcher or watering can to wet the cat, fill it with lukewarm water and place it next to the sink or tub.

- Adopt a calm, nurturing attitude to alleviate your cat's anxiety.

- Bring your cat into the room and secure the door closed.

- Have a partner hold the cat by the scruff of the neck with the other hand under his chest—with the cat's claws pointing away from him.

- Have the partner set the cat in the empty sink or tub, on top of the rubber mat or towel, holding him securely.

- Using a plastic water pitcher, watering can, or hand-held shower attachment, pour water over the cat to wet him thoroughly. Keeping your cat's face dry will help keep your cat relatively calm.

- Apply shampoo and lather well, starting at the neck and working toward the tail.

- Wash the face last, using a soapy sponge or washcloth.

- Rinse thoroughly to remove all traces of the shampoo or soap (remembering that the cat will lick any residue off himself).

- Wrap the cat in a big clean towel, and dry him thoroughly.

- Place your cat in a warm place until he dries completely.

- Once your pet is dry, brush him well.

- **Quaker Oats.** Rub dry Quaker Oats into your pet's coat, work it through with your fingers, and brush it out. Oats absorbs grease and dirt from your pet's fur.

For Dogs Only

- **Johnson's Baby Powder.** To give your dog a dry shampoo, rub Johnson's Baby Powder into your pet's fur, wait a few minutes, and then brush out. The talcum powder absorbs grease and dirt.

Drying

For Dogs and Cats

- **ConAir 1875 Watt Dryer.** After toweling your dog or cat after a bath, use the warm dry air from a blow dryer (on a low setting) to dry your dog or cat, provided your pet will tolerate the noise and blasts of hot air. (Do not aim the dryer at your pet's face, and never use hot air, which can dry out the skin and possibly burn your pet.)

Whitening

For Dogs and Cats

- **Mrs. Stewart's Liquid Bluing.** To whiten white pet fur, just add a couple of drops of Mrs. Stewart's Liquid Bluing—a very fine blue iron powder in a colloidal suspension that optically whitens white fabric—in the rinse water.

Pet Tricks
Cleaning the Bathtub

- **Arm & Hammer Baking Soda.** Once you've given your pet a bath, you may want to give the bathtub a good cleaning as well. Sprinkle Arm & Hammer Baking Soda on a damp sponge, scrub the bathtub, and rinse clean. The abrasive baking soda scours the tub and simultaneously deodorizes.

- **Clorox Bleach.** To clean and disinfect your bathtub after giving your pet a bath, fill the tub with warm water, add three-quarters cup Clorox Bleach, let sit for fifteen minutes, drain, and rinse clean.

- **Country Time Lemonade.** To clean the bathtub thoroughly and get rid of any lingering pet smells, sprinkle Country Time Lemonade drink mix in the bathtub, scrub with a damp sponge, and rinse well. The lemon freshens the tub, and the abrasive granular powder scours it clean.

- **Dawn Dishwashing Liquid.** For an astonishingly effective way to clean grime from a bathtub, pour a few drops of Dawn Dishwashing Liquid on damp sponge and scrub. Then rinse clean with water. Dawn Dishwashing Liquid cuts through grease and leaves the tub sparkling like new.

- **Downy Fabric Softener.** To clean stubborn stains and deodorize the bathtub after giving your pet a bath, fill the bathtub with water, add two tablespoons Downy Fabric Softener, and let sit overnight. In the morning, rinse clean. Downy contains a surfactant that turns water into a powerful solvent, and the fragrance refreshes the entire room.

- **Efferdent.** If you'd like to clean the bathtub and disinfect it at the same time without having to scrub at all, fill a sixteen-ounce trigger-spray bottle with water, and drop in four Efferent denture cleansing tablets. When the water turns blue and the tablets fully dissolve, spray the solution on the inside surface of the bathtub. Let sit for fifteen minutes and rinse clean. The denture cleansing tablets dissolve the soap scum from the tub and kill germs and bacteria.

- **Gillette Foamy.** To clean the bathtub and simultaneously entertain your kids, spray a can of Gillette Foamy shaving cream all over the inside of the bathtub and tell the kids to hop in and play with the shaving cream. When they're all finished scrubbing the tub and tiles for you, rinse the condensed soap off with water for a sparkling clean tub and sparkling clean kids.

- **Heinz White Vinegar.** To disinfect the bathtub after giving your pet a bath, fill the bathtub with hot water, pour in four cups Heinz White Vinegar, and let sit overnight. In the morning, rinse clean with water. The acetic acid in the vinegar cuts through grease and kills germs and bacteria.

- **Hydrogen Peroxide.** To clean any germs left in the bathtub by your pet, mix two tablespoons hydrogen peroxide and one gallon water, wipe down the bathtub with the solution, and rinse clean.

- **L'eggs Sheer Energy Panty Hose.** To clean grime from the bathtub, ball up a clean, used pair of L'eggs Sheer Energy Panty Hose and scrub the bathtub. The nylon is a mild abrasive and doubles as a scouring pad.

- **Listerine.** To disinfect a bathtub after giving your pet a bath, fill a spray bottle with Listerine antiseptic mouthwash, spray the inside surface of the bathtub with the antiseptic, let sit for ten minutes, and rinse clean.

- **Smirnoff Vodka.** Another way to disinfect the bathtub after giving a pet a bath? Fill a spray bottle with equal parts Smirnoff Vodka and water, shake well, and spray the inside surface of the bathtub. Let sit for ten minutes and rinse clean. The alcohol in the vodka kills any germs and bacteria left in the tub by your pet.

- **Tide.** To clean the bathtub, fill the tub with hot water, add two tablespoons Tide liquid laundry detergent, and let stand for approximately fifteen minutes. Use an abrasive sponge to scrub any stains, and then rinse clean with water.

- **20 Mule Team Borax** and **Heinz White Vinegar.** To disinfectant the bathtub easily and effectively, mix one-quarter cup 20 Mule Team Borax, one ounce Heinz White Vinegar, and one gallon hot water. Sponge the solution onto the bathtub surface, rinse clean, and let dry.

- **Wilson Tennis Ball.** To clean soap scum from a bathtub, gently rub the stains with a damp Wilson Tennis Ball, wash the tub thoroughly with soapy water, rinse clean, and dry.

PET PEEVES
ALL WASHED UP

- The more often you groom your dog or cat, the less often you need to bathe him. Brushing removes dirt, dander, and excess oil.

- Dogs and cats need baths only if they appear dirty, smell bad, or get coated with a foul chemical—and never more than once a week.

- Before bathing a dog or cat, make sure the water temperature is around 100 degrees Fahrenheit. Otherwise, your discontented pet will make every effort to escape from the tub.

- Make sure that wherever you chose to bathe a pet is a warm location free of drafts. Wet pets are susceptible to respiratory infections.

- When giving your pet a bath, keep your pet on a leash to avert any surprise escape attempts. Just be sure not to attach the leash to the hot water faucet.

- When giving your dog a bath, prevent your dog from shaking himself dry and splattering you with water by washing his head last. A wet head (not body) prompts the dog to shake himself dry. Immediately after you finish giving your dog a bath, towel your pet dry.

- If your dog fears baths, let him watch you take a bath so he accepts the idea.

- Before giving your dog a bath, let him relieve himself so he doesn't excrete anything into the bath water.

- When bathing your dog or cat, start washing around the neck to discourage fleas—should your pet have them—from racing to his face.

- A plastic wading pool makes the perfect bathtub for large dogs.

- Dogs typically tremble during baths.

- The ideal tool for bathing your dog or cat? A hand-held shower attachment.

- To bathe your dog in the bathtub without getting the floor splashed with water, cut holes to fit your head and arms through a special shower curtain.

- Before giving your pet a bath, place a rubber floor mat in the bathtub so your pet can get a foothold without sliding around and feel more secure and less skittish.

- Use a plant watering can with a perforated pouring piece to gently shower your dog or cat with rinse water.

Bedding

For Dogs and Cats

- **Arm & Hammer Baking Soda.** To clean and deodorize your dog or cat's bedding between launderings, make certain the bedding is dry, sprinkle Arm & Hammer Baking Soda on your pet's bedding, let sit for fifteen to thirty minutes, and then shake out the powder or vacuum clean. Repeat if necessary.

- **Clorox Bleach.** If your pet suffers from ringworm, wash any pet bedding, sheets, or furniture covers in hot water and add one cup Clorox Bleach to the wash load.

- **Concern Diatomaceous Earth.** To kill fleas in your pet's bedding, don a dust mask and goggles and sprinkle Concern Diatomaceous Earth around pet bedding and sleeping areas. Let sit for forty-eight hours and vacuum clean. The finely ground fossils of prehistoric fresh water diatoms, diatomaceous earth kills fleas (and many other crawling insects) by absorbing the waxy coating on the insect. (Be sure to use amorphous diatomaceous earth, not glassified diatomaceous earth, used in swimming pool filters).

Pet Tricks
Washing the Bedding

- **Arm & Hammer Baking Soda.** To boost the cleaning power of your laundry detergent to clean and deodorize pet bedding (unzip the cover and toss it in the washing machine), add one-half cup Arm & Hammer Baking Soda, along with your regular detergent, to your laundry.

- **Cascade.** To whiten pet bedding, unzip the cover and mix two tablespoons Cascade (powder or gel) and one gallon hot water in a bucket. Soak the bedding cover in the solution for one hour. Pour the entire contents of the bucket into your washing machine and launder as usual with your regular detergent.

- **Coca-Cola.** To clean grease or oil stains from pet bedding, saturate the bedding cover with Coca-Cola, let sit for five minutes, and then launder as usual with your regular detergent. The sugars and phosphoric acid in the Coke break down the grease and oil stains.

- **Heinz White Vinegar.** Remove pet odors from bedding by adding one cup Heinz White Vinegar to your regular wash while the machine fills with water. For fierce pet odors on bedding, add one-cup vinegar to a bucket of water and soak the bedding in the mixture for one hour, and then launder as usual.

- **Morton Salt.** To rinse and deodorize a urine stain from pet bedding, dissolve one-half cup Morton Salt in a bucket of water, soak the pet bedding in the salt water for one hour, discard the salt water, and launder as usual with your regular detergent.

- **Spot Shot.** To clean a stubborn urine stain from pet bedding, saturate the stain with Spot Shot Instant Carpet Stain Remover, let sit for one minute, and launder as usual. (Do not use Spot Shot on non-colorfast garments.)

- **20 Mule Team Borax.** To clean mud stains from pet bedding, let the mud dry, brush off as much of the dirt as possible, and dampen the remaining stain with water. Rub 20 Mule Team Borax into the spot, rinse clean, and launder as usual.

- **Listerine.** Another way to kill fleas in your pet's bedding is to fill a spray bottle with Listerine antiseptic mouthwash and spray the bedding. The antiseptic kills the fleas, and the eucalyptol in the Listerine prevents them from returning.

- **McCormick Fennel Seed.** To repel fleas in your pet's bedding, use a mortar and pestle to crush McCormick Fennel Seed and sprinkle the powdered fennel in your pet's bedding. Fennel repels fleas. In fact, an old adage advises planting "fennel near the kennel."

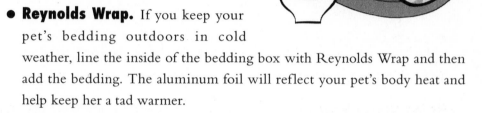

- **Reynolds Wrap.** If you keep your pet's bedding outdoors in cold weather, line the inside of the bedding box with Reynolds Wrap and then add the bedding. The aluminum foil will reflect your pet's body heat and help keep her a tad warmer.

For Dogs Only

- **Coca-Cola.** During hot, humid weather, fill clean, empty two-liter Coca-Cola bottles with water, freeze, and place in a doghouse to keep your dog comfortable.

- **Pine-Sol.** To clean and deodorize a doghouse, mix one-half cup Pine-Sol in a bucket of water and wash the house thoroughly.

PET PEEVES

LET SLEEPING DOGS (AND CATS) LIE

- Make a cat bed by cutting an opening into one side of a clean, empty cardboard box, and then line the box with a pillow, blanket, or towel.

- A square of foam rubber makes excellent bedding for a doghouse.

- A comfortable pet bed lessens pet mess around the house, by confining most of your pet's shedding time to one spot rather than on your carpeting and furniture.

- Cats sleep an average of sixteen hours a day, but usually only a few minutes at a time, thus explaining the origins of the term "catnapping."

- Does your cat wake you up every morning by meowing incessantly outside your bedroom door or by jumping on your bed? Hang a birdfeeder outside a window on the opposite side of the house. The activity of the birds in the early morning will likely keep your cat distracted and entertained.

- When choosing a bed for a dog, select a bed made from material that your dog is less likely to chew. Wicker, for instance, may be a bad choice. To prevent your dog from chewing her bed, give her a suitable chew toy.

- Give your dog a small blanket or towel for her bed. Dogs love arranging them.

- Avoid letting your pet sleep on your bed. Aside from leaving pet hair, your dog or cat may also leave behind fleas, mites, ringworm, ticks, and a variety of diseases. You could also injure your pet when your toss and turn during the night. If you do let your pet sleep on your bed, wash your blankets often and take your pet to the veterinarian for frequent checkups to catch any diseases before you do.

Begging

For Dogs and Cats

- **Coca-Cola.** Put a few pennies in a clean, empty Coca-Cola can and tape the opening shut. To stop your pet from begging while you're trying to enjoy a meal, simply shake the can vigorously. The disturbing sound of coins jangling in a can will send your pet scampering to another room.

- **Jif Peanut Butter.** Fill or coat a rawhide bone or toy with Jif Peanut Butter (crunchy or creamy) and offer the treat to your dog or cat. When the animal starts chewing on the toy, encourage her, repeating the word "Chew!" with enthusiastic praise. Repeating this technique several times will eventually teach your pet to chew her toy whenever you say the word "Chew!"—instead of begging for table scraps.

- **Orville Redenbacher Gourmet Popping Corn.** To make a shaker, place a dozen unpopped kernels of Orville Redenbacher Gourmet Popping Corn in a clean, empty plastic water bottle and seal the cap on tightly. Whenever your pet begs, rattle the homemade maraca. The jarring noise will prompt your pet to seek a quiet room.

- **ReaLemon.** If your dog or cat starts displaying brazen behavior by jumping up on dining room chairs or tables while you're trying to enjoy a meal, fill a spray bottle with water, add one teaspoon ReaLemon lemon juice, and shake well. Whenever your pet leaps into action, spray him with a blast of the lemony water. He'll quickly learn to steer clear of your meals.

- **Scotch Double Sided Tape.** If your pet begs by jumping up on the kitchen counter, apply strips of Scotch Double Sided Tape on trouble spots on the counter. Dogs and cats hate the sticky feeling of the tape on their paw pads and will quickly learn to shun the countertop.

For Cats Only

- **Saran Wrap.** Cats hate the feeling of plastic on their paw pads. Cover your countertop with Saran Wrap until your cat learns to stay off.

PET PEEVES
AIN'T TOO PROUD TO BEG

- To stop your pet from whining, drooling, and climbing up on the table for your food, never give in. Otherwise you're rewarding bad behavior, and your pet will be forever begging for more. Adamantly refusing to feed your pet from the table firmly discourages begging by making it unprofitable.

- Feed your pet on a regular schedule at precise times and right before you eat. Once your pet has a full stomach, she won't come mooching for more.

- To discourage begging behavior, ignore your pet completely while you're eating. Do not make eye contact or speak to your pet.

- Never feed your dog or cat from the dinner table, from your plate, or while you are preparing food in the kitchen. If you want to give your pet table scraps, cut them up and place them in her food bowl after you've finished your meal.

- If your dog or cat won't leave you alone at mealtime, exclaim "No!" firmly and then calmly place him in another room and close the door until you finish eating. Sooner or later, he'll realize that when he doesn't beg, he doesn't get solitary confinement.

- "Ain't Too Proud to Beg," the Top 20 hit single originally recorded by the Temptations in 1966, was covered by the Rolling Stones on their 1974 album "It's Only Rock 'n' Roll".

Birds

Bathing

- **ConAir 1875 Watt Dryer.** After bathing, some birds enjoy the warm, dry air blown from a hair dryer. Set the heat on low and point the nozzle of a ConAir 1875 Watt Dryer toward your bird and keep the nozzle moving to avoid burning your bird.

Bird Food

- **Betty Crocker Cornbread & Muffin Mix** and **Gerber Baby Food.** Prepare Betty Crocker Cornbread & Muffin Mix according to the directions on the box, but add one more egg than the directions require. You may also add the contents of a four-ounce jar of any Gerber Baby Food vegetable, some hulled seeds, some pellets, and the shell of one egg (pulverized in the blender). Bake in a greased muffin pan or a cake pan, following the directions on the box. Break off pieces of the finished bird bread to feed your bird daily.

- **Cheerios.** Give your bird a treat by filling the bird feeder with Cheerios.

- **Kellogg's Raisin Bran.** Birds also love the all-natural goodness of Kellogg's Raisin Bran.

- **Orville Redenbacher Gourmet Popping Corn.** Birds love freshly popped popcorn—without any salt or butter, of course.

- **Quaker Oats.** To jazz up your bird's diet, add some uncooked Quaker Oats to the bird feeder. Your bird will find them nutritious and delicious.

- **Sun-Maid Raisins.** Giving your bird some Sun-Maid Raisins as a treat also adds extra nutrition to your pet's diet.

- **Uncle Ben's Converted Brand Rice.** Birds love cooked Uncle Ben's Converted Brand Rice. Just let the rice cool before feeding it to your bird.

- **Uncle Ben's Whole Grain Brown Rice** and **Green Giant Valley Fresh Steamers Mixed Vegetables.** Cook up one cup Uncle Ben's Whole Grain Brown Rice according to the directions on the box. Thaw one cup Green Giant Valley Fresh Steamers Mixed Vegetables by heating in the microwave oven for one minute. Mix the brown rice and vegetables together and add two finely chopped hardboiled eggs. Feed the treat to your bird.

- **Ziploc Freezer Bags.** Store birdseed in gallon-size Ziploc Freezer Bags to keep it airtight and fresh.

Birdbaths

- **Clorox Bleach.** To remove fungus from an outdoor birdbath, empty the birdbath, lay some clean, old towels to cover the inside of the birdbath, saturate the towels with Clorox Bleach, and let sit for thirty minutes. Remove the towels, rinse the birdbath thoroughly with water, and carefully discard the towels or run them through the regular cycle of your washing machine to remove the bleach.

Winging It
THE SCOOP ON BIRD POOP

- **Colgate Regular Flavor Toothpaste.** To clean bird droppings from any surface, squeeze a dollop of Colgate Regular Flavor Toothpaste onto a clean, used toothbrush (or any hard brush) and scrub the affected spot. Rinse clean with water.

- **Heinz Apple Cider Vinegar.** Fill a trigger-spray bottle with full-strength Heinz Apple Cider Vinegar, spray the bird droppings, and then use a rag or sponge to wipe up the excrement with ease. If you don't have a spray bottle handy, soak a rag with the vinegar and apply it to the spot.

- **Mr. Clean Magic Eraser.** To scour stubborn bird droppings from any surface, rub the splotch with a damp Mr. Clean Magic Eraser, wash with soapy water, and rinse clean.

- **Reynolds Wrap.** In a pinch, a crumpled-up ball of Reynolds Wrap makes a great scrubber for scouring bird droppings from any surface.

- **Frisbee.** To make a simple yet convenient outdoor birdbath, punch three equidistant holes along the circumference of a Frisbee, insert a piece of wire through each hole, and hang the disk upside-down from a tree branch. Fill the plastic saucer with water, or let the rain do it naturally—and you've got a chic birdbath. Replace the water regularly to stay in vogue.

- **Heinz White Vinegar.** To keep cats away from an outdoor birdbath, fill a trigger-spray bottle with Heinz White Vinegar and spray around the base of the birdbath. The bitter smell of vinegar repels cats and simultaneously neutralizes the stench of any cat urine that a cat may have sprayed to his territory.

- **Mrs. Stewart's Liquid Bluing.** Brighten the water in an outdoor birdbath by adding a few drops of Mrs. Stewart's Liquid Bluing. The tiny particles of iron tint the water a glistening blue color without disturbing the clarity of the water. The bluing also helps reduce algae and bacteria buildup.

- **Reynolds Wrap.** To scrub mold, mildew, or bird droppings from a bird-bath, crumple up a sheet of Reynolds Wrap into a ball and use it as an abrasive, disposable scrubber.

Birdcages

- **Arm & Hammer Baking Soda.** To clean and deodorize a birdcage, remove the bird, papers, bowls, and toys from the cage, sprinkle Arm & Hammer Baking Soda on a damp sponge, and scrub. Rinse well and dry.

- **Cascade.** To clean wood, plastic, and stiffened rope perches and toys, place them in your dishwasher, add Cascade to the receptacle dish, and run them through the regular cycle.

- **Clorox Bleach.** Mix one-half cup Clorox Bleach and one gallon water, and use the solution to clean the cage (making sure the bird is another location). Rinse the cage thoroughly with water afterward and let air-dry.

- **Con-Tact Paper.** To make cleaning the bottom of a birdcage less complicated, line the floor of the birdcage with colorful Con-Tact Paper to create a water-resistant surface that's easy to wash clean.

- **Dustbuster.** Use a Dustbuster to vacuum up dust, pellets, feathers, shells, and seeds from the bottom of the birdcage and the floor underneath the cage.

- **Hydrogen Peroxide.** For a simple, nontoxic way to clean and disinfect a birdcage, use full-strength Hydrogen Peroxide. Rinse clean with water and let air-dry.

- **Ivory Dishwashing Liquid.** To clean your bird's toys and dishes, use Ivory Dishwashing Liquid and water.

- **L'eggs Sheer Energy Panty Hose.** To prevent your bird from showering your home with birdseed, use a pair of scissors to cut off one leg from a clean, used pair of L'eggs Sheer Energy Panty Hose, snip off the toe section, and cut the leg open by making one long slice along the length of the hose. Wrap this strip of nylon net around the birdcage, from the bottom up, to thwart your bird from sending seeds flying out of the cage.

Winging It
RUFFLING FEATHERS

- **L'eggs Sheer Energy Panty Hose** and **Oral-B Waxed Floss.** To prevent wild birds from destroying growing fruits and vegetables in your garden, cut off the foot from a clean, used pair of L'eggs Sheer Energy Panty Hose, slip the foot over apples, tomatoes, grapes, broccoli, cabbage, pears, or eggplant, and seal the open end closed with a piece of Oral-B Waxed Floss. The synthetic nylon fibers keep birds away, and the flexible hose expands as the fruit or vegetable grows. You can also cut sections from the leg of the panty hose, tie one end closed with dental floss, cover the fruit or vegetable, and then secure the open end shut.

- **Oral-B Waxed Floss, Reynolds Wrap,** and **Scotch Tape.** To frighten wild birds away from your vegetable garden, run a string of Oral-B Waxed Floss across your garden just a few inches above a row of plants. Using a pair of scissors, cut a dozen or more strips of Reynolds Wrap one-inch wide by five-inches long. Use Scotch Tape to attach the strips of aluminum foil along the string of dental floss every few feet. The strips of reflective foil flapping in the breeze will scare away any birds.

- **Pam Cooking Spray.** To stop wild birds from building nests under the awnings of your house, spray nooks and crannies with nontoxic Pam Cooking Spray. If the birds try to construct a nest in the slick location, the new nesting material will simply slip off.

- **Reynolds Wrap** and **Oral-B Waxed Floss.** To keep wild birds away from fruit trees and berry bushes, use a pair of scissors to cut circles, triangles, or star shapes from cardboard, wrap the cardboard cut-outs in Reynolds Wrap, and then hang the glittering shapes from the trees or bushes with loops of Oral-B Waxed Floss. The silvery shapes, glittering in the sunlight, will shoo away birds.

- **Slinky.** To discourage birds from nesting under the awnings of your house, extend a Slinky across the eaves where the birds like to nest. Or stretch out a Slinky and wrap it into a tangled ball, and then wedge the springy mess into any troublesome crevice.

- **Oral-B Toothbrush.** A clean, used Oral-B Toothbrush makes a great tool for cleaning bird poop off perches, toys, dishes, and cage bars. To clean the toothbrush, run it through the dishwasher along with the dishes.

- **Pam Cooking Spray.** If you don't wish to cover the grid at the bottom of the cage with a layer of newspaper, give the grid a light coat of Pam Cooking Spray (while your bird is out of the cage). The cooking oil prevents droppings from adhering to the bars.

- **Tide.** Toss flexible rope perches in the washing machine along with any towels you use to clean your birdcage, and add the regular amount of Tide laundry detergent to the load.

Birdfeeders

- **Clorox Bleach.** To make a birdfeeder for wild birds, cut a hole approximately two inches in diameter in the side of an empty, clean Clorox Bleach jug opposite the handle. (Be sure to wash the jug thoroughly with water and a few drops of dishwashing liquid, and air-dry for several days.) Fill the bottom of the jug with birdseed and hang the bird feeder from a tree branch.

- **Crisco All-Vegetable Shortening.** To stop rambunctious squirrels from climbing up the pole to an outdoor birdfeeder to devour the cache of food, lubricate the pole with Crisco All-Vegetable Shortening. You'll love watching the squirrels scurry up the greased pole only to slide right back down.

- **Elmer's Glue-All, Reynolds Cut-Rite Wax Paper, Hartz Parakeet Seed, and Oral-B Dental Floss.** Remove the cap from a bottle of Elmer's Glue-All and squeeze out a thick, squiggly line (overlapping itself if you wish) on a sheet of Reynolds Cut-Rite Wax Paper. Using a spoon, sprinkle Hartz Parakeet Seed over the squiggly glue line, covering all the glue. Let dry overnight. Tilt the wax paper to let the excess birdseed spill off, and then carefully peel off the wax paper. Tie a piece of Oral-B Dental Floss to the hardened glue squiggle to hang it inside your bird's cage or outdoors for wild birds.

- **Jif Peanut Butter, Hartz Parakeet Seed, and Oral-B Dental Floss.** Spoon Jif Peanut Butter between the petals of a large pinecone, and then roll the peanut-butter-coated pine cone in the Hartz Parakeet Seed. Use a piece of Oral-B Dental Floss to hang the birdseed-coated pinecone in your bird's cage or outdoors for wild birds.

- **McCormick Ground (Cayenne) Red Pepper.** Here's a devious yet harmless way to keep squirrels out of your outdoor birdfeeder. Sprinkle the birdseed with McCormick Ground (Cayenne) Red Pepper. Birds cannot taste cayenne pepper, but squirrels definitely can and will hastily scamper away.

- **SueBee Honey, Hartz Parakeet Seed, Charmin,** and **Oral-B Dental Floss.** To make a simple birdfeeder, roll an empty cardboard tube from a used roll of Charmin toilet paper in SueBee Honey, and then roll the honey-coated tube in Hartz Parakeet Seed. Use Oral-B Dental Floss to hang the birdseed-coated tube inside your bird's cage or outdoors for wild birds. (Instead of a cardboard tube, you can also use a large pinecone.)

Winging It
OTHER USES FOR BIRD SEED

- **Substitute for rice at weddings.** Instead of throwing rice at the bride and groom after their wedding, give the guests Hartz Parakeet Seed to toss at the newlywed couple. People can easily slip on rice strewn on a hard surface (and the rice is difficult to clean up), but birdseed provides traction, and birds and squirrels will enthusiastically clean up the mess.

- **Decorate artwork.** Draw a design by dispensing Elmer's Glue-All directly from the bottle on construction paper, cover the glue with Harz Parakeet Seed, and let dry.

- **Make a snow angel.** Lie down in the snow and make a snow angel by brushing your extended arms up to your head and back down to your waist with a sweeping motion. Then move your extended legs apart and back together. After making these indentations in the snow, carefully get up without disturbing the imprint. Pour cups of variously colored birdseed (corn, safflower, sunflower, thistle) to fill the head and body of the snow angel with bands of color.

PET PEEVES
IN FINE FEATHER

- Be gentle when holding a pet bird. The slightest pressure can fracture a bird's fragile bones. Unlike human bones, many bird bones are hollow to enable flight.

- To prevent your bird from pecking your hands while you refill the water dish in the cage, use a turkey baster or a long-stemmed watering can to pour the water without having to reach your hands inside the cage.

- To thwart your cat from attacking your bird, suspend the birdcage from the ceiling or set it on a secure pedestal. Position the birdcage far enough away from other furniture so your cat cannot leap onto the cage.

- If your bird escapes from its cage, recapture it by tossing a small lightweight hand towel over it. Then gently pick him up and place him back in the cage. This way, you won't risk harming the bird by frantically clutching for it.

- Buy birds only from reputable dealers. The United States Department of Agriculture requires that all domesticated birds wear identification leg bands, affixed upon entering quarantine. Birds smuggled into the country have not been quarantined and might spread disease to other birds.

- A reputable bird dealer will agree that you can return the bird for a full refund if the bird fails to pass an examination by a veterinarian of your choosing.

- Place your birdcage away from air-conditioning and heating ducts, away from windows that get direct sunshine, and out of drafts.

- Never keep a birdcage in the kitchen (where toxic fumes can kill birds), and never let a pet bird loose in the kitchen (where it may land on a hot pan, pot, or burner).

- Cover the cage when the sun sets. The cover mimics the shelter birds seek amidst trees and bushes, and birds need to stay on a schedule that follows the sun.

- Birds require companionship, otherwise loneliness and boredom prompt them to start plucking out their own feathers. Provide your bird with toys, bells, and mirrors, and when you leave the house, turn on the radio to give the bird some company.

- When buying a birdcage, chose a cage large enough for your birds to fly from one perch to another.

- Protect your bird from fumes from deodorizers, hair spray, insecticide, and paint. Fumes from ammonia, paint, and solvents can harm a bird. Avoid using these products in the vicinity of your bird.

- To prevent birds from being infected by bacteria that can breed in a birdbath, scrub the birdbath with a brush or sponge once a week, and change the water ever few days (daily in the summer). Never use chemical household cleansers to clean a birdbath.

- Clean bird feeders with plain water and a scrub brush, not soap.

- Flush hummingbird feeders clean with very hot water every few days to kill any mold that might harm the birds.

- Avoid the temptation to set your pet bird outside in its cage to enjoy the fresh air. The food in his cage will attract wild birds that might infect your pet bird with parasites or a disease.

- Never feed birds chocolate, which is potentially deadly, and never give birds alcoholic or caffeinated beverages.

- Never let a pet bird loose in a room with a ceiling fan or whirling electric fan. Even if the fan is turned off, the bird can injure itself on the blades.

- You can ascertain the sex of an adult budgie parakeet by noting the color of the skin just above the beak (bluish on males, brownish on females).

- Planting birdseed in your garden yields plants that grow birdseed, attracting birds and freeing you from forever having to refill a birdfeeder.

Birdhouses

- **Dawn Dishwashing Liquid.** Before each new bird season, mix one teaspoon Dawn Dishwashing Liquid in a bucket of water and use the soapy solution to thoroughly clean the birdhouse. Rinse clean with water. Keeping the birdhouse clean helps prevent wild birds from infecting each other with diseases.

Birdseed

- **Bounty Paper Towels.** Pick up spilled or scattered birdseed with a dampened sheet of Bounty Paper Towels.

- **Gatorade.** To keep birdseed fresh and protect it from insects and mice, pour an open box or bag of the seed into a clean, empty Gatorade bottle and secure the lid tightly shut.

- **Morton Salt.** Using a funnel, fill a clean, empty Morton Salt canister with bird feed so you can refill the small food cups in your bird's cage with less fuss and mess.

Bleeding

- **McCormick Alum.** If your bird suffers from a bleeding wound, dissolve one-half teaspoon McCormick Alum in one cup water, saturate a sterilized cotton ball with the solution, and use it to dab the wound to stop the bleeding and disinfect the injury.

Bowls

- **Dawn Dishwashing Liquid** and **Clorox Bleach.** Every day, scrub food and water bowls clean with a few drops of Dawn Dishwashing Liquid and water. Then mix one ounce Clorox Bleach and one quart water, soak the bowls in the bleach solution for thirty minutes, rinse clean, and let air-dry.

Droppings

- **Johnson's Baby Powder.** To prevent wild birds from excreting on patio furniture or fence posts, sprinkle Johnson's Baby Powder wherever the birds perch. Birds dislike the way baby powder feels on their feet and will find other places to roost.

Hummingbirds

- **Domino Sugar** and **McCormick Pure Orange Extract.** To attract hummingbirds to your backyard, mix one part Domino Sugar to four parts water in a hummingbird feeder, add four drops McCormick Pure Orange Extract, and shake well. Once a week, clean out the feeder and refill with a fresh batch of formula.

- **Efferdent.** To clean a hummingbird feeder, fill the bottle with hot water and drop in one Efferdent denture-cleansing tablet. When the fizzy blue solution turns clear, rinse clean.

- **Revlon Red Nail Polish.** Hummingbirds are attracted to the color red. Paint a design on the hummingbird feeder with Revlon Red Nail Polish.

PET PROJECTS
ROCK CITY BIRDHOUSES

During the Depression in the 1930s, Garnet Carter and his wife, Frieda, decided to turn the rock formations on their land on Lookout Mountain, six miles from downtown Chattanooga, Tennessee, into a tourist attraction called Rock City.

To promote Rock City, Carter hired a young sign painter named Clark Byers to travel the country and offer to paint farmer's barns for free in exchange for letting him paint the succinct slogan "See Rock City" on the roof or side of the barn. Byers painted hundreds of barns along major roadways, creating one of the most famous advertising campaigns of all time with just a ladder, paintbrush, and a few hundred buckets of paint.

Carter also designed mailboxes resembling barns painted with his slogan, but when the United States Postal Service rejected the design, he turned his mailboxes into birdhouses. You can buy the birdhouses, designed to resemble the rural barns adorned with the familiar "See Rock City" rooftop painting, at the Rock City Country Store or at Cracker Barrel Restaurants.

- **Vaseline Petroleum Jelly.** If you rub a light coat of Vaseline Petroleum Jelly along the length of the chain or wire from which you hang your hummingbird feeder, ants won't be able to descend into the hummingbird feeder to pilfer the sweet nectar.

Itching

- **Fruit of the Earth Aloe Vera Juice.** To soothe an itchy bird, add one tablespoon Fruit of the Earth Aloe Vera Juice (drinkable for humans, not the gel for topical applications) to a spray bottle filled with one cup water. Mist your bird with the solution.

- **Listerine.** Mix one tablespoon Listerine antiseptic mouthwash in a sixteen-ounce trigger-spray bottle filled with water. Mist your bird with the solution to help bring relief to an itchy bird.

Liners

- **Kleenex Tissues.** In a pinch, you can line the bottom of a birdcage with Kleenex Tissues to catch and absorb any droppings.

- **Reynolds Cut-Rite Wax Paper.** A sheet of Reynolds Cut-Rite Wax Paper makes an excellent liner for the bottom of a birdcage to capture foul matter.

- **USA Today.** Line the floor of your birdcage with several layers of sections from *USA Today* above and below the grid. Remove and replace one section at a time whenever droppings appear.

Toys

- **Bounty Paper Towels.** Place an empty Bounty Paper Towel roll inside the cage as a play toy for your bird, or string a few tubes together with a thick leather cord and hang them in the cage for your bird to shred.

- **Charmin.** An empty Charmin toilet paper roll placed inside the cage creates a terrific toy that your bird can roll around the bottom of the cage.

- **Glad Flexible Straws.** To make an inexpensive toy for your pet bird, weave several straws through the bars of the cage. Parrots, macaws, and cockatiels love to remove them, chew them, and play with them. The birds do not eat the straws, making them inexpensive, easy, and safe toys.

- **Oral-B Toothbrush.** Wash a new or used Oral-B Toothbrush with hot, soapy water, rinse clean, and hang it in the cage from a thick leather cord as a toy for your bird.

- **Slinky.** To make a playful tunnel for a parakeet to explore, stretch a Slinky across the ceiling of parakeet cage.

PET PROJECTS
THE STORY OF HARTZ MOUNTAIN

In 1926, German immigrant Max Stern, age 26, arrived in New York Harbor on the Hamburg American Steamship Line with 2,100 singing canaries from the Harz Mountains, given to him by a childhood friend to settle a debt.

Not knowing a word of English, Stern sold the canaries to the John Wannamaker Department Store at Astor Place in Manhattan and soon founded the Hartz Mountain Company (adding the letter *t* so Americans would pronounce the name Harz properly) at Cooper Square. Stern traveled back and forth to Germany, returning each time with more singing canaries, selling them to stores like R.H. Macy, Sears Roebuck, F.W. Woolworth, W. T. Grant, and S.S. Kresge. He soon expanded to selling packaged bird foods and cages.

Stern's son Leonard joined the company in 1959 and expanded the product line to include goldfish, tropical fish, and aquatic supplies. During the following decade, Hartz Mountain began selling dog and cat products, most notably the Hartz Flea & Tick Collar, the best-selling flea and tick collar to this day. Leonard turned his father's small pet supply company into a major corporation whose products included mirrors for parakeets and plastic palm trees for turtles.

In 2000, a private equity investment firm purchased the Hartz Mountain Corporation, and in 2004, the Sumitomo Corporation acquired the company. Today, Hartz sells 1,500 products—catering to dogs, cats, parakeets, canaries, parrots, cockatiels, finches, goldfish, tropical fish, reptiles, ferrets, chinchillas, guinea pigs, hamsters, and rabbits.

Bites

For Dogs and Cats

- **Betadine Skin Cleanser.** If another animal bites your dog or cat, prevent the bite wound from getting infected by scrubbing it well with Betadine Skin Cleanser and then flushing it clean with lukewarm running water. Pat dry with a towel.

- **K-Y Jelly.** Smear a thin coat of water-soluble K-Y Jelly around the bite wound and use a pair of scissors to trim the hair from around the bite wound. The jelly traps the cut hairs and prevents them from falling into the wound.

- **L'eggs Sheer Energy Panty Hose.** Before treating an injured dog or cat, protect yourself from serious bites by muzzling your pet's mouth closed. Improvise a muzzle by cutting off a leg from a clean, used pair of L'eggs Sheer Energy Panty Hose, wrapping it several times around your pet's mouth, and tying the ends back behind the animal's ears. Do not cover the animal's nostrils and remove the impromptu muzzle if the pet experiences difficulty breathing, starts vomiting, or bleeds from the mouth.

- **Neosporin.** After washing and drying the bite wound (see Betadine Skin Cleanser above), apply Neosporin ointment to the wound to prevent infection, and then bandage the area with gauze, secured in place with first-aid tape.

- To stop two dogs from fighting, make a loud noise by honking a car horn, banging pots and pans together, ringing a bell, or blasting an air horn. If that doesn't work, toss a blanket on top of the dogs, spray the dogs with a garden hose, or toss buckets of water at them.

- Rabies is a deadly virus. A bite from a contaminated dog, squirrel, skunk, raccoon, fox, or bat can transmit rabies to your pet. If your pet has not been vaccinated against rabies, take your pet to the veterinarian immediately.

- An animal bite can cause internal bleeding, resulting in severe blood loss, without any external bleeding.

- If a snake bites your dog or cat (typically in the face, nose, or front legs), take your pet to the veterinarian immediately for treatment. Snakebites, particularly from poisonous snakes, tend to cause lethargy, a slowed blink reflex, severe swelling, and difficulty breathing.

- To make a bite wound easier to clean, use a pair of scissors or a disposable razor to trim some of the hair from around the spot. Fresh air will help the wound heal quickly. If you wrap gauze around the bite, don't make it too tight.

- Animals lick their wounds naturally, which might expedite the healing process.

- To keep your dog or cat from disturbing a wound, have your pet fit with an Elizabethan collar—a conical plastic casing that fits around the animal's neck.

- If you get bitten by a dog or cat, wash the wound with soap and water to remove any saliva, rinse under running water for at least five minutes, apply an antibiotic ointment (such as Neosporin), dress with a bandage, and see a doctor immediately. Dogs and cats carry diseases like cat scratch fever, rabies, and tetanus.

- According to the Centers for Disease Control and Prevention, dogs bite approximately 4.7 million people in the United States each year. Roughly 800,000 of those people, half of them children, seek medical treatment for the bites. Dog bites kill between 15 and 20 Americans during a year.

- Five times more Americans die every year from being struck by lightning than from being bitten by dogs.

Pet Tricks
Stop Biting

For Dogs Only

- **Coca-Cola.** Put a few pennies in a clean, empty Coca-Cola can and tape the opening shut. To stop your dog from biting, simply shake the can a few times. Dogs find the sound of coins jangling in a can disconcerting and gradually will stop biting to avoid the jarring penalty.

- **Orville Redenbacher Gourmet Popping Corn.** To make a shaker, place a dozen unpopped kernels of Orville Redenbacher Gourmet Popping Corn in a clean, empty plastic water bottle and seal the cap on tightly. Whenever your dog bites, rattle the homemade maraca. The jarring noise will prompt your dog to stop biting.

- **ReaLemon.** To train a dog to stop biting, when your dog starts biting, squirt some ReaLemon lemon juice in the dog's mouth (not eyes) and sharply say "No!" The lemon juice is nontoxic and harmless, providing simple and effective behavior modification.

For Cats Only

- **USA Today.** If your cat bites you, immediately give her a swat with a rolled-up section of *USA Today*. This mimics the way another cat would react and gets your message across in an understandable way.

GET YOUR PET TO THE VET

Bite back! Any time another animal bites your dog or cat, take your pet to the veterinarian. Animal saliva contains bacteria, and rather than risk infection or disease, play it safe.

Bleeding

For Dogs and Cats

- **Betadine Solution.** To prevent a wound from getting infected, apply Betadine Solution, and then flush it clean with lukewarm running water. Pat dry with a towel.

- **Hibiclens.** After flushing the wound for at least five minutes with lukewarm running water, wash the affected area with Hibiclens antibacterial soap. Then apply Neosporin (see page 46) and bandage with gauze.

- **Hydrogen Peroxide.** To treat a small wound on a dog or cat, after muzzling the animal (see L'eggs Sheer Energy Panty Hose on page 46), use an electric trimmer or a small pair of safety scissors to cut away all hairs around the wound, and flush the wound with hydrogen peroxide. Place a sterile gauze pad on the wound, apply pressure until the bleeding ceases, and then wrap a roll of gauze around the pad, securing the end of the gauze roll with tape.

- **K-Y Jelly.** After getting the bleeding under control, smear a thin coat of water-soluble K-Y Jelly around the wound and use a pair of scissors to trim the hair from around the bite wound. The jelly traps the cut hairs and prevents them from falling into the wound. Then wash away the jelly. Trimming the hair from around the wound helps to keep the wound clean.

- **L'eggs Sheer Energy Panty Hose.** An injured animal tends to become defensive and may snap at you if you attempt to provide help. Before treating an injured dog or cat, protect yourself from serious bites by muzzling your pet's mouth closed. Improvise a muzzle by cutting off a leg from a clean, used pair of L'eggs Sheer Energy Panty Hose, wrapping it several times around your pet's mouth, and tying the ends back behind the animal's ears. Do not cover the animal's nostrils and remove the impromptu muzzle if the pet experiences difficulty breathing, starts vomiting, or bleeds from the mouth.

- **Neosporin.** After washing and drying the wound (see Hibiclens on page 45), apply Neosporin ointment to the wound to prevent infection by killing any bacteria, and then bandage the area with gauze, secured in place with first-aid tape.

GET YOUR PET TO THE VET

Bad blood! If your dog or cat suffers from a deep wound or severe blood loss, take your pet to the veterinarian immediately. The animal may need stitches, anesthesia, or a transfusion. Signs of internal bleeding include blood in urine or vomit, pale pink or white gums, and lethargy.

● To keep a wound clean and protected, wrap it with gauze, but not too tightly. Change the bandage daily, but first wash the wound and apply antibiotic ointment.

● To protect a paw injury, insert the paw into a clean white sock.

● Use a blanket as a stretcher for your pet. Place your dog or cat in the center of the blanket, and have two people each lift two corners of the blanket to carry the pet.

● Rather than bandaging a minor wound on your dog or cat, trim the hair around the wound to allow air-drying. Hair retains bacteria, dirt, secretions, and debris, hindering the healing process.

● **Stayfree Maxi Pads** and **L'eggs Sheer Energy Panty Hose.** Use a Stayfree Maxi Pad as a compress for wounds or lacerations to control heavy bleeding. In an emergency, you can hold the maxi pad in place by tying it with L'eggs Sheer Energy Panty Hose.

● **Tampax Tampons.** Use a tampon as a compress for wounds or lacerations to control heavy bleeding. In an emergency, you can hold the tampon in place by tying it with L'eggs Sheer Energy Panty Hose.

● **Wesson Vegetable Oil.** If you're unable to bandage a wound on your dog or cat, dab some Wesson Vegetable Oil liberally on the wound. Vegetable oil can stop the bleeding.

Body Odor

For Dogs Only

- **Arm & Hammer Baking Soda.** To reduce your dog's body odor, sprinkle some baking soda on your pet, rub it into his coat thoroughly, and then brush off. This dry shampoo neutralizes odors, leaves your pet smelling fresh, and makes a great way to clean your pet during the cold winter months. (Do not use on dogs restricted to a low-sodium diet.)

- **Bounce.** To mask the repugnant smell of a wet dog, wipe the animal with a Bounce dryer sheet, giving the dog a springtime-fresh aroma.

- **Heinz White Vinegar.** Bad odors may be caused by ear infections. To prevent ear infections, mix one part Heinz White Vinegar and two parts water. Using a bulb syringe, gently flush each ear with the solution. Wipe clean with a cotton ball.

- **Huggies Baby Wipes.** To deodorize a dog, wipe the animal with a hypoallergenic, fragrance-free Huggies Baby Wipe, which eliminates the offending smell along with any loose fur.

- **Johnson's Baby Shampoo.** The best way to eliminate body odor from your dog is to bathe your pet regularly with Johnson's Baby Shampoo. For more ways to bathe your dog, see page 13.

- **L'eggs Sheer Energy Panty Hose.** Your dog's foul odor may be caused by bad breath. Wrap a piece of a clean, used pair of L'eggs Sheer Energy Panty Hose around your forefinger to clean his teeth. For more ways to get rid of a dog's bad breath, see page 9.

- **Listerine Cool Mint.** Mix one capful Listerine Cool Mint in one cup water, pour the solution in a spray bottle, and spray your dog's body. The minty mouthwash will freshen the dog's coat.

- **Skin So Soft Bath Oil.** To deodorize your dog, mix one capful Skin So Soft Bath Oil and two cups water in a sixteen-ounce trigger-spray bottle. Shake well, spray your dog with the fragrant solution, and then rub it into your pet's coat.

- **Vicks VapoRub.** To trick your sense of smell so you can withstand a foul odor emanating from your pet, put a dab of Vicks VapoRub under your nostrils.

Get Your Pet to the Vet

That stinks! If you've brushed and bathed your pet but he still reeks, take him to your veterinarian for a checkup. That nasty smell may be symptomatic of an ear infection, gum or tooth disease, a kidney problem, or skin disease.

PET PEEVES
RAISING A STINK

- Pet odors may be caused by ear infections, anal glad infections, and dermatitis. If the problem doesn't go away after bathing your pet, cleaning his ears, and cleaning his teeth, consult your veterinarian.

- A foul odor emanating from your pet may be a natural hormonal secretion discharged to attract a mate. In that case, the only solution is to have your pet neutered or spayed.

- Bad odors coming from your dog may mean that a pet's natural skin oils have turned rancid or that your pet rolled in something putrid. A simple bath should solve the problem.

- Avoid bathing your dog more than once a month, otherwise you risk stimulating the oil glands to secrete excess oil, worsening the problem.

- Frequent grooming keeps the coat clean, removing odor-causing debris and excess oils.

- If a strange odor permeates your dog, check to see if a foreign object is lodged in your dog's mouth and slowly rotting.

Bowls

Ceramic Bowls

For Dogs and Cats

- **Arm & Hammer Baking Soda.** To clean stubborn stains from a ceramic pet food bowl, sprinkle Arm & Hammer Baking Soda on a damp sponge, rub off the stains, and rinse clean.

- **Coca-Cola.** To do away with stains in a ceramic pet food bowl, fill the bowl with Coca-Cola, let sit for one hour, and rinse clean. The phosphoric acid in the Coke dissolves the grime.

- **Colgate Regular Flavor Toothpaste.** A dollop of Colgate Regular Flavor Toothpaste squeezed on a damp cloth and rubbed into stains in a ceramic pet food bowl scours away the stains. Rinse clean and dry.

- **Efferdent.** To clean a ceramic pet food bowl, fill the bowl with water, drop in two Efferdent denture-cleansing tablets, and let sit overnight in a secure place where your pet cannot drink from it. In the morning, rinse clean.

- **Heinz White Vinegar.** Clean stubborn stains from food and water bowls by scrubbing them with full-strength Heinz White Vinegar.

- **McCormick Cream of Tartar.** To clean stains from a ceramic pet food bowl, sprinkle McCormick Cream of Tartar inside the bowl and scrub with a clean, damp sponge. Rinse thoroughly and dry.

- **Mr. Clean Magic Eraser.** To clean persistent stains from a ceramic pet food bowl, gently rub the stains with a damp Mr. Clean Magic Eraser, wash the bowl thoroughly with soapy water, and rinse clean.

Food Residue
For Dogs and Cats

- **Pam Cooking Spray.** To clean bits and pieces of moist food stuck to the inside bottom of your dog or cat's food bowl, spritz the trouble spots with Pam Cooking Spray, let sit for five minutes, and then scrub with a sponge and soapy water under running water. The vegetable oil loosens the caked-on food.

Impromptu Bowls
For Dogs and Cats

- **Cool Whip.** A clean, empty Cool Whip tub makes a perfect water or food bowl when traveling with your pet. You can even pre-measure one serving of food and keep it stored in the Cool Whip tub.

- **Frisbee.** Turn a Frisbee upside-down to improvise a food or water dish for your dog or cat.

- **Ziploc Freezer Bag.** In a pinch, fill a Ziploc Freezer Bag with water and hold it open with both hands to create an instant water bowl for your pet.

Insects
For Dogs and Cats

- **Arm & Hammer Baking Soda.** To keep insects away from your pet's food bowl, sprinkle Arm & Hammer Baking Soda around the bowl.
- **McCormick Ground Cinnamon.** To keep ants out of pet food left in a dog or cat food bowl, sprinkle McCormick Ground Cinnamon around the pet food. Cinnamon repels ants.
- **Vaseline Petroleum Jelly.** To repel ants from a pet food bowl, rub a small dab of Vaseline Petroleum Jelly around the bottom rim of the bowl.

Plastic Bowls
For Dogs and Cats

- **Arm & Hammer Baking Soda.** To clean the stains from a plastic pet food bowl, sprinkle Arm & Hammer Baking Soda in the bowl, scrub with a sponge, rinse clean, and dry.
- **Colman's Mustard Powder.** To deodorize a plastic pet food bowl, fill the bowl with warm water, dissolve one-quarter teaspoon Colman's Mustard Powder, and let sit for one hour. Wash with soapy water, rinse clean, and dry.
- **Mr. Clean Magic Eraser.** To clean a plastic pet food bowl, gently rub the stains with a damp Mr. Clean Magic Eraser. Wash the bowl thoroughly with soapy water and rinse clean.
- **ReaLemon.** To bleach stains from a plastic pet food bowl, apply ReaLemon lemon juice to the stains and place the bowl in the sun to dry.

Spills

For Dogs and Cats

- **USA Today.** Set both the food and water bowl on a plastic tray with a piece of newspaper underneath to absorb any spills.

Splash Guards

For Dogs and Cats

- **Con-Tact Paper.** Adhere a sheet of Con-Tact Paper on the wall behind the spot where you place your pet food bowls. The laminate makes for easy cleanup anytime you need to sponge splatters off the wall.

Stainless Steel Bowls

For Dogs and Cats

- **Bon Ami.** To clean stubborn stains from a stainless steel pet bowl, apply Bon Ami with a damp sponge or cloth, rub off the stains, and wash as usual.

- **Canada Dry Club Soda.** To wash a stainless steel bowl, pour some Canada Dry Club Soda into the bowl and wipe clean with a soft cloth. The effervescent action shines the steel.

- **Clorox Bleach** and **Calgon Water Softener.** Mix one-quarter cup Clorox Bleach, one-quarter cup Calgon Water Softener, and one gallon hot water and soak the bowl in the solution for thirty minutes. Wash thoroughly with soapy water, rinse clean, and dry.

- **Colgate Regular Flavor Toothpaste.** Squeeze a dollop of Colgate Regular Flavor Toothpaste on a soft, clean cloth and rub the stains from a stainless steel bowl. Wash with soapy water, rinse clean, and dry.

- **Gold Medal Flour.** To polish a stainless steel pet bowl, dry the bowl with a soft, clean cloth; sprinkle one tablespoon Gold Medal Flour in the bowl; and rub with a dry, soft, clean cloth. Rinse clean with water and dry well.

- **McCormick Cream of Tartar** and **Heinz White Vinegar.** Mix two teaspoons McCormick Cream of Tartar and enough Heinz White Vinegar to make a paste and rub the paste on the stainless steel bowl with a soft, clean cloth. Rinse clean with warm water and dry with another soft, clean cloth.

- **Morton Salt.** To clean stubborn stains from a stainless steel pet bowl, sprinkle Morton Salt on a damp sponge and rub. Rinse thoroughly and dry.

- **Murphy Oil Soap.** To clean a stainless steel pet bowl, pour a few drops of Murphy Oil Soap on a wet soft, clean cloth and scrub. Rinse well and dry.

- **ReaLemon** and **Morton Salt.** Mix together enough ReaLemon lemon juice and Morton Salt to make a gritty paste and use a soft, clean cloth to rub the paste on the stainless steel bowl. Rinse clean with warm water and polish dry with another soft, clean cloth.

- **Star Olive Oil** and **Bounty Paper Towels.** To give a stainless steel pet bowl a lustrous shine, polish the steel with a drop of Star Olive Oil, and then buff dry with a sheet of Bounty Paper Towel.

- **20 Mule Team Borax.** Make a paste from 20 Mule Team Borax and water and use a soft, clean cloth to rub the paste on a stainless steel bowl. Wash thoroughly with warm soapy water, rinse clean, and polish dry with another soft, clean cloth.

PET PEEVES

BOWLED OVER

- Keep cat bowls clean and the contents fresh, otherwise your cat will refuse to eat and drink from them.

- Position a rubber placemat, rubber bath mat, or cookie sheet on the floor underneath your pet's food dish to prevent it from sliding around as she eats and to make cleaning up a snap.

- To prevent ants from invading your dog or cat's food dish, place the food dish inside a larger dish, and then fill the larger dish with water, creating a moat that ants will be unable to cross.

- Use an angel food cake pan as an outdoor water dish for your pet, and hammer a stake into the ground though the center hole to keep the bowl in place. This way, your pet won't be able to knock over the water dish or carry it elsewhere.

- When buying a food or water bowl for your pet, choose a heavy, round bowl (without any corners) that your pet can easily lick clean, ideally with a weighted bottom to prevent your pet from knocking it over, sliding it across the floor, or carrying it away.

- Avoid purchasing plastic or aluminum bowls that can be easily chewed.

- Position the water bowl far enough away from the food bowl to prevent your pet from dropping a mouthful of food into the water bowl.

- Buy a bowl that suits the shape of your dog's head. Get a deep bowl for a long-nosed pet, a shallow bowl for a short-nosed pet, and a narrow bowl for a long-eared dog. For tall pets, consider an elevated food bowl.

- Wash your pet's food bowl and water bowl with soapy water once a day.

Cat Flu

For Cats Only

- **Bausch & Lomb Sensitive Eyes Saline Solution.** To soothe your cat's weepy eyes, wash your pet's eyes with Bausch & Lomb Sensitive Eyes Saline Solution.

- **Chicken of the Sea Tuna.** A cat suffering from a stuffy nose has difficulty tasting and smelling food. Tuna fish has a strong smell that will stimulate his taste buds in a big way. Mix a tablespoon of Chicken of the Sea Tuna in with his regular food or simply put a tablespoon or two of tuna on a saucer.

- **Gatorade.** To prevent dehydration, fill your cat's water bowl with fruit punch-flavored Gatorade. Gatorade quickly replaces minerals—including sodium, potassium, and chloride—reenergizing your ailing pet. (If your pet refuses to drink Gatorade, switch back to water.)

- **Huggies Baby Wipes.** To help your cat breathe easier, use a Huggies Baby Wipe to clean any mucus buildup from around her nose. The lanolin in the wipes also helps soothe the skin.

- **Little Noses Decongestant Nose Drops.** To thin coagulated mucus and help clear your cat's nose, give your cat a few drops of Little Noses Decongestant Nose Drops. Simply tip the cat's head back with one hand, and holding the dropper in the other hand, place one or two drops of the saline solution in each nostril. Keep the cat's head tipped back for a minute or two to give the nose drops sufficient time to work. Repeat twice a day.

- **Pedialyte.** Another way to prevent dehydration caused by cat flu is to pour Pedialyte into your cat's water bowl. Drinking an electrolyte solution like Pedialyte, formulated for babies, quickly replaces electrolytes, potassium, and sodium. (Not all pets will drink Pedialyte, so keep another bowl of water available.)

GET YOUR PET TO THE VET

Nothing to sneeze at! Cat flu can lead to pneumonia, anemia, or dehydration. If your cat seems terribly sick, or if the secretions from her eyes and nose seem excessive, take her to your veterinarian immediately.

PET PEEVES

THE COLD FACTS

- Cat flu is essentially a feline version of the common cold that lasts from one week to ten days. Symptoms include runny nose, discharge from the eyes, and, sometimes, abrupt sneezing attacks.

- If your cat suffers from cat flu, rouse her to eat by adding warm water to her kibble or gently warming her food in a microwave oven. Good nutrition helps boost her immune system to fight off the virus. If your cat refuses to eat solid food, liquefy it in a blender.

- Make your congested cat more comfortable by running a humidifier to give the air in your home more moisture.

- When you take a hot bath or shower, bring your congested cat into the bathroom to let the steam provide natural relief.

Chewing

For Dogs and Cats

- **BenGay.** To train your dog or cat to stop chewing on a specific object, coat the object with a dab of BenGay. The smell will repel the animal.

- **Campbell's Beef Broth.** To train your pet to chew on a toy rather than a leather couch, cook up a can of Campbell's Beef Broth according to the directions on the label. Soak a rawhide bone or any other toy in the broth for five minutes, and let it dry. Attach a string to the chew toy and drag it past your pet to arouse his attention. When your pet starts chewing on the toy, warmly shower him with praise and enthusiastically repeat the word "Chew!" After repeating this tactic on several occasions, your pet will soon learn to chew his toy, rather than the furniture, any time you say "Chew!"

- **Heinz Chili Sauce.** To get your pet to stop chewing the furniture, rub wooden furniture legs with Heinz Chili Sauce, and then wipe it off. The smell alone repels the animals.

- **Heinz White Vinegar** and **Heinz Apple Cider Vinegar.** Mix five ounces Heinz White Vinegar, five ounces Heinz Apple Cider Vinegar, and five ounces water in a sixteen-ounce trigger-spray bottle. Shake well. Spray the solution on whatever furniture your dog or cat loves to chew.

- **Jif Peanut Butter.** Fill or coat a rawhide bone or toy with Jif Peanut Butter (crunchy or creamy) and offer the treat to your dog or cat. When the animal starts chewing on the toy, encourage her with enthusiastic praise, repeating the word "Chew!" with zeal. Repeating this technique several times will eventually teach your pet to chew her toy instead of the furniture whenever you say the word "Chew!"

- **Knorr Beef Bouillon.** Bring a cup of water to a boil, and dissolve one Knorr Beef Bouillon cube in the water. Soak a rawhide bone or stick in the broth for five minutes, and then place it on a paper towel to dry. When the animal starts chewing on the toy, reward his behavior with praise and say the word "Chew" repeatedly. Any time you say the word "Chew," your pet will chew his toy instead of the furniture.

- **McCormick Ground (Cayenne) Red Pepper.** To prevent your dog or cat from chewing wood furniture or doors, sprinkle the item with McCormick Ground (Cayenne) Red Pepper.

- **Old Spice Aftershave Lotion.** Mix one part Old Spice Aftershave Lotion with ten parts water in a spray bottle and spray the solution wherever pets are giving you trouble. Pets dislike the smell of Old Spice and will keep away.

- **ReaLemon.** Mix six ounces ReaLemon lemon juice, three ounces water, and one ounce rubbing (isopropyl) alcohol in a sixteen-ounce trigger-spray bottle. Shake well and spray whatever furniture your pet loves to chew.

- **Tabasco Pepper Sauce.** Spray or rub Tabasco Pepper Sauce on the furniture or walls you want your pet to cease chewing. From the time you spot your pet chewing the items tainted with Tabasco Pepper Sauce, prevent the animal from drinking water for an hour to better reinforce the discomfort associated with chewing that particular object. The hot sauce wipes off easily, but test an inconspicuous spot first to make sure it doesn't stain.

For Dogs Only

- **Easy Cheese.** To train your pet to chew on a toy rather than a leather couch, spray some aerosol Easy Cheese inside a hollow chew toy. When

PET PROJECTS
A BITE OF BITTER APPLE

In 1960, a regular customer walked into Grannick's Pharmacy, founded in 1948 in Greenwich, Connecticut, and asked pharmacist Irv Grannick if he sold a product that would stop her anxious show dog from chewing and licking his coat. Unaware of any such product, Grannick decided to concoct his own compound, combining different bitter flavorings until he developed a successful formula. He named the product "Bitter Apple" and gave it to his customer free of charge. Soon after, Grannick was giving "Bitter Apple" to his friends as well.

As word of mouth spread, Grannick, encouraged by friends, began marketing "Grannick's Bitter Apple," mixing up batches of the formula in his kitchen, much to his wife Mary's dismay. Grannick's Bitter Apple quickly grew into a full line of pet products used to prevent excessive licking and chewing and scratching problems.

your dog starts chewing on the toy, warmly shower him with praise and enthusiastically repeat the word "Chew!" After repeating this tactic on several occasions, your pet will soon learn to chew his toy, rather than the furniture, any time you say "Chew!"

- **McCormick Alum.** Dogs dislike the smell and taste of alum. Fill a sixteen-ounce trigger-spray bottle with water, add one teaspoon McCormick Alum, and shake vigorously until the alum dissolves. Spray the solution on your furniture wherever your pet sinks in her teeth or gives you trouble.

- **Pam Cooking Spray** and **McCormick Garlic Salt.** To attract your dog to his chew toys, spray his cloth toys with Pam Cooking Spray. To make the toys even more appealing, sprinkle on some McCormick Garlic Salt.

- **Wilson Tennis Ball.** To distract your dog from chewing your possessions, give him something more satisfying to gnaw—a Wilson Tennis Ball.

For Cats Only

- **Heinz White Vinegar.** To teach a cat to stop chewing certain spots in your home, any time the cat approaches that forbidden area, gently dab a cotton ball dampened with Heinz White Vinegar on your cat's lips. Place the wet cotton ball in the prohibited zone as added discouragement.

- **McCormick Pure Lemon Extract.** To dissuade your cat from chewing any item, saturate a cotton ball with McCormick Pure Lemon Extract and rub it on the object. The smell of lemon repulses cats.

- **Oust Air Sanitizer.** Cats hate the smell of oranges and lemons. Simply spray whatever item the animal loves chewing with Oust Air Sanitizer (Citrus Scent), and the cat will no longer find that item appealing in the least.

- **ReaLemon.** To keep your cat from chewing a certain object, saturate a cotton ball with ReaLemon lemon juice and rub it on the off-limits item. Cats abhor lemon juice.

- **Tang.** Dissolve one-half teaspoon Tang powdered drink mix into two cups rubbing (isopropyl) alcohol in a sixteen-ounce trigger-spray bottle. Spray the solution on whatever items the cat loves chewing. Cats despise the smell of oranges and will give up on that item.

PET PEEVES
CHEW IT OVER

- Never let your pet chew on a forbidden item; otherwise you're rewarding bad behavior. When you spot your pet chewing something off-limits, quickly chastise him with a firm "No!" Confiscate the item, replace it with a chew toy, and when he starts chewing it, praise him.

- To keep your pet interested in her chew toys, give her one or two at a time, rather than bombarding her with a surplus of toys. Every few days, swap the toys for new ones to stoke her attention.

- Pets love to chew on shoes because they are leather and exude your scent. The best way to stop your pet from chewing your shoes is to keep them hidden out of reach in the closet.

Claws

For Dogs and Cats

- **ChapStick.** If you trim your pet's nails too close to the quick, stop the bleeding by rubbing the cut spot with ChapStick lip balm. The wax clogs the unfortunate nick.

- **Gold Medal Flour.** Another way to stop a bleeding nail is to pour a small hill of Gold Medal Flour on the floor or countertop, dip the toenail in the white powder, and then apply mild pressure. The flour helps clot the blood.

- **Ivory Soap.** If you accidentally clip your dog or cat's nails too close, stop the bleeding by inserting the cut nail into a bar of Ivory Soap.

- **Johnson's Baby Powder.** To stop a bleeding nail, sprinkle some Johnson's Baby Powder in your cupped palm, and then dip the nail into the powder.

- **Kingsford's Corn Starch.** If you clip your dog or cat's toenail too short and it starts bleeding, pack cornstarch into the nail bed to clot the blood.

- **Neosporin.** If your pet breaks a nail and starts bleeding, clean the nail with soap and water, pat dry with a towel, and apply a small dab of Neosporin. The anti-bacterial ointment prevents infection.

PET PEEVES
YOUR CLAWS ARE SHOWING

- The best time to trim your dog's nails is immediately after a bath. The warm water softens the nails, making them easier to cut.

- Dogs have dew claws—essentially a thumb located a few inches up your dog's leg.

- Declawing your cat so he won't scratch you or your furniture is cruel and inhumane. This painful operation is like surgically amputating all your fingertips at the first joint. Declawing also lessens a cat's ability to defend against dogs and other animals.

- Cats instinctively protect their feet from being touched. If you wish to trim your cat's claws, get your cat accustomed to having her feet handled at a young age, offering plenty of praise and rewarding the cat with a treat. Gradually introduce your cat to the nail clippers and having her claws trimmed.

- Trimming your cat's claws reduces your pet's desire to scratch furniture and makes handling your cat less menacing.

- Never trim your pet's claws with nail clippers designed for humans.

Cut to the Quick

HOW TO TRIM YOUR PET'S NAILS

To trim your dog or cat's nails, buy a pair of nail trimmers made specifically for your dog or cat. (If trimming a cat's nails, use your fingers to pinch the cat's toe, forcing the claw to extend.) Clip the end of the nail, making sure you don't cut back into the vein that runs about three-quarters of the length of the nail. Cut the nail clear of the quick—the pink line that can be seen running through white nails. To avoid cutting the quick, merely blunt the tip of the nail. File the cut end. Finish by giving your pet a treat.

- **3M Sandpaper.** If your pet scratches on the cabinet door where you store her food or treats, use masking tape to adhere a sheet of 3M Sandpaper to the trouble spot. Instead of scratching the woodwork, your pet will file her own nails.

For Cats Only

- **USA Today.** If your cat scratches you, immediately give her a swat with a rolled-up section of *USA Today*. This mimics the way another cat would react and gets your message across in an understandable way.

GET YOUR PET TO THE VET

A nail-biting experience! If your pet develops an ingrown toenail (with the sharp tip penetrating the pad) or accidentally tears a claw loose, take the animal to your veterinarian.

Constipation

For Dogs and Cats

- **Gatorade.** Failure to drink sufficient amounts of water causes mild dehydration, which withdraws water from the colon, desiccating the feces. To quickly relieve constipation, fill you pet's water bowl with fruit punch–flavored Gatorade. Gatorade quickly rehydrates the body and replaces sodium, potassium, and chloride. (If your pet refuses to drink Gatorade, switch back to water.)

- **Libby's Pumpkin.** Another way to relieve your pet's constipation? Mix one or two tablespoons (depending on the size of the animal) into your pet's food for several days. The natural fiber in pumpkin not only returns your pet to regularity, but dogs and cats also love pumpkin.

- **Metamucil.** To relieve constipation in your pet, mix one-half teaspoon Metamucil with water and pour it on your small pet's food twice a day, and mix two teaspoons Metamucil with water and pour it on your large dog's food twice a day. The psyllium seed husks in this laxative absorb water into the stool, helping it pass through the intestines. Adding water (and giving your pet plenty of water to drink) prevents the Metamucil from congealing in the stomach.

- **Nestlé Carnation NonFat Dry Milk.** To relieve your pet's constipation, dissolve two teaspoons Nestlé Carnation NonFat Dry Milk in one ounce water and place the milky solution in a saucer for your small dog or cat twice a day. For large dogs, mix three tablespoons Nestlé Carnation NonFat Dry Milk in one-half cup water. Once things start moving again for your pet, slowly wean him off the milk over several days.

- **Pedialyte.** If the feces in your pet's colon have been dried and hardened as a result of mild dehydration, pour Pedialyte into your dog or cat's water bowl to quickly replace lost body fluids, electrolytes, and minerals. (Not all pets will drink Pedialyte, so keep another bowl of water available.)

- **Post Grape-Nuts Flakes.** A high-fiber diet prevents constipation. To clear up constipation, give your pet one to three tablespoons of Post Grape-Nuts Flakes several times a day. Once the constipation fades, sprinkle up to three tablespoons of Post Grape-Nuts Flakes on your pet's food. The fiber helps prevent constipation, and it also helps your pet lose weight and improve digestion, increasing your pet's ability to absorb nutrients.

- **Quaker Oats Oat Bran.** Ward off constipation in the first place by sprinkling one-half teaspoon to two tablespoons of Quaker Oats Oat Bran on your pet's food daily, depending on the size of the animal. To help your pet swallow the bran, consider adding warm broth to the food.

- **Reddi-wip.** Dairy products help relieve constipation in cats and dogs. Spray a dollop of Reddi-wip Whipped Cream on a saucer or on top of your pet's food. Don't give your pet too much whipped cream unless you're willing to deal with the other extreme— diarrhea.

For Dogs Only

- **Gerber Baby Food.** To relieve constipation in a dog, feed the animal one jar of Gerber Green Beans.

- **Maxwell House Instant Coffee** and **Vaseline Petroleum Jelly.** Mix two tablespoons Maxwell House Instant Coffee and two cups warm water for a small dog, or four tablespoons Maxwell House Instant Coffee and one quart warm water for a large dog. Using Vaseline Petroleum Jelly, lubricate the stem of a turkey baster or a bulb syringe, fill it with the coffee solution, and insert it into the dog's rectum, slowly flushing out the colon, using half the solution. Let the dog walk around for five minutes and repeat. The coffee enema triggers defecation.

- **Phillips' Milk of Magnesia.** For constipation in dogs, give one teaspoon Phillips' Milk of Magnesia per five pounds of weight every six hours. Do not give Phillips' Milk of Magnesia to any dog with kidney failure.

For Cats Only

- **Chicken of the Sea Sardines.** To ease constipation, feed your cat one Chicken of the Sea Sardine each month.

- **Hain Safflower Oil.** To prevent constipation and lubricate your cat's bowels, occasionally mix one teaspoon of Hain Safflower Oil into your cat's food (unless your cat is obese).

- **Vaseline Petroleum Jelly.** Feeding your cat one-half teaspoon of Vaseline Petroleum Jelly each day, by simply mixing it into her food or placing it on her paw, lubricates the digestive tract and gets her bowels working smoothly again.

- **Wesson Corn Oil.** Another way to prevent constipation? Add one teaspoon Wesson Corn Oil to your cat's food occasionally. The polyunsaturated oil also fortifies your cat with vitamins, lubricates the digestive tract, and helps free impacted hairballs. (Never feed vegetable oil directly into your cat's mouth. Doing so may cause diarrhea.)

PET PEEVES

CLOGGED UP

- For a dog or cat, drinking plenty of water prevents constipation. If your pet isn't getting enough fluid, add water to dry food.

- Walking your dog for twenty minutes several times a day helps keep your pet's digestive system flowing properly.

- A cat or dog forced to refrain himself from defecating for long periods of time winds up with hard, dry stools, which quickly leads to constipation. Walk your dog several times a day, keep the litter box accessible, or install a pet door.

- A natural laxative for a constipated cat is a small serving of raw liver no more than twice a week.

- Feeding bones (especially pork chop bones) to your dog can cause constipation.

- Never feed your dog a commercial laxative made for humans, unless specifically instructed by a veterinarian. Serious problems for your pet may result.

Coprophagia

For Dogs Only

- **Accent Flavor Enhancer.** To prevent a dog from eating his own feces, add one teaspoon Accent Flavor Enhancer to your pet's food twice daily for three days. Accent Flavor Enhancer is actually a digestive enzyme, and it prevents coprophagia, putting an end to the nasty habit.

- **Adolph's Meat Tenderizer.** Sprinkling your dog's food with Adolph's Meat Tenderizer alters the taste of her feces, making them unpalatable to the dog. Adolph's Meat Tenderizer contains papain, which alters the taste of the waste.

- **Clorox.** Cut an empty, clean Clorox Bleach jug in half diagonally. Use the half with the handle as a pooper-scooper to clean up any waste before your dog gets tempted to feast on his own dung.

- **Jif Peanut Butter.** Provide a toy stuffed with Jif Peanut Butter to give your dog a better alternative than feces.

- **Libby's Pumpkin.** To dissuade your dog from eating her own stool, mix one or two tablespoons of Libby's Canned Pumpkin into your pet's food at each meal. The papain in pumpkin will alter the taste of the dung, making it repulsive to your dog. Pumpkin also adds beneficial fiber to your dog's diet.

- **McCormick Ground (Cayenne) Red Pepper.** To keep your dog from eating the contents of your cat's litter box or feces in the yard, sprinkle McCormick Ground (Cayenne) Red Pepper on the dung. Dogs abhor powerful spices.

- **Ziploc Storage Bags.** To get rid of your dog's waste before she decides to gobble it up, turn a Ziploc Storage Bag inside out, put your hand inside the bag like a glove, pick up the mess, pull the bag right-side out again, seal shut, and discard.

GET YOUR PET TO THE VET

Don't let them go to waste! Dogs that eat feces from a cat litter box may accidentally swallow too much cat box litter, resulting in intestinal obstructions. A dog that eats excrement may also contract parasites, resulting in lethargy and weight loss. For a cat, eating feces could be a sign of parasites, pancreatitis, or feline leukemia. If you notice these symptoms, take your dog or cat to your veterinarian immediately.

PET PEEVES

DOG EAT DOG

- The word *coprophagia* stems from the Greek words *copros,* meaning "feces," and *phagien,* meaning "to eat."

- When housetraining a dog, chastise the dog when he urinates or defecates in the house only if you catch him in the act. Dogs have short memories, and your pet will have no idea why you're scolding him later. Do not hold your dog's snout in his own feces. Otherwise your pet may think you want him to eat the feces.

- No one knows for certain why some dogs eat their own feces or the feces of other animals. Veterinarians conjecture that dogs may start eating feces out of boredom, to obtain nutrients missing from their existing diet, or because they truly like the taste.

- If your dog uses your cat's litter box as a buffet, place the litter box in a location accessible only to the cat, perhaps using a door narrow enough for only the cat to slip through. Or purchase a covered litter box.

- Among dogs, a nursing mother instinctively eats her puppies' feces to keep the nest clean and avoid attracting predators.

- Dogs commonly eat the feces of other species, particularly herbivores like rabbits. The behavior, while undesirable to people, is completely normal.

- To rule out the possibility that your dog eats feces to obtain nutrition missing from his diet, add a multivitamin to his food.

- Anthropologists believe that people began domesticating dogs some 12,000 to 15,000 years ago because dogs ate garbage and human feces, helping keep the outer lying areas around human habitations clean.

- To train your dog to stop eating feces, keep him on a leash even when you walk him in the yard, and, if he shows interest in any dung, pull back on the leash and exclaim "No!" firmly.

- Dogs tend to adopt bad habits to alleviate boredom. Giving your dog thirty minutes of playtime twice a day or a different toy each day should negate his need to engage in distasteful activities.

Dandruff

For Dogs and Cats

- **Bayer Aspirin** and **Johnson's Baby Shampoo.** Unless you're allergic to aspirin, grind six Bayer Aspirin into a fine powder using a mortar and pestle, pour the pulverized aspirin into a bottle of Johnson's Baby Shampoo, and shake well. Lather up your pet with the shampoo. Let sit for five minute to allow the salicylic acid in the aspirin time to exfoliate your pet's dead skin cells. Rinse clean with water.

- **Cheerios** and **L'eggs Sheer Energy Panty Hose.** Using a blender, grind  one cup Cheerios into a fine powder. Cut off the foot from a clean, used pair of L'eggs Sheer Energy Panty Hose, fill with the powdered oats, and tie a knot in the nylon. Tie the powdered Cheerios sachet to the spigot, letting it dangle in the flow of water as the tub fills with cool water. Bathe your pet for five to ten minutes in this soothing bath. The powdered Cheerios moisturize your pet's dry skin, which stops dandruff.

- **Downy Fabric Softener.** To reduce dander, add a capful of Downy Fabric Softener to the bath water when washing your pets.

- **Fruit of the Earth Aloe Vera Gel.** Rub Fruit of the Earth Aloe Vera Gel into your pet's skin, let set five minutes, and then shampoo and rinse. Aloe moisturizes the skin, putting an end to the flaking instantly.

- **Hain Safflower Oil.** To boost your pet's metabolism of fats in skin tissue and bring dandruff under control, mix one-half to one teaspoon of Hain Safflower Oil into your dog or cat's food every day.

- **Huggies Baby Wipes.** Wipe down your pet daily with a hypoallergenic, fragrance-free Huggies Baby Wipe to lessen dandruff and shedding.

- **Johnson's Baby Shampoo.** Using warm water, lather Johnson's Baby Shampoo into your pet's skin, massaging well, then rinse thoroughly, and dry with a towel. Bathing your pet regularly (once a month in winter, twice a month in summer) washes away dandruff. For more ways to bathe your animal, see page 13.

PET PEEVES
GETTING FLAKEY

- Dandruff is simply flakey skin.

- To keep dandruff at bay, groom your dog or cat frequently. Brushing your pet's coat distributes the natural oils equally over the skin. After a few grooming sessions, the dandruff should disappear.

- Dandruff may result from a poor diet. Make sure you're feeding your pet a food that provides the proper range of vitamins and minerals.

- Do not use human dandruff shampoos on a dog or cat. Human dandruff shampoos that contain tar can kill a cat, and those that contain pyrithione zinc (such as Head & Shoulders and Selsun Blue) can cause blindness in dogs. Consult your veterinarian before shampooing your pet with a medicated shampoo.

- **Listerine.** After shampooing your pet, rinse with Listerine antiseptic mouthwash. Thymol, one of the active ingredients in Listerine, is a mild antiseptic that helps reduce dandruff. Let sit for five minutes, and then rinse clean with water.

- **Lubriderm.** Rub your dog or cat's coat with Lubriderm moisturizing lotion to moisturize the skin deep down.

- **Quaker Oats** and **L'eggs Sheer Energy Panty Hose.** Using a blender, grind one cup Quaker Oats into a fine powder. Cut off the foot from a clean, used pair of L'eggs Sheer Energy Panty Hose, fill with the powdered oats, and tie a knot in the nylon. Tie the oatmeal sachet to the spigot, letting it dangle in the flow of water as the tub fills with cool water. Bathe your pet for five to ten minutes in this inexpensive and soothing oatmeal bath that moisturizes dry skin and relieves flaking.

- **Wesson Corn Oil.** Mix one-half to one teaspoon of Wesson Corn Oil into your pet's food every day to help improve the metabolism of fats in skin tissue. Animals that get sufficient fat in their diets tend to stay free of dandruff.

Get Your Pet to the Vet

Don't flake out! If shampoos, regular brushing, and a change in diet don't reduce your pet's dandruff, the flaking skin may be a symptom of an allergy, parasite infestation, skin infection, or internal disease. If the symptoms don't go away—or if they worsen—take your pet to a veterinarian.

Dehydration

For Dogs and Cats

- **Coca-Cola.** To prevent dehydration during hot, humid weather, fill clean, empty two-liter Coca-Cola bottles with water, freeze, and place in a doghouse or near your cat's bedding to keep your dog or cat comfortable.

- **Cool Whip.** To avoid dehydration when traveling with your pet, take along a clean, empty Cool Whip tub as a portable water bowl. If you place some ice cubes in the tub before hoping in the car, as the ice melts, your pet will have clean, fresh, cold water.

- **Gatorade.** To quickly revive a dog or cat afflicted with dehydration, fill her water bowl with fruit punch–flavored Gatorade. Gatorade quickly replaces the minerals—sodium, potassium, and chloride—lost from dehydration. (If your pet refuses to drink Gatorade, switch back to water.)

- **Pedialyte.** If your pet suffers from dehydration, pour Pedialyte into your dog or cat's water bowl to quickly replace her electrolytes. Drinking water will replace most electrolytes, but drinking an electrolyte solution such as Pedialyte, formulated for babies, quickly replaces minerals like potassium and sodium. (Not all pets will drink Pedialyte, so keep another bowl of water available.)

PET PEEVES

TAKING THE HEAT

- Never leave your pet in a parked car in warm weather. On a day when the temperature is 85 degrees Fahrenheit, the temperature inside a closed car can rise to 102 degrees Fahrenheit within ten minutes and 120 degrees Fahrenheit within thirty minutes, killing your pet. Do not leave your pet in the car even if you parked in the shade with the windows open.

- In the summer, when the temperature exceeds 80 degrees Fahrenheit, dogs and cats require fresh water every thirty minutes. Keep your pet's bowl filled with fresh cold tap water, or drop in a few ice cubes to keep it cool.

- Never tie your dog to a tree or post in hot weather and leave her there. Heat exhaustion could cause brain damage or kill the animal.

- If your pet has gone too long without drinking water, give her a bowl of water, let her take a few laps, take the bowl away for a minute, and then let her drink a few more laps. Or instead of water, fill your pet's bowl with ice cubes so she can slowly rehydrate. Otherwise, allowing your pet to gulp down an entire bowl of the water at once may trigger vomiting.

- Signs of heat exhaustion for a dog: nonstop panting, agitation, and unconsciousness.

- If your dog suffers from heat exhaustion, use a hose or shower to saturate her with water, place icepacks on her neck and paws to reduce her temperature, and take her to a veterinarian.

- Eager to please their owners, dogs will jog alongside you to the point of heat exhaustion. Never over-exercise your dog on a hot summer day.

- Determine how long you should let your pet outdoors based on how long you would stay outside in such weather.

GET YOUR PET TO THE VET

Too hot too handle! If your dog or cat suffers from a dry mouth, sunken eyes, and extreme exhaustion, gently lift the skin along your pet's back and release it. If the skin doesn't snap back into place, take your pet to the veterinarian immediately.

Diabetes

For Dogs and Cats

- **Karo Corn Syrup.** If, after giving your diabetic pet insulin, your pet's blood sugar drops too low and the animal starts shaking from hyperglycemia, rub some Karo Light Corn Syrup on your pet's lips to temporarily raise her sugar level and immediately take your pet to your veterinarian. Hyperglycemia is a medical emergency, and your veterinarian might need to administer intravenous glucose.

- **Metamucil.** Adding fiber to your pet's diet can keep blood sugar levels more constant by steadying the pace at which fuels enter the body. Mix one teaspoon of Metamucil with water and pour it on your pet's food. The fiber helps your pet's body absorb the carbohydrates in food more slowly.

- **Post Grape-Nuts Flakes.** If you don't want to go to the expense of using Metamucil to add fiber to your pet's diet, sprinkle three tablespoons of Post Grape-Nuts Flakes on your pet's food. The added fiber helps keep your pet's blood sugar levels more constant, and it also helps prevent constipation and improves digestion.

- **Quaker Oats.** Adding cooked Quaker Oats to your pet's food helps regulate insulin levels and provides fiber.

- **SueBee Honey.** If, after giving your diabetic pet insulin, your pet's blood sugar drops too low and the animal starts shaking from hyperglycemia, rub some SueBee Honey on your pet's lips to temporarily raise his sugar level and immediately take your pet to your veterinarian. Hyperglycemia is a medical emergency, and your veterinarian might need to administer intravenous glucose.

- **Uncle Ben's Converted Brand Rice.** Adding cooked Uncle Ben's Converted Brand Rice to your pet's food is beneficial for diabetes. Rice provides fiber and helps control the levels of insulin.

GET YOUR PET TO THE VET

Don't sugarcoat it! If you notice that your dog or cat drinks, eats, and urinates excessively, has developed sweet breath, shakes, seems tired or weak, or constantly loses weight, take your pet to the veterinarian for a urine test right away.

PET PEEVES

SWEET NOTHINGS

● In an animal with diabetes, the pancreas doesn't produce sufficient insulin to enable the cells to metabolize glucose, the body's fuel.

● Dogs with diabetes usually require regular injections of insulin to live. Cats with diabetes may require insulin injections or may be able to overcome the disease by losing weight.

● To prevent your cat from getting diabetes, keep him at a healthy weight by measuring the amount of food you feed him. Obese cats are susceptible to diabetes.

● If you give medication to your pet to control diabetes, do so at the same time every day to stabilize your pet's blood sugar levels.

● To keep diabetes under control, feed your dog two smaller meals a day, rather than one big meal, and give your cat four small meals a day. This levels out the pace at which sugars enter the bloodstream.

● Sustaining a regular exercise regimen helps control your dog or cat's weight and lowers the amount of insulin your pet's body needs.

● After tenderly giving your pet a shot of insulin, reward her with praise, affection, and a small treat—to make the experience more pleasant.

● To reduce the stress placed on the pancreas, strictly avoid giving your pet foods that contain sugar and stick to a low-fat diet.

Diarrhea

For Dogs and Cats

- **Campbell's Beef Broth.** To prevent the possibility of dehydration from diarrhea, feed your pet a small amount of Campbell's Beef Broth every few hours.

- **CharcoCaps Activated Charcoal.** Mix one-half to one teaspoon of activated charcoal (by emptying the contents of CharcoCaps capsules into a measuring spoon) with water, and feed it to your pet in a dish (or by using a turkey baster or bulb syringe) every three or four hours for 24 hours. The charcoal absorbs toxins, drugs, poisons, and other irritants. Charcoal also absorbs nutrients, so be sure to discontinue use after a few days. (Don't confuse activated charcoal with charcoal briquettes. Activated charcoal is a charcoal that has been processed with oxygen to be extremely porous and absorb odors or other substances.)

- **Dannon Yogurt.** Once your dog or cat is on the path to recovery, feed your pet small amounts of plain Dannon Yogurt to help replenish the intestinal tract with beneficial bacteria. The *Lactobacillus acidophilus* in yogurt produces the bacteriocins necessary for proper digestion. Give one-quarter teaspoon to cats and small dogs, one teaspoon to medium-sized dogs (fifteen to twenty pounds), and one tablespoon to large dogs. Cats and dogs generally enjoy yogurt, so there's no need to mix it into their food. Even lactose-intolerant pets can digest yogurt without any ill effects.

- **Gatorade.** Diarrhea quickly depletes vital liquids from a dog or cat's body. Fill her water bowl with fruit punch–flavored Gatorade, which pets seem to love. Gatorade quickly replaces the lost minerals—sodium, potassium, and chloride—and prevents dehydration. (If your pet refuses to drink Gatorade, switch back to water.)

- **Kaopectate.** To cure diarrhea in dogs, use a turkey baster or bulb syringe to give your dog one teaspoon of liquid Kaopectate per five pounds of weight every four hours. Hold your pet's head back, squirt the medicine toward the back of his throat, hold his mouth closed, and stroke his throat until he swallows. Be sure to consult your veterinarian for the precise dosage for your particular pet.

- **Metamucil.** Once you've got your dog or cat on a bland diet, if stools continue coming out soft, mix from one-half to one tablespoon Metamucil with water and pour it on your pet's food. Fiber absorbs water from the stool, and in the large intestine, the fiber ferments and its nutrients are absorbed.

- **Pedialyte.** After your dog or cat experiences a bout of diarrhea, pour Pedialyte into your pet's water bowl to quickly replace her electrolytes. Drinking water will replace most electrolytes, but drinking an electrolyte solution such as Pedialyte, formulated for babies, quickly replaces crucial minerals like potassium and sodium. (Not all pets will drink Pedialyte, so keep another bowl of water available.)

- **Post Grape-Nuts Flakes.** Adding fiber to your pet's diet after the diarrhea subsides helps firm up runny stool. Give your pet one to three tablespoons of Post Grape-Nuts Flakes several times a day. Once the constipation fades, sprinkle up to three tablespoons of Post Grape-Nuts Flakes on your pet's food. The fiber helps improves digestion, increasing your pet's ability to absorb nutrients.

- **Quaker Oats Oat Bran.** An alternative way to add fiber to your pet's food is to sprinkle one-half teaspoon to two tablespoons of Quaker Oats Oat Bran on your pet's food daily, depending on the size of the animal. To help your pet swallow the bran, consider adding warm broth to the food.

- **Uncle Ben's Converted Brand Rice.** Once your pet has gotten over his bout with diarrhea, help him recover by mixing two parts cooked Uncle Ben's Converted Brand Rice to one part boiled hamburger meat (or skinless white meat chicken) and feed him small servings every four hours for two days. Then gradually transition your pet back to his regular diet. White rice soothes the stomach and helps cure diarrhea.

GET YOUR PET TO THE VET

Don't run any risks! Diarrhea can be a symptom of diabetes, worms, distemper, or pancreatitis. If your pet suffers from diarrhea for more than 24 hours (or if your pet also experiences fever, vomiting, abdominal pain, or excessive thirst), take him to your veterinarian immediately.

PET PEEVES

RUNNING ON EMPTY

- Giving a bowl of milk to your dog or cat can cause diarrhea. Surprisingly, many cats and dogs are lactose intolerant. If you've been giving milk to your pet who now suffers from diarrhea, cease immediately.

- Do not give milk to a cat suffering from diarrhea. Her digestive system will likely reject milk, making the situation worse.

- Diarrhea in pets is usually caused by an intestinal virus, consumption of rotten garbage, or a sudden change in diet.

- Stress and anxiety can also cause diarrhea in pets. If your pet has been traumatized by the addition of a new pet in your home or a move to a new house, shower her with compassion and reassurance.

- Resist the temptation to give your pet any over-the-counter medication to stop diarrhea. Let the diarrhea run its course to flush any irritants from your pet's system.

- If your dog or cat suffers from diarrhea, stop feeding any solid food to your pet for 24 hours and give plenty of water to drink. If the animal's condition fails to improve, consult your veterinarian.

- To calm your dog's diarrhea, give your ailing pet a fifteen-minute walk twice a day, provided she has the stamina to accompany you.

Digging

For Dogs Only

- **Coca-Cola.** Put a few pennies in a clean, empty Coca-Cola can and tape the opening shut. To stop your dog from digging, exclaim "No" in a firm voice and shake the can vigorously. The disturbing sound of coins jangling in a can will stop a dog in his tracks.

- **Glad Trash Bags.** Slice open the sides of large plastic Glad Trash Bag to make long sheets and place the plastic over the area where your dog digs. Secure the plastic sheets in place with large stones or bricks. Interfering with your dog's digging should cause him to abandon his habit, and once sufficient time has passes, you can remove the plastic sheets.

- **Tabasco Pepper Sauce and McCormick Ground (Cayenne) Red Pepper.** To stop your dog from digging up your yard, mix four tablespoons Tabasco Pepper Sauce and four tablespoons McCormick Ground (Cayenne) Red Pepper in one quart of water. Sprinkle the spicy solution over the area where your dog digs.

PET PEEVES

CAN YOU DIG IT?

- Giving your dog plenty of exercise (or at least one thirty-minute walk a day) will divert his attention away from digging.

- Dogs tend to dig holes on hot days to create a cool place to rest in the insulated earth. To prevent this, make sure your dog has plenty of drinking water and a shady spot to rest.

- If you dig in the garden, prevent your dog from imitating your behavior by leaving him inside.

- An obvious and simple way to stop your dog from digging up certain areas of your yard is to surround the spot with a tall fence made from chicken wire.

- If your dog digs escape tunnels from your yard, install a fence that penetrates several feet into the ground. Or consider having your dog neutered or spayed to stifle the urge to tunnel out to find a mate.

- To train your dog not to dig up the backyard, when you spot your pet digging, exclaim "No!" firmly and give him a spritz of water from a spray bottle or make disturbing noise to startle him. (See "Coca-Cola" on page 86.) When your dog stops digging, immediately shower him with praise, and then distract him with a chew toy or by playing ball.

- If your dog thrives on digging, fence off an area of the yard to create a digging pen and train your dog to dig only in that allocated space by burying some of his toys under a few inches of soil.

- Cats tend to dig up houseplants to create a new litter box. To prevent this behavior, provide several litter boxes around your house, including at least one on each floor. If you have more than one cat, provide at least one litter box for each cat.

- Make sure the cat box litter you use does not resemble potting soil. Otherwise, your cat may easily mistake houseplant soil for a litter box.

For Cats Only

- **Arm & Hammer Baking Soda.** Cats tend to dig up houseplants in the hopes of finding an adequate substitute for a dirty litter box. Aside from cleaning the litter box daily and changing the litter weekly, sprinkle Arm & Hammer Baking Soda in the litter box and work it into the litter to absorb odors that might send your cat excavating your houseplants.

- **Heinz White Vinegar.** To prevent cats from digging up houseplants, add one teaspoon Heinz White Vinegar to two cups water in a sixteen-ounce trigger-spray bottle and mist the plants with the solution. The smell of vinegar repels cats.

- **L'eggs Sheer Energy Panty Hose.** To keep cats out of your houseplants, cover the soil with a balled up pair (or several pairs) of clean, used, L'eggs Sheer Energy Panty Hose. The nylon repels the cat, and you can still water the plant through the porous panty hose.

- **Maxwell House Coffee.** Fertilizing houseplants and plants around your garden with used Maxwell House Coffee grounds repels cats and prevents them from digging up the soil.

Ears

Burrs and Foxtails

For Dogs Only

- **Star Olive Oil.** If your long-eared dog gets a burr or foxtail stuck in his ear and you can't take him to the veterinarian immediately, put a few drops of warm Star Olive Oil in your pet's ear to soften the foxtail and relieve some of the irritation until you can get proper medical attention.

Cleaning

For Dogs and Cats

- **Heinz White Vinegar.** To prevent your dog or cat from scratching his ears, saturate a cotton ball with Heinz White Vinegar and wipe out the inside of his ears on a regular basis.
- **Johnson's Baby Oil.** To clean ear wax from your dog or cat's ears, moisten a cotton ball with Johnson's Baby Oil and gently wipe the inside of the ear.

- **Smirnoff Vodka** and **Q-tips Cotton Swabs.** Once a month, clean out the visible portion of your pet's ear canal with a Q-tips Cotton Swab saturated with Smirnoff Vodka.

Ear Mites

For Dogs and Cats

- **Hydrogen Peroxide** and **Q-tips Cotton Swabs.** To prevent your dog or cat from getting an ear mite infestation, once a month, dip a Q-tips Cotton Swab in hydrogen peroxide, and gently use it clean out the ear canal. Many dogs enjoy this treatment, which removes ear mites before they can set up shop.

- **Johnson's Baby Oil.** Instead of using medications to treat your dog or cat for ear mites, put one or two drops of warm Johnson's Baby Oil in your pet's ear to simply coat the ear canal without flooding it. The mites drown in the oil, which gives your pet instant relief. Repeat every day or so for a month so the oil drowns any mites that hatch from eggs before they can lay more eggs.

- **Johnson's Baby Oil** and **Heinz White Vinegar.** Before using medications to treat your pet for ear mites, clear away the crumbly, reddish-black waxy debris (that looks like coffee grounds) from inside the ear by using a small dropper to put several drops of Johnson's Baby Oil inside the ear canal. Wait several hours, giving the crust time to soften, and then fill a ball syringe with equal parts Heinz White Vinegar and lukewarm water to gently rinse the ear clean. Wipe the ear clean with a cotton ball. If matter remains in the ear, repeat the entire process as many times as needed.

- **Q-tips Cotton Swabs.** To determine whether your pet has ear mites, gently swab the ear canal with a Q-tips Cotton Swab. Rub the cotton swab on a black sheet of paper, hold the paper under a bright light, and look for small wiggly white specks.

PET PEEVES
PLAYING IT BY EAR

- Dogs have a considerably more acute sense of hearing than people, detecting sounds at higher frequencies and greater distances.

- Dogs alter the position of their ears to communicate emotions, including fear and anger.

- Paul McCartney included an ultrasonic whistle that can only be heard by dogs at the end of the song "A Day in the Life" on the Beatles 1967 album *Sgt. Peppers Lonely Hearts Club Band,* as a secret message to his Shetland sheepdog, Martha, for whom he later wrote the song "Martha My Dear" on the Beatles 1968 *White Album.* McCartney wrote the song "Jet" on the 1973 Wings album *Band on the Run* for his dog Jet, a black Labrador.

- If your dog or cat constantly scratches his ears, check to see if he's suffering from a parasite infestation.

- Ear mites are minuscule, eight-legged pests that nest in the ears and quickly multiply into the thousands, creating a crumbly brown debris in the ears.

- To determine whether your pet has ear mites, shine a flashlight into the ear. Mites prefer darkness, and brightness makes them scurry frantically.

- To combat ear mites, veterinarians typically recommend cleaning the ears and then using an over-the-counter medication containing pyrethrins.

- Ear mites can easily infect other animals. So if you have more than one pet, treat them all simultaneously.

- Ear mites develop from a egg to an adult over a period of three weeks, so, if you wish to wipe out the little devils and their offspring, you need to treat your pet for one month.

- Other common ear problems include yeast infections (a waxy buildup that looks like peanut butter and smells like yeast), bacterial infections (a moist yellow paste that smells fruity), or a punctured eardrum.

- **Star Olive Oil.** If your dog or cat gets ear mites, crush four cloves of garlic and steep them overnight in one cup Star Olive Oil. In the morning, fish out the garlic and discard it. Heat the olive oil until it's warm to the touch, and put several drops into your pet's ears to smother the ear mites and relieve itching. Repeat every other day for several weeks.

- **Wesson Vegetable Oil.** To kill ear mites, put a few drops of Wesson Vegetable Oil into your dog or cat's ear and massage. Use a cotton ball to clean out all debris. Repeat daily for three days. The oil soothes the animal's sensitive skin, smothers the mites, and promotes healing.

Infections

For Dogs Only

- **Heinz White Vinegar.** If your dog suffers from an ear infection, hold your pet's head to the side and use an ear dropper to place eight to ten drops of Heinz White Vinegar in your pet's ear. Hold your pet's head to the side for a few minutes, massaging the area around the ear, and then drain out the vinegar. Repeat for three days. If the infection persists, take your pet to the veterinarian.

- **ReaLemon.** If your dog gets water in his ears during a swim, reduce the chances of a bacterial or fungal infection by flushing out his ears with a solution made from two tablespoons ReaLemon lemon juice and one cup warm water.

GET YOUR PET TO THE VET

Can't believe your ears? If ear mites refuse to disappear after a month of home treatment or your pet develops a painful rash in the ear, take the animal to your veterinarian.

Feeding

Catnip

For Cats Only

- **Ziploc Storage Bags.** Store catnip inside a sealed Ziploc Storage Bag to preserve its potency.

Leftovers

For Dogs and Cats

- **Ziploc Storage Bags.** If your dog or cat loves leftovers from restaurants, take a Ziploc Storage Bag to wrap messy leftover foods when you're finished dining out, which you can then carry home safely without any mess.

Nursing

For Dogs Only

- **Lewis Lab's Brewer's Yeast.** To help a lactating mother dog build milk, sprinkle Lewis Lab's Brewer's Yeast over her food.

- **Uncle Ben's Converted Brand Rice.** To help a lactating mother dog build milk, supplement the protein in her diet by adding cooked Uncle Ben's Converted Brand Rice.

- **Wesson Corn Oil.** To help a lactating mother dog build milk, sprinkle a tablespoon of Wesson Corn Oil over her food.

Pet Food

For Dogs and Cats

- **Knorr Beef Bouillon.** Adding a cup of Knorr Beef Bouillon to your dog or cat's dry food turns the kibble into an enticing delicacy.

- **Pam Cooking Spray.** To prevent leftover bits and pieces of moist pet food from sticking to the bottom of your dog or cat's food bowl, before filling the bowl with pet food, give the inside of the bowl a light coat of Pam Cooking Spray. The vegetable oil will prevent the food from adhering to the bowl, and the oil gives your pet's coat a nice shine.

- **Uncle Ben's Converted Brand Rice** and **Campbell's Beef Broth.** If your dog or cat seems disinterested in eating pet food, break the monotony of the animal's routine by serving cooked Uncle Ben's Converted Brand Rice topped with some heated Campbell's Beef Broth.

For Cats Only

- **Chicken of the Sea Tuna.** If your cat is a finicky eater, pour some of the water or oil from a can of Chicken of the Sea Tuna over her food.

- **Fritos Cheese Dip.** To cover an opened can of cat food and save it in the refrigerator for future use, use the plastic lid from a small can of Fritos Cheese Dip.

- **Kraft Grated Parmesan Cheese.** If your cat refuses to eat the expensive cat food you bought as a special treat, sprinkle a little Kraft Grated Parmesan Cheese on it. Attracted by the cheese, your cat will likely gobble up the cat food.

- **Mr. Coffee Filters.** To keep a cat food bowl clean, place approximately six Mr. Coffee Filters in the empty cat food dish, and then place the food on top of the paper filter. When the cat finishes eating, discard the top filter, revealing a clean filter underneath.

Storage

For Dogs and Cats

- **Cool Whip.** To prevent leftover canned pet food from stinking up the refrigerator, place the open pet food can in a clean, empty Cool Whip tub and seal the plastic lid securely shut to seal in the odors.

- **Glad Trash Bags.** Store that bag of dry dog food inside a Glad Trash Bag to prevent spills and to protect the contents from insects and other pests.

- **Maxwell House Coffee.** To thwart the stench of leftover canned pet food from infusing other foods in the refrigerator, place the open pet food can in a clean, empty Maxwell House Coffee can and seal the plastic lid tightly.

- **Pam Cooking Spray** and **Reynolds Cut-Rite Wax Paper.** If your dry dog food has dried out, line a cookie pan with a sheet of Reynolds Cut-Rite Wax Paper, spread the chunks of dog food on the pan, and spray a light coat of Pam Cooking Spray on the morsels. Store the oiled dog food in a resealable, airtight container. The vegetable oil will moisten and refresh the dog food.

- **Reynolds Wrap.** Stop an open can of pet food in the refrigerator from emitting an odor by capping it with a square of Reynolds Wrap pressed firmly around the can.

- **Ziploc Storage Bags.** Place an opened can of pet food inside a Ziploc Storage Bag and seal it securely shut to prevent pungent odors from wafting through your refrigerator.

- **Ziploc Freezer Bags.** To preserve the flavor and nutritional value of canned pet food (and save money), buy large cans of pet food, spoon the contents into meal-sized portions stored in individual Ziploc Storage Bags, and freeze. Defrost one bag a day to feed the preserved contents to your pet.

Simple Recipes
HOMEMADE DOG TREATS

Basic Biscuits

Ingredients

1 cube Knorr Chicken Bouillon
2 cups Gold Medal Whole Wheat Flour
½ cup Aunt Jemima Corn Meal
6 tablespoons Wesson Vegetable Oil

Directions

Dissolve the bouillon cube in ⅔ cup boiled water. In a large bowl, mix the bouillon and all the other ingredients together. Roll the resulting dough, cut into shapes, and place on a greased cookie sheet. Bake at 350 degrees Fahrenheit for 40 minutes.

Beefy Biscuits

Ingredients

2½ cups Gold Medal Whole Wheat Flour
½ cup Nestlé Carnation NonFat Dry Milk
1 teaspoon McCormick Garlic Powder
1 egg, beaten
1 can Campbell's Beef Broth

Directions

Combine the flour, dry milk, and garlic powder in a medium bowl. Add the egg, and mix well. Add just enough beef broth to flavor the dough while retaining a stiff consistency. Roll to ¼-inch thick logs on a floured surface. Cut into shapes and bake at 350 degrees Fahrenheit for 30 minutes.

CHEESY TREATS

Ingredients

1¾ cups grated Cheddar cheese (grated and room temperature)

1 stick Land O Lakes Margarine

1½ cups Gold Medal Whole Wheat Flour

Directions

Mix the Cheddar cheese, margarine, and flour in a medium bowl. Roll out two logs, about two inches in diameter. Chill in the refrigerator. Cut the logs into ¼-inch slices and place all the chips on a greased cookie sheet. Bake at 375 degrees Fahrenheit for 15 minutes, or until slightly brown.

PEANUT BUTTER TREATS

Ingredients

1 tablespoon SueBee Honey

1 teaspoon Jif Peanut Butter

¾ cup Gold Medal All-Purpose Flour

¼ cup Crisco All-Vegetable Shortening

1 teaspoon Arm & Hammer Baking Soda

¼ cup Quaker Oats

½ teaspoon McCormick Vanilla Extract

1 egg

Directions

Heat the honey and peanut butter in a microwave oven until the peanut butter is melted (about 20 seconds). Add the remaining ingredients. Drop ½ teaspoon of the batter onto a greased cookie sheet at a time, filling the cookie sheet. Bake at 350 degrees Fahrenheit for roughly 10 minutes.

● **Ziploc Freezer Bags.** Use a gallon-size Ziploc Freezer Bag to store an opened bag of dry pet food. The airtight bag keeps the food fresh and protects it from insects.

PET PEEVES
FOOD FOR THOUGHT

● There are three types of commercial dog foods: canned dog food, semi-moist kibble, and dry kibble.

● By law, dog food labeled "beef dog food" must be composed of at least 95 percent beef, and the same rules apply to dog food labeled "chicken dog food," "lamb dog food," and "pork dog food." Dog food labeled "beef dinner," "chicken dinner," or "pork dinner," must be composed of at least 25 percent beef, chicken, or pork. And dog food labeled "with beef," "with chicken," or "with pork," must contain at least 3 percent of that particular meat. The remainder of the product is made from vegetable and grain fillers.

● Unlike meat products purchased for human consumption, dog food made with beef, chicken, or pork contains all parts of the respective animals, including blood, ground-up bones, internal organs, and intestines. While this may seem repulsive, a dog living in the wild devours all parts of its prey.

● Store bags of dry pet food in a plastic garbage pail with a secure lid to prevent insects or rodents from invading the bag.

● Treats, petting, and praise are all positive reinforcement that condition your dog or cat to behave appropriately.

● Never give your dog a real bone to chew. Dogs chip or break their teeth chewing bones, and your dog might swallow a piece of the bone, which will have to be surgically removed from her stomach. Instead, give your dog rawhide bones.

● Never give your dog chicken bones, pork chop bones, or fish bones, which can splinter and puncture the stomach lining or intestines.

● Before feeding the contents of an open can of dog or cat food that you've stored in the refrigerator to your pet, set the can on the countertop and let the food come to room temperature.

Treats

For Dogs and Cats

- **Ziploc Storage Bags.** Keep treats in Ziploc Storage Bags when training or traveling to keep them handy, fresh, and protected from insects.

- If your pet refuses to eat anything but expensive canned food, mix in a little of the bargain food or more affordable kibble, gradually increasing the ratio of the inexpensive food until your pet has switched to the less pricey chow.

- Never feed uncooked meat to your pets. It could contain dangerous parasites.

- Dogs and cat naturally eat grass, which for pets, is similar to eating a salad. Some pets eat grass to ease stomach upset.

- Never feed a dog or cat chocolate. It can be toxic.

- To empty the contents from a can of pet food easily and quickly (without having to excavate with a spoon), open both ends of the can and use one of the tops to push the food from the can.

- If your cat leaves dry food in her bowl in the hopes that you toss it out and pour fresh food, sprinkle some water on the leftovers to bring out the aroma and revive your cat's interest.

- If your cat becomes a finicky eater, stop leaving her food bowl filled all of the time. Instead, put out food only once or twice a day and when your cat finishes eating, toss out the leftover food. The limited dining opportunities should intensify your cat's appetite.

- Do not feed cat food to a dog, and do not feed dog food to a cat. A cat fed nothing but dry dog food will starve to death. Dog food, while high in bulk, will not give a cat sufficient protein and vitamins to stay alive.

- If you have more than one cat, give them each their own food bowls, at least 1 foot apart.

- Never let a cat eat a dead mouse or rat. Your cat will become infected with the rodent's internal parasites, and, if the rodent was poisoned, the poison that killed the rodent might very well kill your cat.

PET PROJECTS
MILK-BONE UNLEASHED

In 1908, the F. H. Bennett Biscuit Co., a small bakery on New York City's Lower East Side, created a bone-shaped dog biscuit under the brand name Maltoid, receiving a trademark in 1911. Since milk was a primary ingredient in the biscuit, the company changed the name to Milk-Bone in 1915.

After acquiring Milk-Bone dog biscuits in 1931, the Nabisco Biscuit Company advertised the treat strictly as "a dog's dessert" and "a nourishing snack for canines." Eventually, the company began to advertise the fact that Milk-Bone biscuits clean a dog's teeth, improve a dog's breath, and nutritionally supplement a dog's regular diet. In 1940, Nabisco made Milk-Bone dog biscuits available in three different sizes. In 1956, Nabisco reconfigured one of its manufacturing plants in Buffalo, New York, to produce only Milk-Bone products. Milk-Bone remained the only dog biscuit commercially available to the public for fifty years.

In 2002, Kraft Food acquired Milk-Bone, and in 2006, Del Monte purchased Milk-Bone. Today, Milk-Bone makes more than thirty varieties of dog treats.

For Dogs Only

- **Easy Cheese.** To give your dog a special chew toy, stuff a sterilized beef bone with this aerosol cheese spread.
- **Jif Peanut Butter.** Another great way to add zing to a chew toy is to fill it with Jif Peanut Butter.

Water

For Dogs and Cats

- **Ziploc Freezer Bags.** To fill an outdoor water bowl, fill a Ziploc Freezer Bag with water, seal it securely shut, carry it outside, and empty the water into the bowl.

Fish

Algae Growth

- **Mrs. Stewart's Liquid Bluing.** To reduce the algae growth in fishponds and fish tanks (and brighten the water with a pleasant blue tinge at the same time), add a few drops of Mrs. Stewart's Liquid Bluing. Mrs. Stewart's Liquid Bluing contains a non-toxic amount of a pH balancer and a biocide to prevent the buildup of algae and bacteria.

Catching Fish

- **Ziploc Storage Bags.** If you need to remove a fish from your tank, use a Ziploc Storage Bag to gently catch the fish without terrifying the small creature. Hold the bag open underwater and stationery in front of the fish's path, allowing the fish to swim into the bag.

Fish Food

- **Cheerios.** All out of fish food? In a pinch, you can feed your fish a few Cheerios. Made from oats, Cheerios doubles as nourishing fish food.

- **Kretschmer Wheat Germ.** Wheat germ makes a highly nutritious diet for fish, including koi and goldfish.

- **Quaker Oats.** Fish love Quaker Oats. Just toss a pinch of these beneficial rolled oats into the tank.

- **Ziploc Storage Bags.** Store brine shrimp in a Ziploc Storage Bag to keep them fresh in your freezer.

Fungus

- **Morton Salt.** According to *The ASPCA Complete Guide to Pet Care*, "Fungus, or saprolegnia, is a slimy, cottony clump of fibers that hangs on the infected areas of the fish, often around the mouth." To cure fungus, isolate the affected fish in a hospital tank (a separate, small tank) and add two teaspoons Morton Salt to the water. After several days, the fungus should go away. If not, add one more teaspoon of salt and wait a few more days. If the fungus does not dissipate, consult your local supplier for a commercial medication.

Gravel

- **L'eggs Sheer Energy Panty Hose.** To wash gravel before placing it in an aquarium, stretch the waistband of a pair of clean, used L'eggs Sheer Energy Panty Hose over the rim of a clean five-gallon bucket. Fill the panty hose with gravel. Pour water over the gravel in the panty hose, gently shaking the gravel, and continue pouring water over the gravel until the water runs clear. Several washings may be necessary. Once the water runs clear, place the gravel in the tank.

GET YOUR PET TO THE VET

Is something fishy? If you notice any abnormal growths, fin damage, changes in scales or body shape, difficulty swimming, or parasites, take the afflicted fish to a veterinarian immediately to prevent any disease from spreading to your other fish.

New Fish

- **Ziploc Storage Bags.** To introduce a new fish to your aquarium, pour the newly purchased fish and its water into a Ziploc Storage Bag and float the bag in your aquarium for fifteen minutes, allowing the water in the bag to gradually reach the same temperature as the water in the tank. Once the new fish has grown accustomed to the water temperature, open the bag, releasing the new fish into the tank.

Pop Eye

- **Parsons' Ammonia.** To treat the abnormal protrusion of one or both of a fish's eyes (caused by hemorrhaging behind the eye that results from stress), place the affected fish in a hospital tank, raise the water temperature to approximately 80 degrees Fahrenheit, and using an eyedropper, add one drop of Parsons' Ammonia (Clear) per gallon of water in the tank. After three or four hours, add new water to the tank. When the pop eye subsides, return the fish to the tank.

Water Color

- **McCormick Food Coloring.** To color the water in a fish tank, add a few drops of McCormick Food Coloring. The non-toxic food coloring makes a colorful environment without harming the fish.

Whiteworms

- **Maxwell House Coffee** and **Wonder Bread.** To culture a supply of live food for your fish, buy a culture of whiteworms for your local aquatic dealer or pet store, place the worms in a clean, empty Maxwell House Coffee can filled with soil, place a slice of wet Wonder Bread on top, and seal the lid shut. The worms feed on the bread and breed quickly.

PET PEEVES
PLENTY OF FISH IN THE SEA

- Watching fish swim in an aquarium for fifteen minutes a day lowers blood pressure and reduces stress and anxiety. That's why so many doctors and dentists have fish tanks in their waiting rooms.

- Sprinkle only enough fish food that the fish can eat within five minutes. Otherwise, uneaten food sinks to the bottom of the tank and decomposes, poisoning the water. To measure out the proper amount of food for each meal, feed your fish only as much food as you can pinch between your thumb and index finger.

- A variety of sea animals (such as snails) eat the algae that grow in fish tanks.

- When choosing fish to fill your tank, select a range of species that occupy different levels of the aquarium. Some fish swim near the surface, a second group swims at mid-level, and a third group swims at the bottom. By choosing fish from all three groups, you'll take full advantage of all the space in your aquarium.

- Different species of fish live to different ages, with coldwater freshwater fish tending to live the longest. Larger fish tend to live longest.

- Use plants, branches, rocks, and gravel in your aquarium to hide technical hardware and provide plenty of hiding places for the fish.

- Give your fish a pinch of food two or three times a day, rather than feeding your fish one large meal once a day. Also, vary the food to prevent the fish from growing bored with their diet.

- The best dried fish food is flake food, which floats long enough to feed surface feeders, sinks slowly to feed mid-water feeders, and then reaches the bottom, where the bottom feeders clean it up.

- Enhance your fish's diet with live treats such as bloodworms, brine shrimp, and waterfleas.

- You can go on vacation for up to two weeks without having to feed your fish—as long as you feed your fish regularly before your departure. Fish can fast for up to two weeks without any problems.

- Handle your fish with care. Harsh treatment causes stress in fish, which can lead to disease or death.

Flatulence

For Dogs and Cats

- **CharcoCaps Activated Charcoal.** To reduce your dog or cat's flatulence, add one-eighth to one-quarter teaspoon of activated charcoal (by emptying the contents of CharcoCaps capsules into a measuring spoon) to your small pet's food for a few days. For larger pets, add one-half teaspoon activated charcoal. The charcoal absorbs the gas that causes flatulence from the digestive track. Charcoal also absorbs nutrients, so be sure to discontinue use after a few days. (Don't confuse activated charcoal with charcoal briquettes. Activated charcoal is a charcoal that has been processed with oxygen to be extremely porous and absorb odors or other substances.)

- **Dannon Yogurt.** The *Lactobacillus acidophilus* in yogurt produces the bacteriocins necessary for proper digestion, decreasing flatulence. Give one-quarter teaspoon of plain Dannon Yogurt to cats and small dogs (under fifteen pounds), one teaspoon to medium-sized dogs (fifteen to twenty pounds), and one tablespoon to large dogs (more than twenty pounds). Cats and dogs generally enjoy yogurt, so there's no need to mix it into their food. Even lactose-intolerant pets can digest yogurt without any ill effects.

- **Wilson Tennis Balls.** To lessen flatulence, place a Wilson Tennis Ball in your dog or cat's food bowl. The ball creates a minor obstacle that forces your pet to nose around the bowl, stop wolfing down his meal, and cease swallowing air, which is one of the causes of flatulence.

PET PEEVES
IT'S A GAS

- Giving your pet plenty of exercise helps reduce gas.

- The soybean content in pet food might be causing gas buildup in your pet. Switching to a pet food with less soy might help fight flatulence. Introduce the new food over a period of four days, replacing one-quarter of the old food with one-quarter of the new food each day. Otherwise, the abrupt change may increase flatulence.

- If flatulence is a problem, make sure your pet isn't getting into the garbage to eat spoiled food scraps.

- Stop serving milk to your flatulent dog or cat. Adult dogs and cats do not produce enough lactase to digest milk, so the undigested milk left in the digestive system ferments, producing large quantities of gas.

- To keep flatulence under control, do not let your pet overeat. Excess food overloads the digestive system, resulting in excess fermentation, which creates gas.

- Unless your dog or cat needs vitamin and mineral supplements for medical purposes, eliminate them from your pet's diet. Supplements can trigger bacteria in the stomach to produce excess gas.

- To prevent flatulence and belching, stop your pet from swallowing air during mealtimes. Raise your pet's food dish off the floor (or buy a stand to hold the bowls at mouth level) so your pet doesn't have to bend his neck down to the floor and swallow so much air. If you have two pets, feed them in separate locations at different times. Otherwise, each animal may ravenously devour his meal to protect it, inadvertently swallowing air.

Fleas

Flea Control

For Dogs and Cats

- **Dawn Dishwashing Liquid.** To kill fleas on dogs or cats without using poisons, add a small amount of Dawn Dishwashing Liquid under running water to fill a sink or bathtub and give the animal a bath in the soapy solution. Work the lather into your pet's coat and let it soak for more than five minutes. The soap penetrates the exoskeletons of the fleas, killing them, working more effectively than some prescribed flea shampoos.

- **Dawn Dishwashing Liquid.** Put a few drops of Dawn Dishwashing Liquid in a bowl of water and run a flea comb through your pet's coat once a day, dipping the comb in the soapy water to kill any fleas. When you're finished, flush the soapy water down the toilet.

- **Heinz Apple Cider Vinegar** and **Dawn Dishwashing Liquid.** To make flea shampoo for your dog or cat, mix equal parts Heinz Apple Cider Vinegar and Dawn Dishwashing Liquid. Lather up the dog or cat with the solution and rinse clean.

- **Johnson's Baby Powder.** To kill fleas, cover your dog or cat with Johnson's Baby Powder, working the powder deep into his coat and skin, avoiding the eyes, ears, nose, and mouth. Start at the head so fleas flee toward the back of your pet. The talcum powder smothers and desiccates the fleas. Veterinarians frequently recommend this technique for puppies or kittens that are too young to be treated with flea powders containing insecticide.

- **McCormick Fennel Seed.** Use a mortar and pestle to crush McCormick Fennel Seed, rub the powdered fennel into the coat of your dog or cat, and then place your pet outside so the displeased fleas jump off into the wild outdoors rather than in your home. For a severe infestation, repeat this treatment several times a week. Also sprinkle the powdered fennel in your pet's bedding. Fennel repels fleas. In fact, an old adage advises planting "fennel near the kennel."

- **Morton Salt.** To fight a flea infestation on your dog or cat, wash your pet with saltwater, which kills fleas by dehydrating them. Dissolve one part Morton Salt to ten parts water in a tub and saturate your pet with the saltwater, rubbing it deep into her coat and avoiding her eyes and ears. Let sit for ten minutes, and then shampoo and rinse clean. If necessary, repeat ten days later to kill any newly hatched fleas.

- **Pam Cooking Spray** and **Dawn Dishwashing Liquid.** Spraying your dog or cat with Pam Cooking Spray (avoiding the eyes, nose, and mouth) kills fleas. The fleas drown in the vegetable oil. The only problem is cleaning the vegetable oil from your pet's fur, which can be done with a few drops of Dawn Dishwashing Liquid and water.

- **Skin So Soft.** After bathing your dog or cat, rinse the animal with two ounces Skin So Soft Bath Oil per gallon of water. Skin So Soft repels fleas, and it also gives your pet a shiny coat. Skin So Soft Bath Oil will not harm your cat if she licks it off her fur. However, other Skin-So-Soft products that contain sunscreen may harm your cat if she licks her fur.

- **Star Olive Oil.** To kill fleas and simultaneously treat dry, itchy skin, dampen a soft cloth or cotton ball with Star Olive Oil and rub it into your

Pet Tricks
Getting Rid of Fleas in Your Yard

- **Concern Diatomaceous Earth.** To kill fleas in your yard, put on a dust mask and goggles and sprinkle the ground with Concern Diatomaceous Earth on a day without any wind. The finely ground fossils of prehistoric fresh water diatoms, diatomaceous earth, kills fleas (and many other crawling insects) by absorbing the waxy coating on the insect. (Be sure to use amorphous diatomaceous earth, not glassified diatomaceous earth used in swimming pool filters). Stay out of the yard for a few days to allow the dust to settle. Repeat ten days later to kill any newly hatched fleas.

- **Pine-Sol** and **Heinz White Vinegar.** Add one cup Pine-Sol and one cup Heinz White Vinegar to a water hose sprayer and spray the yard once or twice a month. The pine oil fertilizes the lawn while simultaneously killing fleas.

dog or cat's entire coat, particularly areas aggravated by flea bites. The fleas drown in the olive oil, which also moisturizes the irritated skin.

- **Wesson Vegetable Oil** and **Dawn Dishwashing Liquid.** Saturating your dog or cat with Wesson Vegetable Oil drowns any fleas infesting the animal's skin. Wash out the oil with Dawn Dishwashing Liquid, famous for cutting through grease.

For Dogs Only

- **McCormick Pure Lemon Extract.** Mix one teaspoon McCormick Pure Lemon Extract and two cups water in a sixteen-ounce trigger-spray bottle, and then saturate your dog with the lemony solution, brushing her coat so the mixture penetrates to the skin. Dry with a towel and give your pet a final brushing. The limonene from the extract kills both fleas and larvae. The lemon also helps heal fleabites. (Don't spray a cat with this solution. Cats detest citrus.)

For Cats Only

- **Kraft Real Mayo.** Rub Kraft Real Mayo into your cat's skin and fur, and then wipe her down with a damp towel. The cat will help clean the mayonnaise off herself by licking. The mayonnaise makes her coat shine, and fleas hate it.

Prevention

For Dogs and Cats

- **Heinz Apple Cider Vinegar.** According to the Vinegar Institute, adding one-half teaspoon Heinz Apple Cider Vinegar for every two cups of your pet's drinking water will keep a dog or cat free of fleas.

- **Lewis Lab's Brewer's Yeast.** Some dog experts claim that sprinkling brewer's yeast into a dog's food on a daily basis causes the animal to emit an odor (undetectable by humans) that repels fleas. The active ingredient in brewer's yeast? Vitamin B_1 (also known as thiamin). For cats, rub Lewis Lab's Brewer's Yeast into your cat's coat. Once the cat grooms her fur and acquires a taste for brewer's yeast, place one-half teaspoon on the side of her food bowl.

- **Lipton Chamomile Tea Bags.** To stop fleas from infesting your dog or cat, place a few Lipton Chamomile Tea Bags in the doghouse or around your cat's bedding. Chamomile repels fleas.

- **McCormick Garlic Powder.** Many people swear by garlic as a flea repellent. To try this, sprinkle your dog or cat's food with McCormick Garlic Powder every day. Supposedly the resulting scent released from your dog's skin repels fleas. To date, studies do not corroborate this anecdotal tip.

- **McCormick Rosemary Leaves.** Combine one teaspoon McCormick Rosemary Leaves and two cups boiling water and steep for ten minutes in a covered pot. Strain out the rosemary leaves and let cool to body temperature. After giving your pet a bath and final rinse, pour the rosemary solution over your pet, rub into her skin, and towel dry. This rosemary tea conditions your pet's coat and helps prevent fleas.

PET PEEVES

WELCOME TO THE FLEA CIRCUS

- Adult fleas live up to four months, during which time the females continuously lay tiny white eggs on your pet. The eggs fall off your pet and hatch, releasing larvae that live in cracks and crevices for up to two weeks, go through a cocoon stage, and emerge one to two weeks later as small fleas that hop back aboard your pet to repeat the endless cycle all over again.

- To determine whether your pet has fleas, rub your hand across your pet's fur and look closely for small insects or small, black coma-shaped specs of flea excrement on the skin. Or place your pet on a sheet of white paper, and as you comb through the animal's hair with a flea comb, look for fleas or their black excrement on the paper.

- To rid your pet of fleas, you must also rid your house of fleas. Comb your pet with a flea comb to remove as many fleas and eggs as possible. Then bathe the animal. Simultaneously, run all your pet's bedding through the washing machine with hot water and your regular detergent. Vacuum the carpets, rugs, baseboards, and upholstered furniture to eliminate flea eggs, larvae, and pupae. Limit the number of rooms in your home where you pet can visit and get rid of any clutter on the floor where fleas can hide.

- Steam cleaning your carpets and mopping floors kill flea eggs.

- Although flea collars are the most popular form of protection against fleas, they are also the least effective. In fact, some pet experts insist that flea collars are completely useless.

- Coping with a severe flea infestation may require a professional exterminator and a visit to your veterinarian to dip your pet in a specially formulated insecticide.

- Never use flea sprays, powders, or dips meant for dogs on a cat. The formulation for dogs could sicken or poison your cat.

- If you're determined to use a flea collar on your pet, buy a collar containing a growth regulating hormone like methoprene that prevents flea larvae from reaching maturity and reproducing.

- Never use a flea collar and flea powder (or flea spray) simultaneously. You'll be giving your pet an overdose of insecticide.

- To get rid of fleas in your yard, buy a canister of nematodes at a gardening store, put them in a hose sprayer, and water the entire lawn. Nematodes are microscopic worms that feed on the larvae and pupae of fleas. Once the fleas are gone, the nematodes will disappear as well.

Pet Tricks
Ridding Your House of Fleas

- **Arm & Hammer Baking Soda.** Sprinkle Arm & Hammer Baking Soda liberally on your carpet, and then use a broom to rub the baking powder deep into the carpet. Let sit for forty-eight hours. Vacuum thoroughly. Remove the bag from your vacuum cleaner, place it in the freezer overnight (to ensure that the eggs cannot possibly hatch), and discard.

- **Concern Diatomaceous Earth.** The finely ground fossils of prehistoric fresh water diatoms, diatomaceous earth, kills fleas (and many other crawling insects) by absorbing the waxy coating on the insect. Wearing a dust mask and goggles, sprinkle the diatomaceous earth on carpeting and upholstered furniture, cracks and crevices in the floor, baseboards, and around pet bedding and sleeping areas. Let sit for forty-eight hours, and then vacuum clean. (Be sure to use amorphous diatomaceous earth, not glassified diatomaceous earth, which is used in swimming pool filters).

- **Dawn Dishwashing Liquid.** To kill fleas in carpeting, mix one tablespoon Dawn Dishwashing Liquid and two cups water in a sixteen-ounce trigger-spray bottle, shake well, and spray the carpet, upholstery, and floors. Let sit for fifteen minutes, and then blot the carpet, upholstery, and floors with a damp towel and vacuum the carpeting. Fleas have exoskeletons, meaning they wear their skeletons on the outside of their bodies. The soap penetrates the exoskeletons, killing the fleas almost instantly.

- **Dawn Dishwashing Liquid.** To trap fleas in your home, fill a shallow pan or dish with water and add a few drops of Dawn Dishwashing Liquid on the water surface. At night, place the pan in the middle of the room, and turn off all the lights except for one lamp suspended over the pan. The fleas, attracted by the light, jump into the water and drown in

- **Skin So Soft.** To prevent fleas on your dog or cat, rinse the animal with two ounces of Skin So Soft Bath Oil per gallon of water. Skin So Soft repels fleas and gives your pet a shiny coat. Skin So Soft Bath Oil will not harm your cat if she licks it off her fur. However, other Skin So Soft products that contain sunscreen may harm your cat if she licks her fur.

the soapy water. Normally, fleas can walk on water, but the detergent breaks the surface tension, causing them to sink. Keep the trap in place for two weeks to catch all the fleas and the next generation that hatch from eggs and spring from larvae.

- **Glad Trash Bags.** Vacuuming the carpets and upholstery and laundering your pet's bedding in hot, soapy water eliminates flea eggs, larvae, and pupae. After vacuuming, remove the bag from your vacuum cleaner, wrap it securely in a Glad Trash Bag, place it in the freezer overnight (to kill the fleas), and discard.

- **Hartz 2 in 1 Flea Collar.** Kill fleas sucked into your vacuum cleaner bag by placing a Hartz 2 in 1 Flea Collar inside the bag. The insecticide on the flea collar will poison any fleas sucked up into the bag.

- **Listerine.** Fill a spray bottle with Listerine antiseptic mouthwash and spray the carpets, upholstered furniture, and pet bedding. The antiseptic kills the fleas, and the eucalyptol in the Listerine prevents them from returning.

- **Lysol Disinfectant.** Spray the carpet and upholstery with Lysol disinfectant spray. The antiseptic kills fleas. Repeat the following day to kill any newly hatched fleas.

- **Morton Salt.** Sprinkle Morton Salt on carpets, let sit for at least three hours, and vacuum thoroughly. The salt dehydrates and kills the fleas.

- **Pine-Sol.** Pour one-quarter cup Pine-Sol into a sixteen-ounce trigger-spray bottle, fill the rest of the bottle with water, shake well, and spray the soapy liquid on your carpets and upholstered furniture. Pine-Sol kills fleas and simultaneously deodorizes pet odors.

For Dogs Only

- **Morton Salt.** To repel fleas from a doghouse, sprinkle Morton Salt into the cracks and crevices inside the doghouse. Or dissolve two tablespoons Morton Salt in two cups water in a sixteen-ounce trigger-spray bottle and spray the inside of the doghouse with the salt water. Salt dehydrates fleas.

Furniture

For Dogs and Cats

- **Glad Trash Bags.** To keep your dog or cat off the furniture, cut open a Glad Trash Bag along the seams and cover your furniture with the plastic. Dogs and cats despise the feeling of plastic and stay away.

- **L'eggs Sheer Energy Panty Hose.** To remove pet hair from furniture, ball up a clean, used pair of L'eggs Sheer Energy Panty Hose and wipe down the furniture. The static cling in the nylon lifts pet hair from furniture. For more ways to remove pet hair, see page 242.

- **McCormick Black Pepper.** To keep your dog or cat off the couch or any furniture, sprinkle McCormick Black Pepper on the surface. Dogs and cats have a keen sense of smell, and the unpleasant scent of pepper will shoo them away.

- **Reynolds Wrap.** To prevent your dog or cat from sleeping on your sofa or comfy chairs, place a sheet of Reynolds Wrap aluminum foil across the cushions. The rustling sound will frighten your pet away and help break the habit.

- **Scotchgard.** If you allow your dog or cat on the furniture, treat your upholstered furniture with Scotchgard Fabric Protector to protect it from any unforeseen accidents.

- **Tabasco Pepper Sauce.** To prevent cats and dogs from scratching dark woodwork, rub the area with Tabasco Pepper Sauce and buff thoroughly. The faint smell of Tabasco Pepper Sauce repels cats and dogs.

For Cats Only

- **Bounce.** To keep cats off furniture, rub a sheet of Bounce (Outdoor Fresh) over the upholstery. The fragrance in Bounce (Outdoor Fresh) is oleander, which is a natural cat repellent.

PET PEEVES
BEING PART OF THE FURNITURE

- To train your dog or cat to cease jumping on tabletops, countertops, beds, and other furniture, use a water pistol or spray bottle to gently squirt your dog or cat with water whenever you see it walking, sitting, or lying on forbidden turf. Eventually, she'll get the idea.

- The only way to keep your pet off the furniture is to consistently forbid her to sit on the furniture, chasing her off anytime you catch her.

- To discourage cats from climbing on kitchen countertops, stack some clean, empty aluminum cans at the edge of the counter. When the cat leaps up, the loud crash of cans will teach the cat to avoid jumping up the counter again.

- Be sure to train your cat to stay off your stove—to avoid unforeseen accidents.

- To vacuum pet hair from furniture, use an attachment with a stiff bristle brush.

- Allowing your dog or cat to lie on your bed can infect your bed with fleas, mites, ringworm, ticks, and any other diseases your pet may contract.

- **Country Time Lemonade.** Dissolve one-half teaspoon Country Time Lemonade Drink Mix and two cups rubbing (isopropyl) alcohol in a sixteen-ounce trigger-spray bottle. Spray the solution on whatever furniture the cat loves scratching or sitting on. Cats despise the smell of lemon and will stay away from that piece of furniture.

- **Heinz Chili Sauce.** Here's a spicy way to stop your cat from scratching furniture. Rub wooden furniture legs with Heinz Chili Sauce, and then wipe it off. Cats can't stand the stuff.

- **Heinz White Vinegar.** To discourage a cat from sitting on furniture, scratching upholstery, or even sitting on a windowsill or countertop, spray the area with Heinz White Vinegar. (Be sure to test the vinegar on an inconspicuous spot on any fabric or carpet for colorfastness.) Or any time the cat approaches that forbidden area, gently dab a cotton ball dampened with Heinz White Vinegar on your cat's lips to teach her to stay off that piece of furniture. Place the wet cotton ball on a saucer on the item as added discouragement.

- **McCormick Pure Lemon Extract.** To dissuade your cat from climbing or lying on any piece of furniture, saturate a cotton ball with McCormick Pure Lemon Extract and rub it on the object. The smell of lemon repulses cats. Repeat once a week until you're satisfied that your cat has gotten the message.

- **Old Spice Aftershave Lotion.** To deter a cat from sharpening its claws on furniture, pour a few drops of Old Spice Aftershave Lotion into the palm of your hand and rub it on the wood or upholstery. The smell repels cats.

- **ReaLemon.** To keep your cat off furniture, any time the cat goes where she shouldn't be, touch her lips lightly with a cotton ball dampened with ReaLemon lemon juice and leave the cotton ball sitting on the off-limits furniture (on a small piece of aluminum foil to avoid any stains).

- **Saran Wrap.** Cats hate plastic coverings. Cover your chair or sofa with Saran Wrap until your cat learns to stay off.

- **Scotch Double Sided Tape.** Cats despise double-side tape. Adhere a few strips to your sofa or any furniture that you don't want the cat using as a bed. The cat will quickly learn to go elsewhere.

PET PROJECTS
SET SAIL WITH OLD SPICE

Old Spice, the world's best-selling men's fragrance, was originally a perfume for women. The Shulton Company, founded in 1934 by William Lightfoot Shultz, created Early American Old Spice in 1937 and soon after starting making products for men, featuring the famous colonial sailing ship on the bottle. By the end of 1938, sales hit $982,000.

In keeping with the aftershave's nautical theme, the Old Spice bottle, originally made from pottery, was made to look like buoys out at sea. The original ships depicted on the bottle were the *Friendship* and the *Grand Turk*. Other ships used on Old Spice packaging include the *Birmingham, Salem Wesley,* and *Hamilton.*

During World War II, American soldiers, needing to protect their skin from infection after shaving on the battlefield, were issued Old Spice Aftershave. When they returned home, many former GIs continued using Old Spice.

The famous Old Spice bottle, now made of plastic, retains its original shape, as a beacon of consistency in an ever-changing world. In 1990, Procter & Gamble bought the Old Spice brand from the Shulton Company.

Garbage Cans

For Dogs and Cats

- **Clorox Bleach.** To make indoor garbage cans less enticing to pets, disinfect and deodorize the pail to minimize odors. Wash the trashcans with a solution made from three-quarter cup Clorox Bleach to one gallon water. Let stand for five minutes, rinse clean, and dry in the sun.

- **L'eggs Sheer Energy Panty Hose.** If your outdoor garbage cans have handles on the sides, you can stop a dog, cat, raccoon, or squirrel from opening the lids by using a clean, used pair of Legg's Sheer Energy Panty Hose like a bungee cord to secure the lid in place by tying the ends of each leg to an opposite handle.

- **Listerine.** To disinfect and deodorize indoor garbage cans to minimize odors and make them less alluring to pets, fill a trigger-spray bottle with equal parts Listerine antiseptic mouthwash and water, shake well, and spray the inside of the garbage pail. Let sit for ten minutes, rinse clean, and dry in the sun. The antiseptic kills odor-causing germs and bacteria.

- **McCormick Black Pepper.** To keep dogs and cats out of your outdoor garbage cans, sprinkle McCormick Black Pepper around the containers. These animals have a keen sense of smell. They catch a whiff of the pepper and take off for someone else's garbage cans.

- **McCormick Ground (Cayenne) Red Pepper.** If black pepper doesn't do the trick, crank it up a notch by sprinkling McCormick Ground (Cayenne) Red Pepper around the garbage cans.

For Dogs Only

- **Jif Peanut Butter, Wonder Bread, *USA Today,* and Tabasco Pepper Sauce.** To train your dog to stay out of the kitchen garbage pail, make a sandwich using Jif Peanut Butter and Wonder Bread and place it in the garbage pail under a few sheets of *USA Today*. Sprinkle the newspaper with Tabasco Pepper Sauce. When your pet sticks his nose into the garbage, the smell or taste of the Tabasco Pepper Sauce will help train him to cease looking in the garbage can. To make sure your pet gets the message, booby-trap the garbage can several times a day for two weeks.

PET PEEVES
TALKING TRASH

- To keep dogs and cats out of your garbage cans, keep your garbage cans inaccessible to pets, seal the garbage cans securely, and never leave filled garbage bags unprotected.

- Pets that knock over garbage cans and scavenge through the trash happen upon broken glass, chicken bones, dead light bulbs, empty containers of poisonous chemicals, jagged can lids, and a host of other potential dangers.

- If necessary, mount garbage cans so a pet can't knock them over.

- Dogs can quickly figure out how to open a garbage can with a lid activated by a step pedal.

- To dissuade your pet from scavenging through the garbage, wrap any smelly foods in plastic before disposing of them and take out the garbage before any foods begin to rot, creating an aroma irresistible to animals.

- To keep your dog or cat (or any neighborhood animal) out of your outdoor garbage cans, mount the garbage cans to a wall, suspend them from the ceiling, or surround your garbage area with a five-foot-tall wire fence with an access gate.

- If you're required to put out your garbage in plastic bags for collection, double-bag your garbage to foil neighborhood dogs and cats.

Gates and Doors

For Dogs and Cats

- **Land O Lakes Butter.** To train your dog or cat to use a pet door, put a dab of Land O Lakes Butter on the bottom edge of the flap, stand on the other side of the door with some treats, and encourage your pet to come to you.

- **Oral-B Dental Floss.** If you're determined to teach your dog or cat to use a pet door, tie a three-foot length of Oral-B Dental Floss to one of your pet's toys and drag the toy through the pet door, encouraging your pet to chase after it.

- **Scotch Packaging Tape.** Another way to help your dog or cat figure out how to use a pet door is to use Scotch Packaging Tape to secure the flap up for a few days. This will get your pet used to the idea of exiting and entering as he pleases. Make sure the raised flap is secure so your pet doesn't get hit unexpectedly by a falling flap.

- **Velcro.** Adhere strips of Velcro along the rims of the pet door, so when your pet enter or leaves the house, it brushes against the Velcro strips, which conveniently groom any loose hairs from its coat—saving you the effort.

PET PEEVES
GETTING A FOOT IN THE DOOR

- Pet doors with plastic flaps that your pet can push open to get into and out of the house on her own can also be used by animals living in the wild, like raccoons, opossums, skunks, rabbits—and neighbors' unleashed pets. And you never know when your cat might bring a maimed rodent or bird inside your home.

- Use a playpen that your child has outgrown as a pet corral.

- To create a durable entrance flap for a doghouse, staple a vinyl floor mat in place and cut a vertical slit in the middle of it. Guide your dog through the flap a few times to teach him how to use it.

- By installing a pet door in the interior door to the room that houses your cat's litter box, you can prevent dogs (larger than the pet door opener) from getting into the litter box.

- Pet doors don't have to lead only to the backyard. You can also install a pet door from your house to a screened porch.

Grooming

Brushing and Combing

For Dogs and Cats

- **Alberto VO5 Conditioning Hairdressing.** To detangle and shine a dog or cat's coat (and tame any static electricity), comb in a small amount of Alberto VO5 Conditioning Hairdressing. (Don't worry if your pet licks her fur; Alberto VO5 Conditioning Hairdressing is natural and nontoxic.)

- **Dustbuster.** Use a Dustbuster with a brush attachment to vacuum shedding hair from your dog or cat (unless the noise from the hand-held vacuum frightens your pet). Many pets love the sensation, which doubles as a massage. To train your pet to tolerate the Dustbuster, first stroke your pet with the Dustbuster turned off, offering constant praise and reassurance. On a second occasion, turn the Dustbuster on, but do not touch your pet with it, again extolling and encouraging the animal. At a later time, once your pet has grown accustomed to the Dustbuster, vacuum the animal's coat.

- **Heinz White Vinegar.** To give your dog or cat a shiny coat, mix three ounces Heinz White Vinegar and twelve ounces water in a sixteen-ounce trigger-spray bottle and mist the solution on your dog.

- **Huggies Baby Wipes.** Wipe down your dog or cat's coat with a hypoallergenic, fragrance-free Huggies Baby Wipe to pick up shedding hair.

- **Johnson's Baby Powder.** Before brushing a longhaired dog or cat, sprinkle Johnson's Baby Powder into her coat, rub it in, and then brush it off immediately. The talcum powder helps the brush glide through the hairs and prevents matting.

- **Ziploc Freezer Bags.** Store your pet's grooming supplies in a Ziploc Freezer Bag.

For Dogs Only

- **Bounce.** To eliminate static electricity, rub a sheet of Bounce fabric softener on your dog's fur before brushing your pet.

Coats

For Dogs and Cats

- **Lewis Lab's Brewer's Yeast.** To give your pet's coat a stunning shine, add two or three tablespoons of Lewis Lab's Brewer's Yeast to her diet every day.

- **Star Olive Oil.** To add a gleam to your dog or cat's coat, add a teaspoon of Star Olive Oil to each food serving.

- **Wesson Corn Oil.** Make your dog or cat's coat shimmer by simply adding a teaspoon of Wesson Corn Oil to each food serving.

Dander

For Dogs and Cats

- **Downy Fabric Softener.** To reduce dander, add a capful of Downy Fabric Softener to the bath water when bathing your pet.

- **Huggies Baby Wipes.** Wipe down your pet daily with some hypoallergenic, fragrance free Huggies Baby Wipes to lessen dander.

- **Johnson's Baby Shampoo.** Bathing your pet with Johnson's Baby Shampoo decreases the amount of dander.

Deodorizing

For Dogs Only

- **Bounce.** Rub a sheet of Bounce over your dog's coat to make him smell fresh and dodge bathing him as often. For more ways to deodorize a dog, see page 13.

Drying

For Dogs and Cats

- **ConAir 1875 Watt Dryer.** After toweling your dog or cat after a bath or a rainstorm, use the warm dry air from a ConAir 1875 Watt blow dryer on a low setting to dry your pet. Hold the nozzle six inches away from your pet, and gently move it around. (Do not aim the dryer at your pet's face.)

Grooming Gloves

For Dogs and Cats

- **Playtex Living Gloves.** To remove shedding pet hair from your dog or cat, put on a pair of Playtex Living Gloves, fill a bucket with water, dip the gloves in the water, and run your fingers and palms along the fur to allow the rubber to collect shedding hair. Dip the hair-covered gloves in the water again. The wet rubber attracts the pet hair, and the water in the bucket rinses it off.

Pet Tricks
Dirty Brushes

- **Arm & Hammer Baking Soda.** To clean pet brushes and combs, dissolve four tablespoons of Arm & Hammer Baking Soda in a glass of warm water and soak the brushes and combs in the alkaline solution for thirty minutes. Then rinse clean.

- **Forster Toothpicks.** To pluck out the hairs from a dog or cat brush, run a Forster Toothpick through the rows of bristles.

- **Heinz White Vinegar.** To clean pet brushes or combs, mix equal parts Heinz White Vinegar and water and soak the brushes or combs in the liquid overnight. In the morning, dry the items with a soft, clean rag.

- **Parsons' Ammonia.** Add three teaspoons Parsons' Ammonia to two cups warm water, soak dirty pet brushes and combs in the solution for thirty minutes, rinse well, and let air-dry.

- **Shout.** Spray dirty pet brushes and combs with Shout stain remover and wash them along with your pet's bedding with your regular detergent in the washing machine. Make sure you remove the brushes and combs before moving any wet items to the dryer.

- **20 Mule Team Borax** and **Dawn Dishwashing Liquid.** Mix one tablespoon 20 Mule Team Borax, one tablespoon Dawn Dishwashing Liquid, and two cups water and soak dirty pet brushes and combs in the solution. Rinse thoroughly with clean water and let air-dry.

Gum

For Dogs or Cats

- **Dawn Dishwashing Liquid.** If your dog or cat gets bubble gum stuck to his paw or fur, you can use a few drops of Dawn Dishwashing Liquid to dissolve it.

- **Jif Peanut Butter.** Rub a dollop of creamy Jif Peanut Butter into the wad of chewing gum stuck in your pet's fur, working it in well, and then comb out the gum. The oils in the peanut butter dissolve the chewing gum.

- **Johnson's Baby Oil.** Pour a few drops of Johnson's Baby Oil into the gum and massage it with your fingers. The mineral oil dissolves the gum, making it easy to comb out of fur. Use soapy water to clean the baby oil from the fur.

- **Miracle Whip.** Rub a dollop of Miracle Whip into the gum, let sit for a few minutes to let the oil dissolve the gum, and comb free. Wash with soapy water and rinse clean.

- **Noxzema.** To remove chewing gum from fur, rub a dollop of Noxzema Deep Cleansing Cream into the gum, and then comb through the hair gently. Wash with soapy water to remove the cold cream from the fur, and then rinse clean.

- **Pam Cooking Spray.** Apply a quick spritz of Pam Cooking Spray to the lump of chewing gum, rub it into the gum, and comb it out.

- **Skin So Soft.** Rub a dollop of Skin So Soft Body Lotion into the chewing gum, and then comb out the dissolved substance.

- **Spray 'n Wash.** Spray the chewing gum liberally with Spray 'n Wash, rub the liquid into the gum, and then comb from the fur. Wash thoroughly with soapy water, and then rinse thoroughly clean.

- **Star Olive Oil.** To get gum out of hair, saturate the gum with Star Olive Oil, rub with your fingers to soften the gum, and comb out. Shampoo hair and rinse.

- **Vaseline Petroleum Jelly** and **Dawn Dishwashing Liquid.** Apply a dollop of Vaseline Petroleum Jelly to the wad of gum and work it in with your fingers until the gum slides off. To remove the petroleum jelly from pet fur, wash gently with a soapy solution made from a few drops of Dawn Dishwashing Liquid in one cup of water. Rinse clean.

- **Wesson Vegetable Oil.** Put a few drops of Wesson Corn Oil over the wad of chewing gum, work it into the gum with your fingers, and then comb free. Wash with soapy water, and then rinse clean.

Mats, Tangles, and Knots

For Dogs or Cats

- **Alberto VO5 Conditioning Hairdressing.** To detangle mats, tangles, or knots in a dog or cat's coat, comb in a small amount of Alberto VO5 Conditioning Hairdressing. (Don't worry if your pet licks its fur; Alberto VO5 Conditioning Hairdressing is natural and nontoxic.)

- **Johnson's No More Tangles.** To free mats from your pet's hair, spray the affected area with Johnson's No More Tangles, try to work the knotted hair free with your fingers, and then comb. Formulated for babies and toddlers, Johnson's No More Tangles is safe to use on your pet.

- **Kingsford's Corn Starch.** To untangle your pet's matted hair, sprinkle the mats with Kingsford's Corn Starch, and then work the mat apart with your fingers, eventually running a comb through the hair. The cornstarch makes the hairs glide free from the mat. Add more cornstarch as needed.

- **Lubriderm.** Rub a few drops of Lubriderm moisturizing lotion into any unmanageable snarl. Lubriderm contains lanolin, the fatty substance found on sheep's wool, which will help free the tangled hairs from the mat.

- **Velcro.** Adhere strips of Velcro along the rims of the pet door, so when your pet enter or leaves the house, it brushes against the Velcro strips, which conveniently groom any loose hairs from its coat—saving you the effort.

For Dogs Only

- **Downy Fabric Softener.** If your dog's fur tangles when wet, mix one capful of Downy Fabric Softener in one-half gallon of water and use as a final rinse when bathing your dog. Rinse your pet again after applying the Downy Fabric Softener. This treatment leaves your pet's coat feeling soft and smelling fresh.

- **Johnson's Baby Powder.** You can untangle your pet's matted hair by dusting the mats with Johnson's Baby Powder. Work the mat apart with your fingers until you can run a comb through the hair. The talcum powder makes the hair glide free from the mat.

Sap

For Dogs and Cats

- **Crisco All-Vegetable Shortening.** If your pet gets sap stuck to her coat, rub a dab of Crisco All-Vegetable Shortening into the sticky mess, wipe clean with a cloth, and wash with soapy water. The vegetable shortening dissolves the gums in the sap.

- **Jif Peanut Butter.** To remove tree sap from your dog or cat's fur, rub Jif Peanut Butter into the sap to dissolve the gums, and then comb it out. The dog or cat will gladly lick off the remaining peanut butter.

- **Miracle Whip.** Rubbing a dollop of Miracle Whip into the tree sap on your pet's coat dissolves the sticky mess. Wipe clean with a cloth.

- **Star Olive Oil.** To clean sap or pine pitch from your pet's fur, rub a few drops of the Star Olive Oil into the affected area. The oil magically melts the sap, letting you comb it right out. Wash clean with soapy water.

Silly Putty

For Dogs and Cats

- **De-Solv-It.** To remove Silly Putty from a dog or cat's fur, spray some De-Solv-It (Citrus Solution)—the non-toxic, biodegradable, and organic degreaser used to clean up the Valdez oil spill without hurting the environment—into the Silly Putty. Comb out the Silly Putty and rinse clean.

- **Jif Peanut Butter.** Rub a dollop of Jif Peanut Butter into the Silly Putty, let sit for a few minutes, and then comb out the resulting gooey mess. The oils in the peanut butter dissolve the Silly Putty. Wash with soapy water and rinse clean.

- **Pam Cooking Spray.** Comb out as much Silly Putty as possible, and then spray the remaining mess with Pam Cooking Spray. Let sit for a few minutes to allow the vegetable oil to dissolve the Silly Putty, and then comb out the mess. Wash with soapy water and rinse clean.

- **Purell Instant Hand Sanitizer.** Squirt some Purell Instant Hand Sanitizer into the Silly Putty, work it in as best you can, and then use a comb to free it from the fur. Use soap and water to wash out any residue and rinse clean.

- **Miracle Whip.** Rub a dollop of Miracle Whip into the Silly Putty, let sit for a few minutes to allow the oils to penetrate the putty, and then comb free. Wash with soapy water and rinse clean.

- **Wesson Vegetable Oil.** Add a few drops of Wesson Vegetable Oil to the fur laden with Silly Putty, work it in with your fingers, and run a comb through the affected fur. Wash with soapy water and rinse clean.

Static Electricity

For Dogs Only

- **Bounce.** To eliminate static electricity from your dog's fur before brushing, rub down your pet with a clean, used sheet of Bounce. The antistatic agent in the fabric softener sheet adds a conducting surface layer that evenly distributes any excess electrical charge.

Tar

For Dogs or Cats

- **Johnson's Baby Oil.** To remove sticky road tar from your dog or cat's fur, saturate the area with Johnson's Baby Oil, let sit for fifteen minutes, wipe with a rag, and then wash clean with warm water and shampoo. Rinse thoroughly.

- **Vaseline Petroleum Jelly** and **Dawn Dishwashing Liquid.** Apply a dollop of Vaseline Petroleum Jelly to the tar, work it in with your fingers, let sit for fifteen minutes, and wipe clean with a rag. To remove the petroleum jelly from pet fur, wash gently a soapy solution made from a few drops of Dawn Dishwashing Liquid in one cup water. Rinse clean.

- **Wesson Corn Oil.** To remove tar from your dog or cat's fur, saturate the affected area on your dog's coat with Wesson Corn Oil, let sit for fifteen minutes (distracting your dog so he doesn't lick the oil), apply a few drops of dog shampoo and lather. Rinse clean immediately.

PET PEEVES

BRUSHING UP

- Get your dog or cat used to regular brushing as young as possible. Talk and play with your pet and praise the animal during grooming sessions to make the experience pleasurable and desirable.

- Brush your cat in the direction the fur grows, not against the grain, which may agitate the animal.

- Cracking a raw egg over your dog's food every once in a while will help give your pet a shiny coat.

- Cats groom themselves to improve the ability of the fur to insulate, distribute the oils from his skin to improve waterproofing, nibble free any mats or tangles, spread their scents across their entire bodies, and control parasites.

- All cats groom themselves in the same order, starting by wetting their paws to wash their faces, and then licking their front legs, shoulders, and sides, followed by their genitals, hind legs, and tails (starting with the base and working to the tip).

- Grooming your cat removes shedding hair, reduces hairballs and odors, helps you bond with your pet and detect early signs of illness, and reduces dander that triggers allergic reactions in people.

- Never trim a cat's whiskers. Cats use their whiskers to sense tight spaces and discern the directional source of odors.

Hairballs

For Cats Only

- **Alberto VO5 Conditioning Hairdressing.** To prevent cat hairballs (and also static electricity on your cat's coat), rub in a dab of Alberto VO5 Conditioning Hairdressing and brush. (Don't worry if your cat licks her fur; Albert VO5 Conditioning Hairdressing is natural and nontoxic.)

- **Chicken of the Sea Sardines.** To thwart hairballs, feed your cat one Chicken of the Sea Sardine each month. The fish oil keeps swallowed clumps of hair gliding through your cat's digestive system.

- **Chicken of the Sea Tuna.** When you open a can of Chicken of the Sea Tuna packed in oil, drain out some of the oil over your cat's food. The oil lubricates your cat's digestive tract, averting hairballs.

- **Hain Safflower Oil.** To prevent hairballs and lubricate your cat's innards, occasionally mix one teaspoon of Hain Safflower Oil into your cat's food (unless your cat is obese).

- **Huggies Baby Wipes.** After grooming your cat to remove shedding hair that she might otherwise swallow, wipe down your cat's coat with a hypoallergenic, fragrance-free Huggies Baby Wipe to remove any loose hairs.

GET YOUR PET TO THE VET

Hair-raising! If your cat continues hacking and retching for more than three days, or if your cat doesn't eat for more than 24 hours and seems constipated, a hairball may be blocking the intestinal tract or about to cause choking. Take your cat to the veterinarian right away.

- **Land O Lakes Butter.** To stop a cat from expelling hairballs, add one-half to one teaspoon Land O Lakes Butter to the cat's food once a day for a week. The butter helps push the fur through the cat's digestive system, preventing hairballs from forming. The butter also makes the gallbladder contract and empty bile, a mild laxative, into the cat's digestive tract, speeding hairballs through the cat's inner workings.

- **Libby's Pumpkin.** To help hairballs pass through your cat's system, mix one or two tablespoons Libby's Canned Pumpkin to your pet's food each day. The natural fiber in pumpkin keeps your cat regular.

- **Metamucil.** To accelerate the passage of hairballs through your cat's system, mix one-half teaspoon of Metamucil with water and pour it on your small pet's food twice a day. The psyllium seed husks in this laxative absorb water into the stool, helping it pass through the intestines.

- **Post Grape-Nuts Flakes.** A high-fiber diet improves digestion, allowing hair to pass swiftly through your cat's digestive tract. To keep those hairballs moving along, give your pet one to three tablespoons of Post Grape-Nuts Flakes several times a day. Once the hairballs pass, continue sprinkling up to three tablespoons of Post Grape-Nuts Flakes on your pet's food. The fiber keeps the digestion tract lubricated, increasing your pet's ability to absorb nutrients.

- **Star Olive Oil.** To prevent your cat from vomiting up hairballs, add one teaspoon Star Olive Oil to your cat's food once a week. The oil lubricates the cat's digestive system, allowing the hairballs to glide through unnoticed.

- **Vaseline Petroleum Jelly.** To stop your cat from getting hairballs, place a dab of Vaseline Petroleum Jelly on one of the cat's paws. The cat will lick off the petroleum jelly, which lubricates her digestive track, allowing hairs to travel naturally out the proper end. Apply the petroleum jelly once a day for four days.

- **Wesson Corn Oil.** Another way to prevent hairballs? Add one teaspoon Wesson Corn Oil to your cat's food occasionally. The polyunsaturated oil also fortifies your cat with vitamins, lubricates the digestive tract, and helps prevent constipation.

PET PEEVES
BAD HAIR DAYS

- Cats get hairballs from licking their coats and swallowing hair, which accumulates in the stomach and eventually forms a wad. The accompanying discomfort prompts the cat to vomit up the hairball.

- To veterinarians, hairballs are called trichobezoars, from the suffix *tricho-*, meaning "pertaining to hair" and the word *bezoar,* meaning "a mass trapped in the gastrointestinal system."

- Brushing and combing your cat's fur on a daily basis removes shedding hairs, eliminating the possibility of your cat swallowing them and helping prevent the subsequent hairballs.

- Aside from the hairball remedies listed here, pet stores sell several tasty lubricants specifically to prevent hairballs.

- A cat infested with fleas tends to groom himself more frequently, swallowing more hair. To minimize the hairballs, treat the fleas.

- If your cat constantly grooms herself, play with your pet more often to reduce any stress she may be experiencing and distract her from compulsive licking.

Hamsters and Gerbils

Cages

- **Arm & Hammer Baking Soda.** To clean a hamster or gerbil terrarium, fill the tank with a half-inch of water, add two tablespoons Arm & Hammer Baking Soda, and using an abrasive sponge, scrub the bottom and sides. Rinse clean. The baking soda deodorizes the tank and makes the glass sparkle.

- **Bounty Paper Towels.** Give your hamster or gerbil plenty of digging and nesting material by adding a few shredded sheets of Bounty Paper Towel to the cage.

- **Dawn Dishwashing Liquid.** To clean your hamster or gerbil's domicile (at least once every six months), add a few drops of Dawn Dishwashing Liquid to a bucket of warm water and wash the cage and furnishings with the soapy liquid. Rinse clean with water, and then dry thoroughly.

- **Johnson & Johnson Cotton Balls.** Placing a handful of Johnson & Johnson Cotton Balls in the cage gives your hamster or gerbil warm, cozy material to use for building a nest.

- **Kleenex Tissues.** Provide your hamster or gerbil with shredded Kleenex Tissues to use as nesting material in the cage.

Constipation

- **Star Olive Oil.** Constipation can be caused by a lack of exercise or a lack of fresh fruits in your hamster or gerbil's diet. The signs of constipation? A distended belly, arching of the back, and lethargy. Use an eyedropper to feed the hamster a few drops of Star Olive Oil. The oil helps lubricate the digestive tract, and then introduce lettuce and fruits to the hamster's diet.

Escapees

- **Reynolds Cut-Rite Wax Paper** and **Kleenex Tissues.** To capture an escaped hamster or gerbil, place a piece of Reynolds Cut-Rite Wax Paper over the hole in the top of an empty Kleenex Tissues box, and place a piece of food on top of the wax paper. When your pet races for the food, he will drop into the box. Place a few crumpled-up tissues in the bottom of the box to cushion the animal's fall.

- **Sun-Maid Raisins.** To find an escaped hamster or gerbil in your home, place a handful of Sun-Maid Raisins in the center of every room in the house. You'll soon find your pet sitting in the middle of one of the rooms eating the treat.

Exercise Wheels

- **Pam Cooking Spray.** To lubricate a squeaky hamster or gerbil exercise wheel, spray the joint with Pam Cooking Spray. Even if the hamster licks off the oil, it won't hurt the critter because Pam Cooking Spray is simply non-toxic vegetable oil.

- **Wesson Vegetable Oil** and **Glad Flexible Straws.** If you don't have any Pam Cooking Spray, dip one end of a Glad Flexible Straw into Wesson Vegetable Oil, hold one finger over the opposite end of the straw, bring the open end of the straw to touch the axle of your hamster or gerbil exercise wheel, and then release your finger, allowing the oil to flow from the improvised eyedropper to lubricate the joint.

Food

- **Chicken of the Sea Tuna.** As a special treat, hamsters and gerbils love eating a half-teaspoon of Chicken of the Sea Tuna.

- **Dannon Yogurt.** To add protein to your hamster or gerbil's diet, feed the critter a teaspoon of fresh Dannon Yogurt mixed with fruit (at room temperature).

- **Kellogg's Corn Flakes.** An easily digestible food for hamsters and gerbils is Kellogg's Corn Flakes.

- **Milk-Bone Dog Biscuits.** Oddly, hamsters and gerbils love to gnaw on Milk-Bone Dog Biscuits. Give your hamster a small piece of a biscuit. Gnawing on the biscuit helps wear down the hamster's sharp teeth.

- **Sun-Maid Raisins.** Hamsters and gerbils love a treat like a few Sun-Maid Raisins fresh from the box.

- **Uncle Ben's Converted Brand Rice.** A teaspoon of cooked Uncle Ben's Converted Brand Rice makes an irresistible feast for a hamster or gerbil.

- **Wonder Bread.** Another delicacy for hamsters and gerbils is a piece of Wonder Bread.

Grooming

- **Oral-B Toothbrush.** Hamsters and gerbils groom themselves, but you can help your hamster remove excess cage bedding or litter from its coat by delicately brushing off the particles with a clean, used Oral-B Toothbrush.

Toys

- **Bounty Paper Towels.** Place an empty Bounty Paper Towel roll inside the cage as a hideaway that the hamster or gerbil can also gnaw on.

- **Charmin Toilet Paper.** An empty Charmin Toilet Paper roll placed inside the cage creates a perfect hideaway for your hamster or gerbil that satisfies her chewing impulses.

- **Cool Whip.** A clean, empty Cool Whip tub makes a great hiding place for a hamster or gerbil.

- **Elmer's Glue-All.** Use nontoxic Elmer's Glue-All to create mazes by connecting the ends of empty cardboard rolls (see Bounty Paper Towels and Charmin Toilet Paper on page 138) and empty cardboard boxes (see Kleenex Tissues below).

- **Huggies Baby Wipes.** Cut some holes in a clean, empty Huggies Baby Wipes container to make a shelter for your hamster or gerbil.

- **Kleenex Tissues.** Place an empty box of Kleenex Tissues in your hamster or gerbil's cage to create a popular hiding place for your pet. Or cut holes of various sizes in empty Kleenex Tissue boxes and glue the boxes together with nontoxic Elmer's Glue-All (see above), to create mazes for your hamster.

- **Maxwell House Coffee.** Place a clean, empty Maxwell House Coffee can on its side inside your hamster or gerbil's cage to create a grotto.

- **Quaker Oats.** A clean, empty Quaker Oats canister makes an excellent addition to your hamster or gerbil's habitat. Hamsters and gerbils love gnawing on the cardboard and hiding in the canister.

PET PEEVES

CREATURE COMFORTS

- The most popular hamster is the Syrian hamster. The most popular gerbil is the Mongolian gerbil.

- Hamsters are larger than gerbils and, unlike gerbils, lack tails. Gerbils, unlike mice, have hairy tails.

- Hamsters should be caged alone. Gerbils are social animals, so consider getting two gerbils of the same sex.

- Never use cat box filler as bedding for hamsters. The dust and chemical additives in cat box filler can cause skin and respiratory problems for hamsters.

- Native to the deserts of Mongolia and China, gerbils, like camels, can regulate water reserves in their bodies, requiring very little water on a daily basis.

- In captivity, hamsters live an average of two years. Gerbils live an average of four years.

- Hamsters are nocturnal, sleeping during the day. Gerbils are active during both the day and night.

- Hamsters tend to bite when awoken during the day.

- Hamsters frequently try to escape. Gerbils rarely attempt to flee.

- Avoid the temptation to use printed newspaper or shredded newspaper as bedding. The chemicals and ink in the paper can be toxic to hamsters and gerbils.

- Line the bottom of your hamster or gerbil's cage with aspen shavings, timothy hay, or commercial rodent bedding. Do not use pine or cedar chips, which emit fumes that can harm your pets.

- For your gerbil, select a exercise wheel without any openings that might accidentally injure his tail.

- Keep the temperature around 70 degrees Fahrenheit for your hamster or gerbil.

- Never pick up a gerbil by his tail or you risk pulling off the skin covering the tail.

- Never bathe a hamster or gerbil. These creatures groom themselves thoroughly, and bathing a hamster or gerbil creates extreme stress for the animal. Plus the chill from a simple bath can cause respiratory problems.

- Hamsters and gerbils love seeds and nuts, such as sunflower seeds. Although these seeds and nuts add diversity to their diet, seeds or nuts alone will lead to malnutrition, and being high in fat, can also lead to obesity.

- Clean your hamster or gerbil's cage at least once a week, removing the old shavings and replacing with fresh shavings.

- Change the water in your hamster or gerbil's water bottle every day and remove soiled bedding, droppings, and any uneaten food as well.

- To keep your hamster or gerbil safely confined while you clean his cage, place the rodent in the bathtub (with the drain closed, of course). The little fellow won't be able to scurry up the slippery sides of the tub.

- Never use plastic bowls or dishes for a hamster or gerbil. The rodent will gnaw the plastic and devour the bowl or dish.

- Do not subject your hamster or gerbil to direct sunlight for a great length of time. Too much sunlight could give the little fellow heatstroke. As nocturnal creatures, hamsters favor soft light.

Health Care

Acne

For Dogs and Cats

- **Fruit of the Earth Aloe Vera Gel.** If your dog or cat develops acne pimples on the chin or around the face, do not squeeze the pimples or apply acne medications formulated for people, which can worsen the problem for pets. Instead, soothe the pain by applying a thin coat of Fruit of the Earth Aloe Vera Gel to the affected area.

- **Ivory Soap.** Gently scrub your pet's face with Ivory Soap and a washcloth dampened with warm water to clean off bacteria and loosen any substance plugging up the oil glands. Rinse off the soap with warm water.

Anal Sacs

For Dogs and Cats

- **Bounty Paper Towels.** Before manually expressing fluids from your pet's anal sacs, have plenty of Bounty Paper Towels on hand to clean up the mess.

- **Huggies Baby Wipes.** Clean up the mess made by releasing the fluids from your pet's anal sacs with Huggies Baby Wipes.

- **Playtex Living Gloves.** Dogs and cats have anal sacs under the skin on both sides of the anus (at the four and eight o'clock positions for cats and at the five and seven o'clock position for dogs). These sacs discharge a pungent liquid that other dogs and cats find attractive (explaining why cats and dogs often sniff each other's behinds) and humans find repulsive. Certain breeds of dog experience difficulty with their anal sacs, which occasionally get clogged. Wearing a pair of Playtex Living Gloves, feel the skin on both sides of the anus. If the sac feels like a hard grape, gently press firmly on the outer sides of the "grapes," drawing outward, toward you, forcing the sacs to discharge the smelly grey matter. If you cannot empty the sacs, or if the discharge contains blood, pus, or a black paste, take your pet to the veterinarian immediately.

Anemia

For Dog and Cats

- **Geritol.** To help raise your pet's energy level, give you dog or cat a daily dose of Geritol, fortified with iron and B vitamins. Consult your veterinarian for the proper dosage for your particular pet.

Arthritis

For Dogs and Cats

- **Uncle Ben's Converted Brand Rice.** To soothe arthritis pain, fill a sock with uncooked Uncle Ben's Converted Brand Rice (not too compactly), tie a knot in the end, and heat it in the microwave for one minute. Place the warm sock directly over painful joints twice a day for fifteen minutes. The reusable heating pad conforms wherever applied, and the rice lasts inside the sock for years.

For Dogs Only

- **Bufferin.** To relieve arthritis pain, after mealtimes give your dog one-quarter of a 325-milligram tablet of Bufferin per ten pounds your dog weighs—twice a day. For instance, a 40-pound dog will require one tablet twice a day. Bufferin is aspirin buffered (with magnesium oxide) to maintain the pH of the aspirin and prevent stomach upset. (Do not give a cat aspirin without first consulting your veterinarian, because the dose of aspirin for a dog can kill a cat.)

Back Problems

For Dogs and Cats

- **Uncle Ben's Converted Brand Rice.** To soothe back pain and minor muscle stiffness, fill a sock with uncooked Uncle Ben's Converted Brand Rice (not too compactly), tie a knot in the end, and heat it in the microwave for one minute. Place the warm sock directly on the affected area and hold it in place for up to fifteen minutes three times a day. To keep your pet still, gently rub her ears. The heat can boost circulation and potentially speed up the healing process. The reusable heating pad conforms wherever applied, and the rice lasts inside the sock for years.

For Dogs Only

- **Bufferin.** To relieve mild back pain, after mealtimes give your dog one-quarter of a 325-milligram tablet of Bufferin per 10 pounds of dog twice a day. For instance, a 40-pound dog will require one tablet twice a day. Bufferin is aspirin buffered (with magnesium oxide) to maintain the pH of the aspirin and prevent stomach upset. (Do not give a cat aspirin without first consulting your veterinarian, because the dose of aspirin for a dog can kill a cat.)

Bladder Control

For Dogs Only

- **Pampers.** If your dog experiences incontinence and needs help staying dry, consider using disposable diapers. If you don't wish to spend extra money on pet diapers, use a pair of scissors to cut a small opening for the pet's tail about one inch below the waistline of the front of the diaper. Using masking tape, cover the edges of the cut opening to prevent seepage. Secure the disposable diaper on the pet backward for a better fit.

Broken Bones

For Dogs and Cats

- **USA Today** and **Scotch Packaging Tape.** Before transporting an animal with a broken bone to a veterinarian, muzzle the animal to avoid being bitten (see Muzzles on page 149) and, only if absolutely necessary, splint the leg. Roll up two copies of *USA Today* (or magazines) place one roll on opposite sides of the broken limb, roll a sheet of newspaper around the entire limb, and tape from top to bottom. Get the animal to the veterinarian immediately.

PET PROJECTS
SLINKY DOG

In 1952, seven years after the introduction of the Slinky, Helen Malsed, a homemaker living in Seattle, Washington, sent an idea to Richard and Betty James, the founders of James Industries, the company that manufactured the Slinky. Later that year, Slinky Dog appeared on toys store shelves across America. Slinky Dog was eventually discontinued, but reappeared after he made a strong supporting role in the 1995 Disney movie *Toy Story* and the 1999 Disney sequel *Toy Story 2*. The voice of Slinky Dog was provided by Jim Varney, better known as Ernest P. Worrell in the movies *Ernest Goes to Camp, Ernest Saves Christmas,* and *Ernest Goes to Jail.*

Coughing

For Dogs and Cats

- **Benadryl.** If your pet's coughing results from hay fever, ask your veterinarian to suggest the proper dosage of Benadryl to give your dog or cat. Expect to give your pet one to three milligrams of Benadryl for every pound she weighs. Benadryl contains the antihistamine diphenhydramine.

- **Robitussin Maximum Strength Cough Syrup.** To suppress a cough in a dog or cat, ask your veterinarian to suggest the proper dose of Robitussin Maximum Strength Cough Syrup for your pet. The active ingredient in Robitussin is dextomethorphan. Never give a pet any cough medicine that contains aspirin, acetaminophen, or ibuprofen, which can be dangerous for pets.

Electrical Cords

For Dogs and Cats

- **Con-Tact Paper.** To prevent your dog or cat from chewing through electrical cords and getting electrocuted, save the cardboard tubes from your wrapping paper (or buy thin cardboard mailing tubes), cover the unsightly cardboard with attractively designed Con-Tact paper, and run your electrical cords through the tubes.

- **Fels-Naptha Soap.** To prevent cats or dogs from chewing electrical cords and risking shocks or electrocution, rub the cords with Fels-Naptha Soap.

- **Scotch Packaging Tape.** To dog or cat from chewing through electrical wiring and getting a deadly shock, use a few strips of Scotch Packaging Tape to organize cables and extension cords together and secure them to the floor.

Fever

For Dogs and Cats

- **Bufferin.** To help lower your dog's fever, split a 325-milligram tablet of Bufferin into quarters and give your dog one-quarter of a tablet for every ten pounds of weight. Bufferin is aspirin buffered (with magnesium oxide) to maintain the pH of the aspirin and prevent stomach upset. (Do not give a cat aspirin without first consulting your veterinarian, because the dose of aspirin for a dog can kill a cat.) Be sure to consult your veterinarian before giving aspirin to your pet. Never give your pet ibuprofen (Advil) or acetaminophen (Tylenol) because either one can be lethal to cats and dogs.

- **Pampers.** Saturate a Pampers disposable diaper with cool water, allowing the super-absorbent polymer flakes inside the diaper to absorb as much liquid as possible. The super-absorbent polymer flakes in the Pampers hold three hundred times their weight in liquid, enabling you to wrap the water-logged diaper around your small dog or cat's body to lower your pet's fever.

Heart Problems

For Dogs and Cats

- **Bufferin.** To thin your pet's blood and reduce the chances of blood clots, which can cause heart attacks, split a 325-milligram tablet of Bufferin into quarters and give your dog one-quarter of a tablet for every ten pounds of weight on a regular basis. Bufferin is aspirin buffered (with magnesium oxide) to maintain the pH of the aspirin and prevent stomach upset. (Do not give a cat aspirin without first consulting your veterinarian, because the dose of aspirin for a dog can kill a cat.) Be sure to consult your veterinarian before giving aspirin to your pet. Never give your pet ibuprofen (Advil) or acetaminophen (Tylenol) because either one can be lethal to cats and dogs.

- **Chicken of the Sea Tuna.** Feeding Chicken of the Sea Tuna to your dog or cat several times a week provides omega-3 fatty acids, which studies suggest might lower blood pressure and reduce the incidence of blood clots, which can trigger heart attacks.

Hip Dysplasia

For Dogs Only

- **Bufferin.** To relieve the pain from hip dysplasia, split a 325-milligram tablet of Bufferin into quarters and give your dog one-quarter of a tablet for every ten pounds of weight—twice a day. Bufferin is aspirin buffered (with magnesium oxide) to maintain the pH of the aspirin and prevent stomach upset. Be sure to consult your veterinarian before giving aspirin to your pet. Never give your pet ibuprofen (Advil) or acetaminophen (Tylenol) because either one can be lethal to dogs.

- **Uncle Ben's Converted Brand Rice.** To ease the ache of hip dysplasia, fill a sock with uncooked Uncle Ben's Converted Brand Rice (not too compactly), tie a knot in the end, and heat it in the microwave for one minute. Place the warm sock directly over painful joints twice a day for fifteen minutes. The reusable heating pad conforms wherever applied, and the rice lasts inside the sock for years.

Hives

For Dogs and Cats

- **Benadryl.** To easy itchiness of hives, you can give your pet one to three milligrams of Benadryl for every pound your pet weighs. Consult your veterinarian for precise dosage for your particular pet. Diphenhydramine, the active ingredient in Benadryl, blocks the effects of histamine, a chemical released by the body that causes itching.

Muzzles

- **L'eggs Sheer Energy Panty Hose.** Before providing first aid to a wounded animal, muzzle the animal's mouth to avoid being bitten. If a muzzle is unavailable, use a clean, used pair of L'eggs Sheer Energy Panty Hose to create a makeshift muzzle and secure the jaws firmly closed. Do not cover the animal's nostrils and remove the impromptu muzzle if the pet experiences difficulty breathing, starts vomiting, or bleeds from the mouth.

Pain Relief

For Dogs and Cats

- **Bufferin.** To provide relieve for pain, split a 325-milligram tablet of Bufferin into quarters and give your dog one-quarter of a tablet for every ten pounds of weight. Bufferin is aspirin buffered (with magnesium oxide) to maintain the pH of the aspirin and prevent stomach upset. (Do not give a cat aspirin without first consulting your veterinarian, because the dose of aspirin for a dog can kill a cat.) Be sure to consult your veterinarian before giving aspirin to your pet. Never give your pet ibuprofen (Advil) or acetaminophen (Tylenol) which one can be lethal to cats and dogs.

Pink Eye

For Dogs and Cats

- **Bausch & Lomb Eye Relief.** Wash the surface of your pet's eyes with these artificial tears, which relieve irritation caused by conjunctivitis and clear away particles that may be triggering the problem.
- **Johnson & Johnson Cotton Balls.** If your dog or cat comes down with conjunctivitis, dampen a Johnson & Johnson Cotton Ball with lukewarm water and use it to gently wipe away the pus or tears from your pet's crusty eyelids. Repeat as often as necessary.

- **OCuSOFT Lid Scrub Original.** Although these pre-moistened pH-balanced eye scrub pads are made for humans, they work equally well on pets. Follow the directions on the box to clean the crusty buildup from your pet's eyelids.

Porcupine Quills

For Dogs and Cats

- **Betadine Solution.** If a porcupine quill skewers your dog or cat, put on a pair of thick leather gloves. Using a pair of needle-nose or blunt-nose piers, grasp the quill firmly close to the fur and remove the quill very slowly, allowing the flesh to release its grip on the barbs. To prevent the wound from getting infected, apply Betadine Solution. For more ways to treat a wound, see page 310.

Prostate Problems

For Dogs and Cats

- **Bufferin.** To provide relieve for prostate pain, split a 325-milligram tablet of Bufferin into quarters and give your dog one-quarter of a tablet for every ten pounds of weight. Bufferin is aspirin buffered (with magnesium oxide) to maintain the pH of the aspirin and prevent stomach upset. (Do not give a cat aspirin without first consulting your veterinarian, because the dose of aspirin for a dog can kill a cat.) Be sure to consult your veterinarian before giving aspirin to your pet. Never give your pet ibuprofen (Advil) or acetaminophen (Tylenol) because either one can be lethal to cats and dogs.

Roundworms

For Dogs Only

- **Purell Instant Hand Sanitizer.** To avoid becoming infected with roundworms, train your children to wash their hands with Purell Instant Hand

Sanitizer after playing with young puppies. Roundworms are common in puppies. However, by two to three months of age, most puppies begin to develop a strong immunity.

- **Ziploc Storage Bags.** Canine roundworms can be passed on to people and other dogs. To prevent other dogs from being contaminated, turn a Ziploc Storage Bag inside out, put your hand inside the bag like a glove, scoop up your dog's poop, pulling the bag right-side out again, seal shut, and discard.

Scratches and Abrasions

For Dogs and Cats

- **Bag Balm.** Quicken healing of cuts, scratches, skin irritations, and paw abrasions by rubbing on Bag Balm, the salve created to relieve cracking in cow udders.

Snakebites

For Dogs and Cats

- **Green Giant Sweet Peas.** If a snake bites your dog or cat, use a plastic bag of frozen Green Giant Sweet Peas as an icepack and take your pet to the veterinarian immediately. If the bag of peas feels too cold, wrap the bag in a sheet of paper towel. The sack of peas conforms to the contours of your pet's body, and you can refreeze the peas for future ice-pack use—just label the bag for ice-pack use only. If you want to eat the peas, cook them after they thaw the first time, never after refreezing.

Stomach Upset

For Dogs Only

- **Phillips' Milk of Magnesia.** To relieve stomach upset in dogs, give one teaspoon per five pounds of weight every six hours.

Ulcers

For Dogs and Cats

- **Bufferin.** If you dog or cat suffers from ulcers and your veterinarian prescribes aspirin, give your pet Bufferin with food so the aspirin won't aggravate the stomach lining. Bufferin is aspirin buffered (with magnesium oxide) to maintain the pH of the aspirin and prevent otherwise acidic aspirin from causing stomach upset. (Do not give a cat aspirin without first consulting your veterinarian, because the dose of aspirin for a dog can kill a cat.) Be sure to consult your veterinarian before giving aspirin to your pet. Never give your pet ibuprofen (Advil) or acetaminophen (Tylenol) because either one can be lethal to cats and dogs.

Urinary Tract Infections

For Dogs and Cats

- **Ocean Spray Cranberry Juice Cocktail.** To cure a urinary tract infection, pour an ounce of Ocean Spray Cranberry Juice Cocktail on your dog or cat's food. Cranberry juice boosts the acidity of urine, killing much of the bacteria and relieving pain from a urinary tract infection. Unfortunately, most pets do not like cranberry juice.

For Cats Only

- **Heinz White Vinegar.** To prevent bladder stones (also known as feline urinary calculi) in cats, add one teaspoon Heinz White Vinegar to your cat's water each day. The vinegar helps increase the acidity of urine, preventing stones from forming.

Worms

For Dogs and Cats

- **Kaopectate.** If your pet suffers from diarrhea from worms, use a turkey baster or oral syringe to give your pet one teaspoon of Kaopectate for every ten pounds your pet weighs two or three times a day. Hold your pet's head back, squirt the medicine toward the back of his throat, hold his mouth closed, and stroke his throat until he swallows. Be sure to consult your veterinarian for the precise dosage for your particular pet.

Yarn and String

For Cats Only

- **Vaseline Petroleum Jelly.** If your cat swallows yarn or string, put a dab of Vaseline Petroleum Jelly on her paw. Your cat will lick off the petroleum jelly, which will lubricate her digestive tract, helping the material to pass through her system. If your cat is hacking, choking, or vomiting from ingesting the yarn or string, take her to a veterinarian immediately.

PET PEEVES

TAKE GOOD CARE

- The first sign of sickness in a dog is usually seen in the animal's eyes. Be aware of any excessive discharge from the tear ducts, puffiness, redness, or a glazed look.

- Use a blanket as a stretcher for your pet. Place your dog or cat in the center of the blanket, and have two people each lift two corners of the blanket to carry the pet.

- If you live in a high-rise apartment building, don't let your cat walk out on the balcony or on windowsills. Cats commonly fall off balconies and out windows.

- Contrary to popular belief, you cannot determine a dog's health based on whether its nose is wet and cold.

- During the Middle Ages, Europeans considered cats evil and associated them with witchcraft and the devil. They killed hundreds of thousands of cats, which may have led to the huge increase in the rat population in Europe and the resulting spread of bubonic plague that killed a quarter of the European people in the fourteenth century.

- Contrary to popular belief, one dog year is not equal to seven human years. A one-year-old puppy has reached approximately the same stage of development as a fifteen-year-old human. A two-year-old puppy is roughly equivalent in development to a twenty-four-year-old human. After that, each dog year equals four human years. These numbers differ between breeds.

- Every United States president since Warren G. Harding has had a dog while in the White House, with the exception of Calvin Coolidge, who had two pet raccoons named Rebecca and Horace.

- Millie, the family dog owned by President George Bush while he lived in the White House, earned more money in 1991 than the president did. Millie is credited as the author of the book *Millie's Book: As Dictated to Barbara Bush*.

Heartworms

For Dogs and Cats

- **Easy Cheese.** If you have trouble getting your dog or cat to take heartworm pills, place the pill in the palm of your hand, smother it with Easy Cheese (from an aerosol can), and let your dog or cat lap up the cheese, oblivious to the fact that he has also consumed the pill.

- **Heinz Apple Cider Vinegar.** Mosquitoes spread heartworms, so eliminating swarms of mosquitoes lowers the possibility of infection. Fill a large bowl with Heinz Apple Cider Vinegar and set it outside. Mosquitoes, attracted by the sweet smell of the apple, drown in the vinegar.

- **Ivory Dishwashing Liquid.** One teaspoon of Ivory Dishwashing Liquid per gallon of water in rain barrels and other pools of still water kills any developing mosquito larvae.

- **Jif Peanut Butter.** If your dog or cat refuses to eat heartworm pills, put Jif Peanut Butter on a cracker and bury the pill in it. The pet, unable to separate the pill from the peanut butter, will devour the nightly snack.

- **Land O Lakes Butter.** If you're having difficulty getting a pill down your dog or cat's throat, coat the pill with Land O Lakes Butter so it slides down.

- **Pam Cooking Spray.** A bite from in infected mosquito passes parasitic heartworms to dogs and cats. You can reduce the risk of infection by reducing the mosquito population in your yard. Mosquito eggs, larvae, and pupae incubate in still water. Eliminating pools of still water helps reduce the proliferation of mosquitoes. If you can't drain pools of still water from fountains, birdbaths, or holes in large tree trunks, spray the water surface with a fine coat of Pam Cooking Spray. The vegetable oil smothers any developing mosquito larvae.

- **Philadelphia Cream Cheese.** To get your dog or cat to take heartworm pills, bury the pills in a spoonful of Philadelphia Cream Cheese and feed it to your pet.

- **Skin So Soft.** This bath oil also happens to double as the best mosquito repellent available, according to *Outdoor Life, Field and Stream,* and "Dear Abby." Put one tablespoon Skin So Soft Bath Oil in a sixteen-ounce trigger-spray bottle and fill with water. Shake well, and then spray on your pet to keep mosquitoes away.

- **Star Olive Oil.** To drive away the mosquitoes that spread heartworm, add a few drops of Star Olive Oil to the puddles of still water around your yard, until a fine film of oil coats the surface. The oil slick will smother any developing mosquito larvae.

- **Wesson Vegetable Oil.** Another nontoxic, biodegradable oil you can use to eradicate developing mosquito larvae in puddles of water around your yard is Wesson Vegetable Oil. Simply add a few drops to coat the water surface with a thin skin of oil.

GET YOUR PET TO THE VET

Don't eat your heart out! Heartworms cause coughing, rapid breathing, fatigue, and weight loss. If you notice these symptoms in your pet, take her to the veterinarian for immediate treatment.

PET PEEVES

HAVE A HEART

- Just like their name suggests, heartworms are parasitic worms living in the right side of the heart and the arteries of the lungs of dogs, cats, and other mammals. The disease can be fatal.

- Mosquitoes spread heartworms by taking blood from one infected animal and then biting another animal.

- The American Heartworm Society recommends year-round preventative heartworm medication by daily or monthly pills, monthly topical treatments, or a six-month inoculation. Have your pet tested for heartworms by a veterinarian before administering any heartworm medication. Giving preventative heartworm medication to an infected pet can imperil the animal.

- To prevent mosquitoes from getting into your home, install tight-fitting window and door screens.

- Heartworms can grow up to eleven inches long.

Heat

For Dogs and Cats

- **Pampers.** To protect a dog or cat in heat, use a pair of scissors to cut a small opening for the pet's tail about one inch below the waistline of the front of the diaper. Using masking tape, cover the edges of the cut opening to prevent leakage. Secure the disposable diaper on the pet backward for a better fit.

- **Vicks VapoRub.** To ward off unwelcome, prowling males eager to mate, rub a dab of Vicks VapoRub near your female dog or cat's tail. The pungent smell of eucalyptus and menthol mask the odor that attracts males. To calm a libidinous male dog, simply put a dab of Vicks VapoRub on his nose.

For Dogs Only

- **Gerber Baby Food.** To compensate for your dog's waning appetite during heat, entice her to eat and maintain her energy by feeding her Gerber Baby Food in such flavors as beef, chicken, or turkey. These special treats are sure to grab her attention.

- **Glad Trash Bags.** To keep your dog from leaving a bloody discharge on your sofa or other upholstered chairs, cut open a Glad Trash Bag along the seams and cover your furniture with the plastic. Dogs dislike the feeling of plastic and stay away.

- **Huggies Baby Wipes.** To reduce the odor that attracts male dogs, use a hypoallergenic Huggies Baby Wipe to regularly clean away any discharge.

- **Johnson's Baby Shampoo.** To hinder your dog from attracting lascivious males, use Johnson's Baby Shampoo to bathe your pet's posterior and hind legs on a daily basis, minimizing the luring odor.

- **Pampers.** During heat, which generally lasts about three weeks, a female dog produces a bloody discharge. To prevent your dog's discharge from messing up the carpet or furniture, use a pair of scissors to cut a small opening for your pet's tail about one inch below the waistline of the front of the diaper. Using masking tape, cover the edges of the cut opening to prevent leakage. Secure the disposable diaper on the pet backward for a better fit. Hypothetically, the disposable diaper also doubles as a cumbersome birth control device.

PET PEEVES

HOT TO TROT

- Female dogs go into heat for two to three weeks once every six months, and female cats go into heat for six to ten days once every three weeks from late winter to early fall.

- When in heat, female dogs become agitated, and female cats become loud and rambunctious. Both animals try everything possible to escape and attract noisy males. The best solution is to have your female pet spayed.

- Male dogs can smell the odor of a female dog in heat from three miles away. Male cats can detect a female cat in heat a mile away.

- If you haven't had your pet spayed and prefer to endure your pet in heat, give your pet additional attention: affection, grooming sessions, playtime, and treats.

- Playing soothing classical music, such as Mozart, Chopin, or Brahms, can calm pets in heat.

- While your dog or cat is in heat, keep the windows closed to prevent her scent from wafting outside and attracting noisy suitors.

- If your amorous dog discharges blood on the furniture or carpeting, or if your ardent cat starts spraying urine around the house, keep the libidinous pet isolated in a bathroom or crate until the unbridled passion subsides.

Horses

Bathing

- **Simple Green.** To bathe a horse, mix one cup Simple Green All-Purpose Cleaner and ten cups of water in a bucket. Wet the horse with water, and apply the solution with a cloth or soft scrub brush, working in sections so the Simple Green solution doesn't stay on the horse's skin for too long (and dry it out). Rinse the cleaned section thoroughly with water. (To treat stubborn stains, put a few drops of Simple Green on a damp cloth, rub the area, and rinse immediately.) When finished, rinse the horse with water and apply a coat conditioner. (Do not get the solution into the horse's eyes, nose, or mouth. If the solution does get in the horses eyes by accident, rinse and flush the eyes with cool water, lifting the upper and lower lids and rinsing for fifteen minutes. Also, do not leave buckets or puddles of Simple Green solution where horses or another animals might drink.)

Burrs

- **Johnson's Baby Oil.** To remove burrs from a horse's mane and tail, wear work gloves (to avoid getting pricked by the burrs), work Johnson's Baby

Oil into the affected areas, and pry the burrs loose. Shampoo the animal to remove the mineral oil.

- **WD-40.** To remove burrs from a horse's mane and tail, spray WD-40 on the burrs. The lubricant lets you slide out the burrs without tearing out the hair or having to cut it.

Chewing

- **McCormick Ground (Cayenne) Red Pepper and Vaseline Petroleum Jelly.** To prevent your horse from chewing wood in his stall, mix one ounce McCormick Ground (Cayenne) Red Pepper and the contents of a thirteen-ounce jar of Vaseline Petroleum Jelly. Paint this mixture on whatever wood your horse has been chewing. The cayenne pepper stops the horse in his tracks, and the mixture won't wash off in the rain.

Coat

- **Bounce.** To clean dust from a horse's coat before entering a show arena, wipe down the horse with a sheet of Bounce. The dryer sheet collects the dust from the horse.

- **Efferdent.** To clean yellow stains from the coat of a white horse, dissolve two Efferdent denture cleansing tablets in a glass of water and use the solution to scrub off the discoloration.

- **Heinz White Vinegar.** To give your horse a shiny coat, mix three ounces Heinz White Vinegar and twelve ounces water in a sixteen-ounce trigger-spray bottle and mist the solution on your horse.

- **Preparation H.** To prevent shaved horse hair from growing back white, apply Preparation H to the shaved skin of the horse every day.

- **Wesson Corn Oil.** To give a horse's coat a shine, add one-quarter cup Wesson Corn Oil to your horse's grain daily.

Flies

- **Bounce.** To repel flies from a horse, tie a sheet of Bounce to the brow band of the horse's bridle. The oleander fragrance in classic Bounce wards off insects.

- **Domino Sugar** and **Heinz White Vinegar.** To kill flies in a barn, fill a clean empty jar with one-quarter cup Domino Sugar, one-quarter cup Heinz White Vinegar, and three cups water. Punch large holes in the lid and set it where appropriate. The sugar water attracts the flies, and the vinegar kills them.

- **Heinz Apple Cider Vinegar.** Pour two ounces Heinz Apple Cider Vinegar into a sixteen-ounce trigger-spray bottle, fill the rest of the bottle with water, shake well, and spray the horse with this safe solution to shoo flies away.

- **Scope** and **Johnson's Baby Oil.** To keep flies off horses, mix equal parts Scope Original Mint Mouthwash with Johnson's Baby Oil in a sixteen-ounce trigger-spray bottle, and spray the minty solution on your horse.

- **Skin So Soft.** Mix four ounces Skin So Soft Bath Oil and twelve ounces water in a sixteen-ounce trigger-spray bottle. Shake well and spray liberally on your horse. This solution repels flies and simultaneously softens your horse's coat.

Hooves

- **Alberto VO5 Conditioning Hairdressing.** To give your horse's hooves a glimmering shine, rub in a dab of Alberto VO5 Conditioning Hairdressing.

- **Bag Balm.** To soften hardened, dry, pinched, or contracted horse hoofs and quarter cracks, rub in a few dabs of Bag Balm.

- **Pam Cooking Spray.** To prevent snow from sticking inside a horse's hooves, spray the bottom of the horse's hooves with Pam Cooking Spray before going for a ride in snow.

Injuries

- **Bag Balm.** To help heal small injuries or rash chapping on a horse, rub in a dab of Bag Balm.

Mane

- **Alberto VO5 Conditioning Hairdressing.** Detangle a horse's mane and tail by rubbing in a dollop of Alberto VO5 Conditioning Hairdressing before brushing.

Medicine

- **Grandma's Molasses.** To get your horse to swallow a paste wormer, dip the end of the syringe halfway into a jar of Grandma's Molasses. Open your horse's mouth and insert the syringe as if slipping in the bit and inject the paste swiftly, as far back on your horse's tongue as possible. Horses love molasses, which makes the process easier for you and more palatable to the horse.

Ringworm or Thrush

- **Clorox Bleach.** To relieve ringworm or thrush, mix one tablespoon Clorox Bleach and two quarts water and sponge the solution on the fungus-infected area. The mild bleach solution will kill the fungus.

Saddles

- **Alberto VO5 Conditioning Hairdressing.** To prevent a leather saddle from drying out, rub in a few dabs of Alberto VO5 Conditioning Hairdressing. The vital organic nutrients revitalize the leather.

- **Bag Balm.** If you experience saddle sores from horseback riding, rub a dab of Bag Balm on the tender area.

Supplies

- **Ziploc Freezer Bags.** To keep supplies in the stable organized, store brushes, powders, shampoos, hoof polish, and first aid kits in Ziploc Freezer Bags.

Swollen Legs

- **Saran Wrap.** To reduce swollen legs, paint them with liniment, and then wrap them lightly with Saran Wrap, causing the horse to sweat. Check your horse's skin for any reaction to this strong treatment before proceeding for a significant length of time.

Tack

- **Coca-Cola.** To clean rust off tack, pour a two-liter bottle of Coca-Cola into a bucket, soak the tack in the Coke for five minutes, and rinse clean with water. Coca-Cola removes rust.

Tail

- **Listerine.** To stop a horse from rubbing his tail, pour some Listerine antiseptic mouthwash in a spray bottle and saturate the horse's tailbone.

Ticks

- **Jif Peanut Butter.** To remove a tick from a horse, cover the tick with a thick glob of Jif Peanut Butter. The peanut butter suffocates the parasite, causing it to back out of the skin. (Do not let the horse lick off the peanut butter and swallow the tick.)

Warts

- **Oral-B Dental Floss.** To remove a wart from your horse's skin, tie off the wart tightly with a piece of Oral-B Dental Floss. The dental floss will strangulate the wart, causing it to fall off after roughly a week, typically without leaving a scar.

Wounds

- **Hydrogen Peroxide.** Disinfect a minor puncture wound by filling a turkey baster with one-half cup hydrogen peroxide and flushing the injury.

PET PEEVES

HORSING AROUND

- The horse is actually native to North America. The western horse (*Equus occidentalis*), roughly the size of a mustang and resembling the modern Burchell's zebra in build, inhabited North America as early as three million years ago during the Ice Age. Horses migrated to Europe, Asia, and Africa before becoming extinct in the western hemisphere 11,000 years ago. In the early sixteenth century, Europeans reintroduced horses to the Americas. Remains of more than two hundred western horses have been found in the La Brea Tar Pits in Los Angeles, California.

- Contrary to popular belief, Russian empress Catherine the Great was not crushed to death in 1796 when attendants lost their grip on ropes supporting a stallion in a truss that was being lowered on her with pulleys from the ceiling. In truth, the sixty-seven-year-old Catherine suffered a stroke while sitting on the toilet in the Winter Palace of Saint Petersburg and died in bed. There were no horses involved. Historians believe the horse myth originated among the French upper classes to defame the powerful, intelligent, witty, and strong-willed woman who expanded the Russian Empire. This vindictive rumor was based on Catherine's freely confessed sexual appetite for virile young men—primarily soldiers in the royal cavalry— and from her widely known skill as an equestrian.

- The Pony Express operated for less than nineteen months. Starting on April 3, 1860, Pony Express horseback riders relayed mail between St. Joseph, Missouri, and Sacramento, California, where a streamer ship brought it to San Francisco, covering 1,966 miles in less than ten days. A Pony Express rider would ride seventy-five miles to a station, where he would change horses. He would continue riding and changing horses at stations until he covered an average of 250 miles in one day. Roughly eighty riders and 400 horses traversed the Pony Express route, dotted by more than 190 stations. Established by John Butterfield, a founder of American Express, the Pony Express ceased operations on October 26, 1861, two days after the completion of the nation's first coast-to-coast telegraph line, which made the Pony Express obsolete.

Hot Spots

For Dogs and Cats

- **Betadine Solution.** To clean a hot spot (wet, red skin eruptions) and kill any bacteria, saturate a cotton ball with Betadine Solution and dab the area two or three times a day.

- **Cortaid.** Applying a thin coat of Cortaid to the hot spot twice a day helps reduce the swelling and relieve the irritation. Distract your pet to give the hydrocortisone cream enough time to penetrate the skin before your pet can lick it off. There's no need to be concerned if your pet licks off the cream later; ingesting a small amount of hydrocortisone cream is not detrimental to pets.

- **Dove Unscented Soap.** Keep the hot spot clean by washing it regularly with Dove Unscented Soap. This gentle soap eradicates any bacteria causing the problem.

- **Dr. Bronner's Unscented Pure Castile Soap.** Another great soap to use to clean a hot spot is Dr. Bronner's Unscented Pure Castile Soap. Keeping the hot spot clean by regularly washing the area kills whatever may be irritating the skin.

- **Fruit of the Earth Aloe Vera Gel.** Rubbing Fruit of the Earth Aloe Vera Gel into the hot spot relieves the pain, moisures the skin, and speeds healing.

- **Lipton Tea.** To relieve hot spots, saturate a Lipton Tea bag with cold water and hold it against the hot spot to provide relief. The tannic acid in the tea will help reduce secretions, dry the skin, and soothe any irritation. Or brew a strong cup of Lipton Tea, let cool to room temperature, and then wash the hot spot with the tea.

- **Murphy Oil Soap.** To clean a hot spot, use a few drops of Murphy Oil Soap and warm water. The mild vegetable oil–based soap works like an antiseptic, killing whatever creature or bacteria may be irritating the skin.

- **Nestea.** To expedite the healing of a hot spot, mix up a glass of Nestea ice tea according to the directions on the side of the jar (without adding any ice and making sure to dissolve the powdered mix sufficiently), and wash the hot spot with the tea. The tannic acid dries the skin and soothes the inflammation.

- **Stayfree Maxi Pads.** Wet a Stayfree Maxi Pad with cool water, wring it well, and then apply it as a soothing compress to the hot spot for ten to fifteen minutes, several times a day. The cool compress soothes the itchiness and softens up any crust to allow for better cleaning.

GET YOUR PET TO THE VET

Hit the spot! If the hot spot fails to improve after twenty-four hours of your home treatment, take your pet to the veterinarian to get a prescription for a topical or oral antibiotic.

For Dogs Only

- **Listerine** and **Johnson's Baby Oil.** Mix equal parts Listerine antiseptic mouthwash, Johnson's Baby Oil, and water in a sixteen-ounce trigger-spray bottle and spray the solution on your dog's hot spots and massage it into your pet's skin. The thymol, eucalyptol, menthol, and methyl salicylate in Listerine seem to work as a fungicide. The baby oil moisturizes the spot, providing relief.

PET PEEVES
TOO HOT TO HANDLE

- A hot spot is a bare, circular area where your pet has scratched, rubbed, licked, or bitten all the hair away in an attempt to soothe irritation caused by bacteria or fleas. Without treatment, hot spots tend to get larger and may start discharging pus and exuding a foul odor.

- To treat a hot spot, trim the hair away from the entire affected area and clean it with a mild fragrance-free soap.

- To keep your dog or cat from disturbing a hot spot, have your pet fit with an Elizabethan collar—a conical, plastic casing that fits around the animal's neck.

- If fleas are the cause of the hot spot, treat your pet for fleas (see page 107).

- Hot spots may also be caused by food allergies or hay fever.

House-breaking

For Dogs and Cats

- **Clorox Bleach.** To make a handy pooper-scooper, cut an empty, clean Clorox Bleach jug in half diagonally. Use the half with the handle to scoop up any mess.

- **Heinz White Vinegar** and **Dawn Dishwashing Liquid.** If your dog or cat stains the carpet, chances are good that your pet, with his keen sense of smell, will return to the same spot again—unless you clean and deodorize the area thoroughly. To do so, mix one-quarter cup Heinz White Vinegar and a few drops of Dawn Dishwashing Liquid in a quart of warm water. Scrub the affected area thoroughly with the soapy solution and blot dry. For more ways to clean and deodorize pet stains from carpet, floors, and furniture, see page 259.

- **Ziploc Storage Bags.** To scoop up poop hygienically, turn a Ziploc Storage Bag inside out, put your hand inside the bag like a glove, pick up the mess, pull the bag right-side out again, seal shut, and discard.

For Dogs Only

- **Arm & Hammer Baking Soda.** When using newspaper to housebreak a puppy, before discarding the soiled newspaper, sprinkle the wet stains with Arm & Hammer Baking Soda to minimize the offending odor.

For Cats Only

- **Arm & Hammer Baking Soda.** Cats tend to soil the carpet or other areas in the house when confronted by a dirty litter box. Aside from cleaning the

IT'S A DOG'S LIFE
HOW TO HOUSEBREAK A PUPPY

Crate Training

To housebreak a puppy using a crate, make the crate comfortable and homey by adding a blanket and a toy. At night, have the puppy sleep in the crate, and during the day, have the puppy use the crate for naps and play. Take the puppy outside every two hours during the day and every four hours at night to relieve himself so he never has an accident in the crate. Animals refrain from soiling their sleeping area, and the dog will quickly associate the outdoors with doing his business. Reward your puppy with a treat and praise every time he does his thing outside.

Paper Training

To paper-train a puppy, cover the floor of a small room in your home (ideally one with tile floor) with two or three layers of newspaper. Confine your puppy to the room and let him outside every two hours during the day (and every four hours at night) to do his business, praising him enthusiastically and rewarding him with a treat when he does. You can place a sheet of soiled newspaper in the area so the puppy will recognize the scent and instinctively use that spot. If the puppy accidentally relieves himself in the room, he will select one spot in the room for relieving himself (and the newspaper will absorb the mess). Once the puppy has selected that one spot, place the newspaper only in that location. Gradually move the newspaper toward the door. Then remove the newspaper entirely. The dog will realize that he should only do his business outside.

litter box daily and changing the litter weekly, sprinkle Arm & Hammer Baking Soda and work it into the litter to absorb odors that may send your cat seeking a more comfortable and convenient local. For more ways to deal with a litter box, see page 194.

- **Land O Lakes Butter.** To make a grown cat feel more comfortable in your home, place a dab of Land O Lakes Butter on his paws.

- **McCormick Onion Powder.** If your cat decides to use a spot outside his litter box, after cleaning and deodorizing the area, sprinkle some McCormick Onion Powder around the location. Onion repels cats.

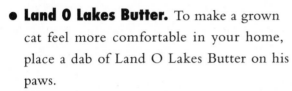

THE CAT'S MEOW
HOW TO HOUSEBREAK A KITTEN

Litter-Box Training

To train a kitten to use a litter box, simply pick up the cat and show him the litter box. Cats instinctively find a place to bury their excrement to fend off predators. To train a kitten, place the litter box in the bathroom and confine the kitten to the same room after meals. Praise the cat for using the box correctly.

PET PEEVES

- Don't bring home a puppy or kitten less than eight weeks old. A puppy or kitten should not be separated from his mother until eight-weeks old. Otherwise, behavior problems may arise.

- When picking up a puppy or kitten, take along a piece of fabric and rub it against the fur of the animal's mother and siblings to catch their scent. Place the fabric in your pet's bed to provide comfort.

- To prevent your new pet from missing her mother, wrap a hot water bottle in a towel for the animal to cuddle against in her bed or wrap a ticking clock in a towel and put it in the bed to remind the pet of her mother's reassuring heartbeat.

- When your dog relieves himself outside, give him positive reinforcement, like praise, petting, or a treat.

- When walking a puppy, keep him away from other dog excrement. Dog feces may contain parvovirus, a common disease that kills large numbers of puppies under five months of age. Older dogs are immune to the disease. Your veterinarian can vaccinate your puppy against parvovirus beginning at six to eight weeks of age, revaccinating every three weeks until the puppy reaches sixteen to twenty weeks of age, followed by a booster at one year of age and every one to three years thereafter.

- When housebreaking a dog, always get the dog outside quickly as soon as you suspect an impending need. Hurried dogs tend to paw the ground, crouch, or circle around sniffing the floor in search of an appropriate spot.

- The key to avoiding dog accidents in the house is to let your dog outside on a regular schedule, at least once every ten hours.

- If you dog stains the carpet, don't yell at the dog or rub his nose in the mess. This will only scare and confuse your pet.

- If your cat decides to use the bathtub rather than the litter box, fill the bathtub with a half-inch of water to convince her otherwise. Do not leave water in a bathtub if you have infants or toddlers in the house.

Houseplants

For Cats Only

- **Bounce.** To keep your cat away from your houseplants, hang fresh sheets of Bounce from the branches or tuck them into the soil. The fragrance (oleander, a natural repellent) keeps cats away. Misting the Bounce sheets with water every so often revives the scent.

- **Dawn Dishwashing Liquid.** How can you thwart a cat that loves chewing on the leaves of your houseplant? Add a few drops of Dawn Dishwashing Liquid to a sixteen-ounce trigger-spray bottle, fill the rest of the bottle with water, shake well, and mist the plant leaves. The soapy taste will convince the cat to find another source of entertainment.

- **Forster Clothespins.** To keep cats out of houseplants, insert several Forster Clothespins into the soil, roughly six-inches apart.

- **Heinz White Vinegar.** To prevent cats from digging up houseplants, add one teaspoon Heinz White Vinegar to two cups of water in a sixteen-ounce trigger-spray bottle and mist the plants with the solution. The smell of the vinegar repels cats.

PET PEEVES

GROWING PAINS

- Many household plants are poisonous to cats, including airplane plant, azalea, caladium, cyclamen, dieffenbachia, dragon tree, English ivy, elephant ear, foxglove, holly, Jerusalem cherry, mistletoe, monstera, oleander, philodendron, poinsettia, rhododendron, spider plant, and yew. Place these plants securely out of reach of your pets.

- Another way to stop cats from digging up the soil of houseplants is to cover the soil with pinecones or marbles (provided you don't have any small children who might swallow the marbles).

- Cats love to lie in sunlit windows, and dogs enjoy looking out windows. Do not block windows with plants.

- To train your cat to stay away from houseplants, fill a spray bottle or squirt gun with water and spritz your cat anytime she approaches a houseplant. The cat will quickly learn to avoid those spots.

- Cats tend to dig up houseplants in the hopes of finding an adequate substitute for a dirty litter box. Keeping the litter box clean and providing at least one litter box on each floor or your house prevents cats from seeking other outlets, such as houseplants.

- To provide your cat with adequate roughage (so he won't disturb the houseplants), add some chopped raw or cooked green vegetables to his food or grow a pot of lawn seed mix especially for your cat.

- Prevent your pets from knocking over houseplants by using heavy pots and planters with enough weight to remain secured to the floor.

- **L'eggs Sheer Energy Panty Hose.** To keep cats out of your houseplants, cover the soil with a balled-up pair (or several pairs) of clean, used, L'eggs Sheer Energy Panty Hose. The nylon repels the cat, and you can still water the plant through the porous panty hose.

- **Maxwell House Coffee.** Fertilizing houseplants with used Maxwell House Coffee grounds repels cats and prevents them from digging up the soil.

- **McCormick Ground (Cayenne) Red Pepper.** To keep cats away from your houseplants, mist the plants with water and then sprinkle McCormick Ground (Cayenne) Red Pepper over the leaves and soil. The cayenne pepper also repels insects.

- **McCormick Ground Ginger.** Here's another pungent spice you can use to get cats to stay away from your houseplants. Mist the tips of the most accessible plant leaves with water, and then sprinkle McCormick Ground Ginger over the dampened leaves.

- **Old Spice Aftershave Lotion.** Cats despise the smell of Old Spice Aftershave Lotion. Mix three tablespoons Old Spice Aftershave Lotion and one cup water in a sixteen-ounce trigger-spray bottle and mist the lower plant leaves with the solution.

- **Reynolds Wrap.** Place a few sheets of Reynolds Wrap in front of your plants. Cats hate walking on aluminum foil.

- **Scotch Double Sided Tape.** Placing strips of Scotch Double Sided Tape around your houseplants will annoy the cat and convince the animal to find a less distressing playground.

- **Tabasco Pepper Sauce.** Need another spicy way to stop cats from nibbling on houseplants? Mix one teaspoon Tabasco Pepper Sauce and two cups water in a sixteen-ounce trigger-spray bottle, let the solution sit for a few hours, shake well, and mist your plants. If the smell alone doesn't deter your cat, the taste will.

GET YOUR PET TO THE VET

Shaking like a leaf? If your pet munches on a plant and displays signs of poisoning, take him (and a sample of the plant he ate) to your veterinarian immediately.

Insect Stings

For Dogs and Cats

- **Adolph's Original Unseasoned Tenderizer.** To relieve bee, hornet, and wasp stings, mix Adolph's Original Unseasoned Tenderizer with water to make a paste and apply directly to the sting, making sure you have removed the stinger (see MasterCard on page 180). The enzymes in meat tenderizer break down the proteins in bee venom. Repeat if necessary.

- **Arm & Hammer Baking Soda.** Make a paste from Arm & Hammer Baking Soda and water and apply it to the sting several times a day. The baking soda draws out the venom, and the alkalinity neutralizes the sting.

- **Cortaid.** Applying a thin coat of Cortaid to an insect sting once a day helps reduce the swelling and relieve the irritation. Distract your pet to give the hydrocortisone cream enough time to penetrate the skin before your pet can lick it off. There's no need to be concerned if your pet licks off the cream later; ingesting a small amount of hydrocortisone cream is not detrimental to pets.

- **Domino Sugar.** To soothe an insect sting, make a paste from a teaspoon of Domino Sugar and water and rub the sticky mixture over the bite for a few minutes. The sugar neutralizes the poison from the sting.

- **Fruit of the Earth Aloe Vera Gel.** To help ease discomfort, apply Fruit of the Earth Aloe Vera Gel directly to the bee, hornet, or wasp sting. Aloe Vera tends to speed healing of skin irritations.

- **Green Giant Sweet Peas.** Applying an ice pack to a bee, hornet, or wasp sting reduces the inflammation and soothes the irritation. Use a plastic bag of frozen Green Giant Sweet Peas as an icepack. If the bag of peas feels too cold, wrap the bag in a sheet of paper towel. Apply the ice pack for five to ten minutes. The sack of peas conforms to the contours of your pet's body, and you can refreeze the peas for future ice-pack use—just label the bag for ice-pack use only. If you want to eat the peas, cook them after they thaw the first time, never after refreezing.

- **Heinz White Vinegar.** Use a cotton ball to apply full-strength Heinz White Vinegar to a bee, hornet, or wasp sting. The acetic acid in the vinegar neutralizes the venom and eases the stinging pain.

- **Jell-O** and **Ziploc Freezer Bags.** Applying an ice pack to a bee or wasp sting constricts the blood vessels, slowing the venom, relieving the swelling, and easing the pain. Prepare Jell-O according to the directions on the box and let cool enough to pour into a Ziploc Freezer Bag until three-quarters full. Seal the bag securely and freeze, and you have a homemade, flexible ice pack. When the Jell-O melts, simply refreeze.

- **Lipton Tea.** To cut the pain from bee, hornet, or wasp stings, place a dampened Lipton Tea Bag over the affected area and hold it in place for ten minutes. The tannic acid in the tea numbs the stinging sensation and also draws the stinger to the surface of the skin, making it easier to remove.

GET YOUR PET TO THE VET

Bite back! If an insect sting causes your pet's nose or throat to swell up and the inflammations threatens to impede the animal's breathing, get your pet to a vet right away.

- **Listerine.** Dab the bee, hornet, or wasp sting with a cotton ball saturated with Listerine antiseptic mouthwash. The antiseptic kills the proteins in the bee venom, disinfects the sting, and relieves the pain instantly.

- **MasterCard.** Remove the stinger and venom sack from a bee sting by lightly scraping the skin with the corner of a MasterCard to flick it out.

- **Orajel.** Applying a dab of Orajel to a bee or wasp sting anesthetizes the pain immediately. Distract your pet to give the numbing ointment enough time to suppress the pain before your pet can lick it off. If your pet licks off the ointment later, fear not. Safe enough to put in a baby's mouth to ease teething, Orajel won't hurt your pet.

- **Parsons' Ammonia.** Use a cotton ball to dab Parsons' Ammonia on the sting. No one knows why it works, but ammonia seems to neutralize the acids in bee venom, relieving the pain quickly.

- **Phillips' Milk of Magnesia.** Use a cotton ball to apply a coat of Phillips' Milk of Magnesia to any insect sting several times a day. The magnesium hydroxide minimizes the pain.

- **Quaker Oats** and **L'eggs Sheer Energy Panty Hose.** To soothe your pet's discomfort, use a blender to grind one cup Quaker Oats into a fine powder. Cut off the foot from a clean, used pair of L'eggs Sheer Energy Panty Hose, fill with the powdered oats, and tie a knot in the nylon. Tie the oatmeal sachet to the spigot, letting it dangle in the flow of water as the tub fills with cool water. Bathe your pet for five to ten minutes in this inexpensive and soothing oatmeal solution.

- **Skin So Soft.** To repel stinging and biting insects from your pet (and make your pet smell good), pour one-quarter capful of Avon Skin So Soft Bath Oil in a sixteen-ounce trigger-spray bottle, fill the rest of the spray bottle with water, shake vigorously, and spray this solution on your pet. Gently rub the Skin So Soft solution into your pet's skin. Avoid getting any of the solution in your pet's face. Brush your pet well.

- **Star Olive Oil.** Rubbing some Star Olive Oil into your pet's insect bites soothes the pain, reduces inflammation, and promotes healing.

PET PEEVES

- Dogs and cats tend to get stung in the nose, in the mouth, or on the face because they stick their noses into everything first.

- Bees pollinate fruit trees, vegetable plants, and flowers. One simple way to get rid of an abundance of bees is to call a local beekeeper.

- According to entomologists, at least 95 percent of the insects in our yards and gardens are beneficial or harmless.

- Scientists estimate the existence of more than thirty million species of insects.

- The heaviest insect in the world is the Goliath beetle of Equatorial Africa, which measures up to 4.33 inches in length and weighs up to 3.5 ounces—or slightly more than the weight of three size AA batteries.

- In the 1998 Walt Disney movie *A Bug's Life,* an inventive ant named Flik, determined to fight off invading tyrannical grasshoppers, joins forces with a circus of insects, including a walking stick, caterpillar, and ladybug.

Itching

For Dogs and Cats

- **Benadryl.** Incessant itching can be triggered by an allergy, such as hay fever. Giving your dog or cat one to three milligrams of Benadryl for every pound your pet weighs can relieve the itching. Consult your veterinarian for the proper dosage for your pet. Benadryl contains the antihistamine diphenhydramine, which thwarts the effects of histamine, a compound released by the body that causes itching. For more ways to combat allergies, see page 1.

- **Dawn Dishwashing Liquid.** Itching can be caused by a flea allergy, which can be caused by just one flea bite. Or your pet may be suffering from a flea infestation. To kill fleas on dogs or cats without using poisons, add a small amount of Dawn Dishwashing Liquid under running water to fill a sink or bathtub and give the animal a bath in the soapy solution. The soap penetrates the exoskeletons of the fleas, killing them, working more effectively than some prescribed flea shampoos. For more ways to fight fleas, see page 107.

- **Epsom Salt.** If your pet suffers from itchy feet, fill the bathtub with one to two inches of water (enough to cover your pet's paws) and dissolve three cups of Epsom Salt in the water. Stand your dog or cat in the tub for five to ten minutes, allowing the Epsom Salt to relieve the itch. Do not let your pet drink the water, since Epsom Salt can have a laxative effect. Remove your pet from the tub and gently pat her feet dry.

- **Heinz Apple Cider Vinegar.** To provide relief from itching and burning caused by a mild skin irritation, dab Heinz Apple Cider Vinegar on the affected area.

- **Quaker Oats** and **L'eggs Sheer Energy Panty Hose.** To relieve itchy, dry skin and alleviate constant scratching, use a blender to grind one cup Quaker Oats into a fine powder. Cut off the foot from a clean, used pair of L'eggs Sheer Energy Panty Hose, fill with the powdered oats, and tie a knot in the nylon. Tie the oatmeal sachet to the spigot, letting it dangle in the flow of water as the tub fills with cool water. Bathe your pet for five to ten minutes in this inexpensive and soothing oatmeal solution.

- **Skin So Soft.** Dry skin generally causes itchy skin, so moisturizing your pet's skin can instantly relieve the itch. Pour one-quarter capful of Avon Skin So Soft Bath Oil in a sixteen-ounce trigger-spray bottle, fill the rest of the spray bottle with water, shake vigorously, and spray this solution on your pet. Gently rub the Skin So Soft solution into your pet's skin. Avoid getting any of the solution in your pet's face. Brush your pet well to help distribute the Skin So Soft evenly and thoroughly.

- **Star Olive Oil.** Rubbing some Star Olive Oil into your pet's itchy skin soothes the pain, reduces inflammation, and promotes healing.

- **Vaseline Petroleum Jelly.** A coating of Vaseline Petroleum Jelly will provide your pet with temporary relief from itchy, irritated skin. If your pet licks off the petroleum jelly, don't fret. It helps lubricate the digestive tract, preventing hairballs.

For Dogs Only

- **Kingsford's Corn Starch.** If your dog is plagued with an itchy belly rash, dust your dog's belly with Kingsford's Corn Starch. The cornstarch absorbs moisture, keeping the area dry, and it's perfectly safe should your dog lick it off.

PET PEEVES

UP TO SCRATCH

- Itching is typically caused by dry skin, fleas, or allergies, and the resultant scratching can produce hair loss, skin damage, and severe infections.

- A cool, ten-minute bath provides fast, temporary relief from itchy skin for at least several hours.

- Which itch is which? Pets with fleas tend to scratch the back half of their body, usually above the tail and down the back of their legs. Dogs with hay fever scratch the front half their body, while cats with hay fever scratch their entire body. Food allergies cause dogs to itch all over and cats to itch around the face and neck.

Kennel Cough

For Dogs Only

- **Huggies Baby Wipes.** Use a hypoallergenic, fragrance-free Huggies Baby Wipe to clean any mucus buildup from your dog's eyes and nose.

- **Hydrogen Peroxide** and **SueBee Honey.** To combat kennel cough, sterilize your dog's water bowl with boiling water. In the sterilized water bowl, mix three drops 3 percent hydrogen peroxide, two teaspoons SueBee Honey, and one cup water. Feed this solution to your dog three times a day until the kennel cough subsides.

- **Lipton Peppermint Tea.** Brew a strong cup of Lipton Peppermint Tea, let cool to room temperature, and give your ailing dog a few drops of the liquid every hour until the coughing subsides. Peppermint relieves coughs.

- **Pedialyte.** To keep your dog well hydrated, give your pet Pedialyte to drink. If the animal refuses to drink, use a turkey baster or bulb syringe to give the dog the liquid. (Not all pets will drink Pedialyte, so keep another bowl of water available.)

- **Robitussin Maximum Strength Cough Suppressant.** To subside a constant cough, consider giving your dog a cough suppressant. Consult your veterinarian for the appropriate dosage of Robitussin Maximum Strength Cough Syrup for your dog (generally one-half teaspoon or less for a small dog, one teaspoon for a twenty-pound dog, and two teaspoons for a dog weighing more than forty pounds). The active ingredient in Robitussin is dextomethorphan. Never give a pet any cough medicine that contains aspirin, acetaminophen, or ibuprofen, which can be lethal for pets.

- **SueBee Honey.** Give your dog one teaspoon of SueBee Honey three times a day. Or add one teaspoon SueBee Honey to a warm cup of water and either lure your dog to drink it or use a turkey baster or bulb syringe to squirt the solution into the back of his mouth. Honey soothes your dog's throat and simultaneously works as an antiseptic.

GET YOUR PET TO THE VET

Can't hack it? If kennel cough does not clear up after a week to ten days, or if your dog starts spitting up white foam or has a loss of appetite, take your pet to the veterinarian.

PET PEEVES

COUGHING IT UP

- Dogs tend to catch kennel cough, a highly contagious virus, from being boarded in—you guessed it—kennels.

- Before boarding your dog in a kennel, make sure the kennel requires proof of immunization to safeguard against kennel cough (and heartworms), or else find a kennel that does.

- Kennel cough is formally called canine infectious tracheobronchitis.

- The symptoms of kennel cough are a dry, hacking cough followed by retching, watery discharge from the eyes and nose, and loss of appetite.

- To determine if your dog has kennel cough, press gently on your dog's throat directly above the collar. If this triggers a coughing fit, your dog may have kennel cough.

- To help relieve your infected pet, keep the air inside your home free from cigarette or fireplace smoke and moist with a humidifier. Clean, moist air prevents your pet's throat from drying out and helps ease coughing.

- To temporarily soothe your dog's throat and airways, bring your dog into the bathroom while you take a hot shower. The steam helps break up any phlegm, allowing the congestion to drain.

- Left untreated, kennel cough can develop into pneumonia.

Lice

For Dogs and Cats

- **Benadryl.** To relieve the relentless itching from lice, give your dog or cat one to three milligrams of Benadryl for every pound your pet weighs. Consult your veterinarian for the proper dosage for your pet. The antihistamine diphenhydramine, the active ingredient in Benadryl, inhibits the effects of histamine, a compound released by the body that causes itching.

- **Clorox Bleach.** After treating your pet for lice, add two teaspoons Clorox Bleach to a sink full of water and soak all combs, brushes, and grooming tools in the solution to kill any residual lice or nits.

- **Glad Trash Bags.** Place all pet bedding in a Glad Trash Bag, tie it shut, and store in the garage for two weeks. Lice cannot survive without a host. The eggs take roughly one week to hatch, so after two weeks all the lice will be dead.

- **Heinz White Vinegar.** To kill the lice on your dog or cat, fill a bathtub or sink with one part Heinz White Vinegar to twenty parts water, and soak your pet in the solution for five minutes. Female lice lay tiny white eggs, called nits, which stick like glue to the hair shafts. The vinegar dissolves the glue, allowing you to comb the nits from hair easily with a nit comb. Repeat this treatment ten days later to kill any hatched nits.

- **Vaseline Petroleum Jelly.** When using a medicated shampoo to kill lice, avoid getting the lather in your pet's eyes by smearing Vaseline Petroleum Jelly around the eyes.

PET PEEVES
GETTING NIT-PICKY

- Lice are tiny parasitic insects that burrow into the skin to feed on the host's blood. A chemical in their saliva stops blood from clotting. This chemical causes the persistent itching.

- Female lice lay up to ten eggs a day and attach them along the hair shafts of their host with a gummy substance. The lice eggs, called nits, hatch around six days later, and grow to adult lice in eighteen days.

- Lice shampoos contain the pesticide pyrethrin (derived from chrysanthemums) or permethrin (a synthetic form of pyrethrin). Recent studies indicate that lice are becoming pyrethrin-resistant. If you decide to use a medicated lice shampoo on your pet, wash your pet with the shampoo once a week for three weeks.

- Lice that feed on dogs or cats do not feed on humans, so if your pet has lice, there's no need to treat everyone in your family.

- Lice that feed on dogs do not feed on cats, and lice that feed on cats do not feed on dogs. If you have several dogs and one of them gets lice, treat all the dogs for lice. The same goes if you have more than one cat.

GET YOUR PET TO THE VET

Don't louse it up! A pet with lice may also have fleas and ticks, and the blood loss from the parasites could cause anemia. If your lice-infested, flea-ridden pet seems fatigued or the inside of her mouth turns stark white, take her to a veterinarian immediately.

Limping

For Dogs and Cats

- **Green Giant Sweet Peas.** If you have a sneaking suspicion that your pet's limp stems from a strained muscle that will heal on its own in a few days, use a plastic bag of frozen Green Giant Sweet Peas as an icepack to relieve the pain and reduce swelling. If the bag of peas feels too cold, wrap the bag in a sheet of paper towel. Apply the ice pack to the affected area for five to ten minutes at least four times daily. The sack of peas conforms to the contours of your pet's body, and you can refreeze the peas for future ice-pack use—just label the bag for ice-pack use only. If you want to eat the peas, cook them after they thaw the first time, never after refreezing.

- **Jell-O** and **Ziploc Freezer Bags.** Another way to make a cold compress? Prepare Jell-O according to the directions on the box and let cool enough to pour into a Ziploc Freezer Bag until three-quarters full. Seal the bag securely and freeze, and you have a homemade, flexible ice pack. When the Jell-O melts, simply refreeze.

- **Jif Peanut Butter.** If your pet is limping, he might have bubble gum stuck between his toes. Rub a dollop of creamy Jif Peanut Butter into the wad of chewing gum stuck in the paw, work it in well, and then comb the gum out.

The oils in the peanut butter dissolve the chewing gum. For more ways to remove gum, see page 127.

- **Playtex Living Gloves.** Heat relieves muscle pain. Fill a Playtex Living Glove with warm water, tie the cuff securely to prevent leaks, and use the warm glove as a heating pad. The rubber glove conforms to the shape of the leg.

- **Uncle Ben's Converted Brand Rice.** To soothe a sore leg, fill a sock with uncooked Uncle Ben's Converted Brand Rice (not too compactly), tie a knot in the end, and heat it in the microwave for one minute. Place the warm sock directly over the affected area twice a day for fifteen minutes. The reusable heating pad conforms wherever applied, and the rice lasts inside the sock for years.

- *USA Today* and **Scotch Packaging Tape.** A limp might indicate a fractured leg. If so, you may wish to immobilize the injured leg with a splint before taking your pet to the vet. Roll up a section of *USA Today* into a tube. Using a pair of scissors, cut the length of the tube to match the length of your pet's leg. Slip your pet's leg through the tube, and use Scotch Packaging Tape to secure the tube in place. Regardless if you have the time and supplies to create a splint, carefully pick up your pet, keeping the injured leg still, place him in the car, and take him to the vet immediately for treatment.

GET YOUR PET TO THE VET

Don't get lost in the shuffle! If your dog or cat continues limping for more than forty-eight to seventy-two hours, your pet may be suffering from a fractured bone. Take the animal to your veterinarian for treatment.

PET PEEVES

OUT OF STEP

- If your dog or cat is limping around the house, he most likely strained a muscle or has a sore paw. The tenderness typically heals after a few days.

- A limp may be symptomatic of a foreign object embedded in your pet's paw. Check for a thorn, nail, or piece of glass.

- Use a blanket as a stretcher for your pet. Place your dog or cat in the center of the blanket, and have two people each lift two corners of the blanket to carry the pet.

- To help a limping dog or cat recover, allow your pet to rest and restrict walks for two to three days to give the leg time to heal.

- Aside from using newspaper and tape to immobilize a fractured leg (see *USA Today* on page 192), you can wrap a washcloth or hand towel around the leg and then wrap that with an elastic bandage.

- Cats usually limp after getting into a catfight. If your cat limps, check her carefully for bite wounds and treat them appropriately (see page 42).

Litter Boxes

- **Arm & Hammer Baking Soda.** To help control odors in a cat litter box, cover the bottom of the litter box with one-quarter inch Arm & Hammer Baking Soda, and then add the litter. The baking soda absorbs and neutralizes offending odors. If you're too busy to empty the used litter until later, sprinkle Arm & Hammer Baking Soda over the used litter and stir gently. The baking soda will deodorize the stench for a few hours.

- **Bounce.** To deodorize a covered cat litter box, use one or two sheets of Bounce as air filters in the top of the box.

- **Dawn Dishwashing Liquid and Clorox Bleach.** To clean and disinfect a litter box, wash the box with a few drops of Dawn Dishwashing Liquid and water. Then mix one-half cup Clorox Bleach in a gallon of water and use a sponge to wipe down the litter box with the solution. Rinse thoroughly with water and let air-dry.

- **Glad Trash Bags.** Tired of cleaning the cat litter box? Open a Glad Trash Bag, place the cat litter box inside, and pour litter on top of the plastic covering the open side of the box. To clean, lift out the bag, turn it inside-out, and throw it away. Or slice open the sides of a large Glad Trash Bag and cut the bag into four large rectangular pieces to make litter-pan liners.

THE CAT'S MEOW
OTHER USES FOR TIDY CATS

- **Make ankle weights.** Fill a pair of socks with clean Tidy Cats, and tie them shut, leaving enough room in the toe so you can tie each weighted sock around your ankles. Lying on your back with your legs straight, bend one knee and raise the straight leg as high as you can, and then lower it back to the floor. Then repeat with the other leg.

- **Clean oil stains from a driveway or garage floor.** Spread a layer of Tidy Cats over the stain, let sit overnight until it soaks up the oil, and sweep clean.

- **Deodorize garbage cans.** Sprinkle a one-inch layer of Tidy Cats inside the bottom of a garbage can to absorb foul odors.

- **Seal drafts.** If cold air is getting into your home through the crack at the bottom of a door, fill several socks three-quarters full of Tidy Cats, knot the tops, and place them along the bottoms of the door as insulation.

- **Preserve flowers.** Pour a two-inch layer of Tidy Cats in an airtight container, place flowers on it, and seal the container shut for seven to ten days.

- **Stuff toys.** Tidy Cats makes excellent filler for beanbags, stuffed animals, and dolls.

- **Deodorize a musty suitcase or trunk.** Fill a clean, empty tin can with Tidy Cats, set it inside a musty suitcase or trunk, close the luggage, and let it sit overnight.

- **Make icy sidewalks safer.** Sprinkle Tidy Cats on an icy sidewalk to improve traction.

- **Create traction.** If your car gets stuck in snow or ice, pour some Tidy Cats under the tires to create traction to get out of the situation.

- **Make drainage for a potted plant.** When bedding a plant, fill the bottom of the plant pot with styrene peanuts to within ten inches of the top, cover with a two-inch layer of Tidy Cats for drainage, and top with an eight-inch layer of potting soil.

- **Deodorize a fireplace.** Sprinkle Tidy Cats in the fireplace to absorb the odors.

- **Heinz White Vinegar.** To clean a litter box, discard the used litter and fill the box with a half-inch layer of Heinz White Vinegar. Let stand for three hours, rinse thoroughly with water, and dry.

- **Huggies Baby Wipes.** To clean a cat filler box, wipe down the plastic container with Huggies Baby Wipes.

- **Murphy Oil Soap.** To clean a litter box, use Murphy Oil Soap to wash and rinse the box in warm water. The mild vegetable oil–based soap won't leave the plastic box smelling like perfume, which could repel the cat from using the litter box.

- **Playtex Living Gloves.** Wear a pair of Playtex Living Gloves when changing the cat box filler and wash your hands and the gloves thoroughly afterward.

- **20 Mule Team Borax.** To control the odors generated by a cat litter box, mix one part 20 Mule Team Borax to six parts cat box filler.

- **Uncle Ben's Converted Brand Rice.** Before filling the litter box with cat box filler, pour a one-quarter inch layer of uncooked Uncle Ben's Converted Brand Rice in the box. The rice absorbs excess moisture and odors.

- *USA Today.* If you don't use plastic liners in your cat's litter box, place a section of *USA Today* on the bottom of the litter box to make dumping out the litter easier.

- *USA Today.* To make emergency cat box litter, use a shredded copy of *USA Today* in your cat's litter box.

- *USA Today.* To prevent your cat from scratching through the bottom of a plastic litter box liner, place a section of *USA Today* in the bottom of the liner before filling the box with cat box filler. The newspaper acts as a padded barrier.

- *USA Today* and **Scotch Tape.** If your cat makes a mess of the wall behind the litter box, use Scotch Tape to hang a sheet of *USA Today* to the wall to protect it from any flying muck.

PET PROJECTS
THE SCOOP ON KITTY LITTER

After serving in the Navy during World War II, Ed Lowe joined his father's company in Cassopolis, Michigan, selling industrial absorbents, including sawdust and a kiln-dried and granulated absorbent clay called Fuller's Earth, for cleaning up grease and oil spills. In 1947, Lowe's neighbor, Kaye Draper, tired of using ashes in her cat's box and dealing with the resulting sooty paw prints across her floors and carpets, asked him for some sand. Instead, Lowe suggested that she take home some of the absorbent clay. Soon Drape came back for more granulated clay, delighted by its absorbency and the fact that her cat did not track it all over the house.

Realizing that other cat owners might love his new cat box filler, Lowe filled ten brown bags with five pounds of the granulated clay, wrote the name "Kitty Litter" on them, and urged a local pet store owner to try selling the bags of clay for 65 cents—despite the fact that the same amount of sand sold for a nickel. When the owner laughed, Lowe suggested he give it away for free and see how customers liked it. When enthusiastic customers asked for more Kitty Litter, the storeowner started charging for it.

Lowe demonstrated his Kitty Litter at cat shows across America, visited local pet shops, and sold Kitty Litter Brand from the back of his 1943 Chevy Coupe.

In 1990, Edward Lowe Industries, Inc. was the nation's largest producer of cat box filler with retail sales of more than $210 million annually. Lowe died in 1995.

- **Ziploc Freezer Bags.** Store your cat's pooper-scooper in its own Ziploc Storage Bag to prevent feces or urine from coming into contact with the floor or sides of your cabinet.

- **Ziploc Storage Bags.** To sift out clumped litter from the litter box, turn a Ziploc Storage Bag inside out, put your hand inside the bag like a glove, pick up the mess, pull the bag right-side out again, seal shut, and discard.

PET PEEVES
THINKING OUTSIDE THE BOX

- The three types of cat box filler are clay litter (which must be replaced entirely on a weekly basis), clumping litter (which dissolves around urine or feces to form a clump that can be scooped or sifted out, minimizing odors and only requiring replacement of the scooped litter), and alternative litter (made from corn cobs, peanut hulls, alfalfa, wheat, oat hulls, recycled newsprint, or other materials).

- If you're pregnant or immunodeficient, do not change, clean, handle, or touch a cat litter box. The parasitic disease toxoplasmosis can be transmitted through cat feces to the fetus in pregnant women (causing birth defects, including loss of vision, mental retardation, and loss of hearing, and death) and to immunodeficient individuals (causing enlargement of the lymph nodes, ocular and central nervous-system disturbances, respiratory disease, heart disease, and relapses of cancer).

- Substitutes for commercial cat box litter? Try sand, wood shavings, or peat.

- You can make your own litter box from a Rubbermaid container, a baking pan, or a plastic dishpan.

- To prevent your cat from tracking litter around the house, place a carpet remnant or the lid from a Rubbermaid container as a mat under the cat box.

- Once your cat becomes accustomed to one brand of cat box filler, you may encounter difficulty switching to another brand and your cat may refuse to use the box. To avoid this problem, introduce the new litter gradually to wean your cat off the old litter. Fill the box with one part new litter and three parts old litter. Next time, mix equal parts old litter and new litter, followed by three parts new litter and one part old litter. Finally use only the new litter. Your cat will greet this slow introduction will far less resistance.

- If your cat starts using another spot in the house instead of his litter box, move his litter box to that spot, and each day gradually move it back to the spot you prefer.

- Never use products containing phenol to clean, disinfect, or deodorize a litter box. Phenol is toxic to cats.

Mange

For Dogs and Cats

- **Benadryl.** To reduce the persistent itching caused by mange, give your dog or cat one to three milligrams of Benadryl for every pound your pet weighs. Consult your veterinarian for the proper dosage for your pet. The antihistamine diphenhydramine, the active ingredient in Benadryl, relieves itching.

- **Dannon Yogurt.** Let a cup of plain Dannon Yogurt warm to room temperature and place two tablespoons of the yogurt inside each ear affected with mange. Let sit for ten minutes, rinse clean with water, and dry. The acidophilus in the yogurt heals the ears.

- **Palmolive Dishwashing Liquid.** Mix one part Palmolive Dishwashing Liquid and nine parts warm water, saturate your pet with the soapy water, and let sit for ten minutes. Palmolive kills the mites on the skin and helps stop the mange from spreading to other parts of the body.

- **SueBee Honey.** Apply SueBee Honey to the reddened skin from demodectic mange. Honey is hygroscopic, meaning it absorbs moisture, smothering the mites while simultaneously relieving the itching.

- **Wesson Vegetable Oil.** Apply a few drops of Wesson Vegetable Oil on the patchy areas of skin to soothe the irritation, soften the waxy deposits created by scabies mites, and smother the mites themselves.

For Dogs Only

- **Hydrogen Peroxide** and **20 Mule Team Borax.** To treat mange on dogs, mix two cups 1 percent hydrogen peroxide, four cups water, and eight tablespoons 20 Mule Team Borax, making sure the borax dissolves completely. Soak the dog with the solution, and let it dry on the skin of the animal. Repeat every three days for no longer than two months.

- **McCormick Pure Lemon Extract.** Mix one tablespoon McCormick Pure Lemon Extract and one cup water, and then apply the mixture to your pet's coat using a sponge. The limonene from the extract kills the mites. (Don't dampen a cat with this solution. Cats detest citrus.)

GET YOUR PET TO THE VET

You're just scratching the surface! Only a veterinarian can tell the difference between demodectic and sarcoptic mange. If you notice hair loss, reddened skin, sores, and scabs, take your pet to a veterinarian right away.

PET PEEVES

THAT MANGY MUTT

- There are two types of mange: demodectic mange (caused by a population explosion of microscopic demodex mites that normally live in your pet's hair follicles) and sarcoptic mange (caused by sarcoptic mites that burrow into the skin).

- Demodectic mange, the most common form of mange, can result in hair loss, skin irritation, and scaling.

- On puppies, demodectic mange tends to disappear within a month without any treatment whatsoever.

- The word mange originates from the Middle French word *mangene,* which means "itching."

- Demodectic mange tends to affect undernourished pets. Keeping your pet on a healthy diet keeps his immune system strong, warding off demodectic mange.

- Humans and cats cannot catch demodectic mange from dogs. Dogs can, however, pass sarcoptic mange to humans.

Medication

For Dogs and Cats

- **Easy Cheese.** If you're experiencing trouble getting your dog to take pills or you're tired of shoving your fingers into your cat's throat, put the pill in the palm of your hand, smother it with aerosol Easy Cheese, and offer your pet the treat. Your dog or cat will gobble up the cheese along with the cleverly concealed pill.

- **Jif Peanut Butter.** If your dog or cat refuses to eat heartworm pills or other medication, put Jif Peanut Butter on a cracker and bury the pill in it. The dog or cat, unable to separate the pill from the peanut butter, will devour the daily snack.

- **Land O Lakes Butter.** If you're having difficulty getting a pill down your dog or cat's throat, coat the pill with Land O Lakes Butter, slip it as far back in your pet's mouth as possible, hold his mouth shut with his muzzle pointed upward, and gently stoke the underside of his neck.

- **Philadelphia Cream Cheese.** To get your dog or cat to take pill medication, bury the pills in Philadelphia Cream Cheese.

For Dogs Only

- **Jet-Puffed Marshmallows.** Trick your dog into taking a pill by pushing the pill into a Jet-Puffed Marshmallow, which your dog will gladly gobble up.

PET PEEVES

SWEETENING THE PILL

- If your cat refuses to take liquid medicine, pour some on her fur. She'll instinctively lick it off.

- If you place a pill as far back in your cat's mouth as possible and then immediately touch his nose with something wet, he'll instinctively try to lick his nose, inadvertently causing the pill to slide down his throat.

- To avoid getting scratched while giving your cat a pill, tightly bundle her in a towel.

- To administer a pill into a dog's mouth, gently grasp your dog's head by placing your hand on top of the muzzle with your thumb on one side and your fingers on the other. Raise his nose toward the ceiling and firmly squeeze just behind the upper canine teeth, prompting the mouth to involuntarily drop open. With your free hand, quickly place the pill as far back on your dog's tongue as possible. Close your dog's mouth, hold it shut, and blow lightly on his nose, causing him to swallow. Praise your dog lavishly and give him a treat.

- To give liquid medicine to a dog, pull out the corner of the animal's lower lip to form a pocket, use the dropper to dispense the medicine into the pocket, and hold his jaw closed and rub his throat until he swallows.

Obesity

For Dogs and Cats

- **McCormick Garlic Powder.** Adding garlic to your dog or cat's diet helps regulate the liver and gallbladder, fine-tuning your pet's digestive system and facilitating weight loss.

- **Metamucil.** To help your pet lose weight, mix one teaspoon of Metamucil with water and pour it on your pet's food. Fiber helps your pet lose weight, prevents constipation, and improves digestion, strengthening your pet's ability to absorb nutrients.

- **Orville Redenbacher Gourmet Popping Corn.** To give your pet a high-fiber, low-calorie snack, air pop some unbuttered, unsalted Orville Redenbacher Gourmet Popping Corn. Cats and dogs love all-natural popcorn, the fiber helps improve digestion, and the delicious snack won't fatten up your pet.

- **Post Grape-Nuts Flakes.** Another way to add fiber to your pet's diet? Sprinkle three tablespoons of Post Grape-Nuts Flakes on your pet's food. Again, the fiber helps your pet lose weight, prevent constipation, and improve digestion, improving your pet's ability to absorb nutrients.

PET PEEVES

FAT CATS AND HOT DOGS

- Obesity in pets can lead to diabetes, high blood pressure, and musculoskeletal problems.

- If you can't feel your pet's ribs when you run your hand along his side, your pet is overweight.

- Taking your pet for regular walks or having vigorous playtime at home provides exercise that raises the metabolic rate and burns off calories.

- If your pet is overweight, switch to a pet food high in fiber and low in fat (or add more fiber to his diet).

- To put your dog or cat on a diet, feed your pet one-quarter less food for two weeks. After that time, if you still can't feel his ribs, reduce his food by another quarter. If, two weeks later, you still can't feel his ribs, take your pet to the veterinarian for an examination and consultation.

- Instead of feeding your dog or cat one or two big meals each day, serve your pet four to six small meals over the course of the day.

- To help your pet savor smaller portions, slow down his food consumption by putting the food in several bowls spread around the room.

- To combat obesity, stop feeding your pet snacks or treats. If you pet begs vehemently, give him a few small slices of carrot or apple.

- Make sure your dieting pet can't get into the garbage and stays off the dining room table.

- To weigh your pet, simply hold your pet in your arms and step onto your bathroom scale. Then weigh yourself alone and subtract your weight from the weight of the two of you together.

GET YOUR PET TO THE VET

Throw your weight around! If your pet gains weight without eating more than usual, consult your veterinarian before putting your pet on a diet to rule out the possibility of diabetes or congestive heart failure.

Odors

Air Fresheners

For Dogs and Cats

- **Arm & Hammer Baking Soda, Parsons' Ammonia, and McCormick Pure Vanilla Extract.** To create an inexpensive yet powerful homemade air freshener, mix one tablespoon Arm & Hammer Baking Soda, one-half tablespoon Parsons' Ammonia, one-eighth teaspoon McCormick Pure Vanilla Extract, and two cups water in a sixteen-ounce trigger-spray bottle. Shake well and spray the air with the solution.

- **Downy Fabric Softener.** Mix one tablespoon Downy Fabric Softener and two cups water in a sixteen-ounce trigger-spray bottle, shake well, and spray the solution to freshen the air in your home.

- **Heinz White Vinegar.** For a potent, natural air freshener, mix equal parts Heinz White Vinegar and water in a trigger-spray bottle. Shake well and mist the air in your home with the pungent solution. The vinegar swiftly neutralizes any foul odors in your home. For persistent odors, use Heinz White Vinegar full strength.

- **McCormick Pure Vanilla Extract.** To freshen the air around your house, mix two teaspoons McCormick Pure Vanilla Extract and two cups water in a trigger-spray bottle and spray the air in your home. Or saturate a cotton ball with vanilla extract and place it in your vacuum cleaner bag before cleaning to fragrance the air.

- **Nestea.** Mix up two cups Nestea according to the directions on the jar, pour the solution into a sixteen-ounce trigger-spray bottle, and spray around your home to freshen the air. Tea is a natural air freshener.

- **Old Spice Aftershave Lotion.** Place a cotton ball dampened with Old Spice Aftershave Lotion in the vacuum cleaner bag. As you vacuum your home, the vacuum cleaner will blast the scented air throughout your home.

- **ReaLemon** and **Arm & Hammer Baking Soda.** Mix one teaspoon ReaLemon lemon juice, one teaspoon Arm & Hammer Baking Soda, and two cups hot water in a sixteen-ounce trigger-spray bottle. Shake well and spray the air in your home to make it lemon fresh.

Bedding

For Dogs and Cats

- **Arm & Hammer Baking Soda.** To clean and deodorize your dog or cat's bedding between launderings, make certain the bedding is dry, sprinkle Arm & Hammer Baking Soda on your pet's bedding, let sit for fifteen to thirty minutes, and then shake out the powder or vacuum clean. Repeat if necessary. For more ways to clean and deodorize pet bedding, see page 26.

Body Odor

For Dogs and Cats

- **Arm & Hammer Baking Soda.** To reduce your pet's body odor, sprinkle some baking soda on your pet, rub it into his coat thoroughly, and then brush off. This dry shampoo neutralizes odors, leaves your pet smelling fresh, and makes a great way to clean your pet during the cold winter months. (Do not use on dogs or cats restricted to a low-sodium diet.) For more ways to deodorize your pet, see page 13.

Bowls

For Dogs and Cats

- **Colman's Mustard Powder.** To deodorize a plastic pet food bowl, fill the bowl with warm water, dissolve one-quarter teaspoon Colman's Mustard Powder, and let sit for one hour. Wash with soapy water, rinse clean, and dry. For more ways do clean and deodorize pet food bowls, see page 51.

Carpets and Upholstery

For Dogs and Cats

- **Arm & Hammer Baking Soda.** To deodorize pet odors from carpeting and upholstery, sprinkle Arm & Hammer Baking Soda lightly over the dry carpet or upholstery, let sit for fifteen minutes, and then vacuum up. The baking soda neutralizes odors.

- **Arm & Hammer Clean Shower.** Clean Shower removes pet odors from carpets and upholstery. Simply spray the area, let sit for a few minutes, blot up with a damp sponge, and then dry with a paper towel.

- **Downy Fabric Softener.** To refresh your musty carpet and upholstery with a more pleasant fragrance, mix two ounces Downy Fabric Softener and fourteen ounces water in a sixteen-ounce trigger-spray bottle, shake well, and spray a fine mist of the solution over your carpet after vacuuming or on your upholstery. The antistatic elements in the Downy Fabric Softener also make vacuuming up pet hair effortless.

- **Heinz White Vinegar.** To deodorize rank pet smells from carpets, add one cup Heinz White Vinegar to your carpet cleaner when shampooing your carpets. The carpet will smell like vinegar for an hour or two after

PET PROJECTS
THE MIRACLE OF NATURE'S MIRACLE

In 1981, Joe Weiss of Rolling Hills Estates, California, created Nature's Miracle as a simple cleaning product for preschools. After a preschool teacher telephoned him and explained that she had used Nature's Miracle to clean her dog's vomit from her brand-new carpet, Weiss produced twenty-four bottles of Nature's Miracle, repackaged as Pet Mess Easy Clean-Up. The repackaged product sold out within forty-eight hours.

Soon afterward, the Weiss family's cat urinated on the carpet. When stain and odor removers purchased at the local pet store failed to work, Weiss decided to attempt to clean the urine stain with a new organic formula containing enzymes that he and chemist friend Van Vlahakis had concocted as a nontoxic drain cleaner. The formula liquefied the enzymes in the urine stain and neutralized the smell, prompting Weiss to repurpose and package the drain cleaner as Nature's Miracle Stain & Odor Remover. The product became a huge seller, and the company developed an entire line of pet products.

In 2003, the Weiss family sold Nature's Miracle to 8 in 1 Pet Products.

cleaning, but once the carpets dry, the smell of the vinegar and the pet's odors will evaporate.

- **Kingsford's Corn Starch.** Deodorize animal odors from carpets and upholstery by sprinkling Kingsford's Corn Starch on the carpet. Let sit for thirty minutes, and then vacuum clean. The mild, all-natural cornstarch absorbs strong odors.

- **Pine-Sol.** To deodorize pet odors from your carpeting and upholstered furniture, pour one-quarter cup Pine-Sol into a sixteen-ounce trigger-spray bottle, fill the rest of the bottle with water, shake well, and spray the soapy liquid on your carpets and upholstered furniture.

Cat Box Litter

For Cats Only

- **Arm & Hammer Baking Soda.** To help control odors in a cat litter box, cover the bottom of the litter box with one-quarter inch Arm & Hammer Baking Soda, and then add the litter. The baking soda absorbs and neutralizes offending odors. For more ways to clean and deodorize a cat litter box, see page 194.

Doghouses

For Dogs Only

- **Pine-Sol.** To clean and deodorize a doghouse, mix one-half cup Pine-Sol in a bucket of water and wash the house thoroughly.

Food

For Dogs and Cats

- **Maxwell House Coffee.** To thwart the stench of leftover canned pet food from infusing other foods in the refrigerator, place the open pet food can in a clean, empty Maxwell House Coffee can and seal the plastic lid tightly. For more ways to handle smelly pet food, see page 95.

Room Deodorizers

For Dogs and Cats

- **Arm & Hammer Baking Soda.** To deodorize stale animal odors from any room in your home, place an open box of Arm & Hammer Baking Soda on a shelf in the room.

- **Bounce.** To mask pet odors in a room, tape a sheet of Bounce to the front of a fan or over an air-conditioning vent (or weave it through the louver slats), and then turn on the fan or air-conditioner to fill the room with fragrance. Or place a sheet of Bounce in your vacuum cleaner bag before vacuuming the carpet and let the vacuum cleaner blow the fragrance throughout the room. You can also place a Bounce sheet in the wastebasket, in a drawer, or behind books on the shelf.

- **Heinz White Vinegar.** Place a glass of Heinz White Vinegar on a table or countertop of any room in the house that needs deodorizing. The vinegar neutralizes odors.

- **Ivory Soap.** To cover up the musty smell of animals, unwrap a bar of Ivory Soap and place it on a desk, table, or countertop to fill the room with a calming, familiar scent.

- **Kingsford Charcoal Briquets.** Fill a clean, used coffee can with untreated Kingsford Charcoal Briquets, and place the container on a shelf to absorb odors.

- **Lipton Chamomile Tea** and **L'eggs Sheer Energy Panty Hose.** To keep the air smelling fresh in the room where you keep your cat's litter box (or any room where you confine your pets), cut off the foot off a clean, used pair of L'eggs Sheer Energy Panty Hose, fill it with Lipton Chamomile Tea bags, and hang the sachet to imbue the room with a pleasant fragrance.

- **Maxwell House Coffee.** Fill a bowl with one-half cup fresh Maxwell House Coffee grounds, and set the bowl on a shelf in whatever room reeks of animal odor. The coffee grounds absorb the musky smells.

- **Speed Stick.** To mask animal odors in any room in your home, rub a Speed Stick on an incandescent light bulb in a lamp and turn on the light. The heat from the bulb spreads the brisk smell of the deodorant stick throughout the room.

- **Tidy Cats.** To eliminate stuffy smells in any small room where pets have been confined, place a bowl filled with unused Tidy Cats cat box filler on a shelf beyond the reach of your pet. The cat box litter absorbs unpleasant odors.

PET PEEVES

THAT STINKS!

- To help prevent carpeting and upholstery from absorbing pet odors, keep pet beds, toys, and litter boxes in rooms with tile or wood floors and non-upholstered furniture.

- Always strive to eliminate the source of the odor rather than simply attempting to mask the odor.

- Many commercial air fresheners contain a nerve-deadening agent or a nasal-lining oil to weaken your sense of smell so your nose can no longer detect the existing odor.

- Opening the doors and windows ventilates a room, drying up and clearing away the source of the odor (unless there's humidity in the air). Running a fan also helps.

- Some commercial powdered carpet deodorizers, sprinkled on carpets and then vacuumed up, cause dermatitis on the bellies of dogs that lie on the carpet.

- Before buying an air freshener in a grocery store, most shoppers pick a can off the shelf, remove the cap, and spray the air or their fingers or into the air, and breathe deeply to test whether they like the fragrance. Air fresheners contain chemicals that no one in their right mind should be inhaling.

Paws

For Dogs and Cats

- **Alberto VO5 Conditioning Hairdressing.** To protect your dog or cat's paw pads, rub in a little Alberto VO5 Conditioning Hairdressing before sending your pet outdoors.

- **Bag Balm.** Moisturize tender paw pads by rubbing on Bag Balm, the salve created in Vermont to relieve cracking in cow udders.

- **ChapStick.** Rubbing ChapStick into dry paw pads seals in moisture and heals rough, dry skin.

- **ConAir 1875 Watt Dryer.** If your pet gets balls of ice stuck between her toes, set a ConAir 1875 Watt blow dryer on a low warm setting, hold the nose six inches away from your pet's feet, and gently move it around to melt the ice.

- **Crisco All-Vegetable Shortening.** To soothe sore paw pads, soak your pet's paws in warm water for five minutes, and then seal in the moisture by coating the pads with a small dab of Crisco All-Vegetable Shortening. To prevent your pet from licking off the vegetable shortening, apply the Crisco right before mealtime, so your pet will be distracted by food long enough to let the soybean and cottonseed oils penetrate the thick pads.

- **Dawn Dishwashing Liquid** and **Star Olive Oil.** If your dog or cat steps in motor oil, antifreeze, or any caustic cleaners, use a few drops of Dawn Dishwashing Liquid on a damp sponge or washcloth to remove the corrosive chemicals from your pet's feet. Applying Star Olive Oil with a washcloth may also help remove any untoward substance. Otherwise, the acidic matter may damage the skin, or your pet may risk his health by licking it off. Rinse clean with water. If you have difficulty removing the harsh chemicals, contact your veterinarian for guidance.

- **Fruit of the Earth Aloe Vera Gel.** Rub Fruit of the Earth Aloe Vera Gel into your dog or cat's sore paw pads to soothe and moisturize them.

- **Heinz Apple Cider Vinegar.** If your dog or cat licks her paws obsessively, saturate a cotton ball with Heinz Apple Cider Vinegar and wipe it on her paws to make them less appetizing.

- **Huggies Baby Wipes.** To clean mud, salt, and chemical de-icers from your dog or cat's paws and feet (and between her toes), use Huggies Baby Wipes.

- **Ivory Soap.** If your dog or cat burns his paw pads by standing on a hot sidewalk, driveway, street, or patio, clean the burn by washing with Ivory Soap and water, and pat dry with a towel. Then apply an antibiotic ointment (see Neosporin on page 215). To prevent the salt used to melt snow from sidewalks from irritating your dog's paws, wash off the salt with Ivory Soap and water, pat the pads dry with a towel, and apply a few drops of moisturizer (see Lubriderm on page 215).

- **Jif Peanut Butter.** To remove bubble gum stuck to a paw or between toes, rub a dollop of creamy Jif Peanut Butter into the wad of chewing gum, working it in well, and then comb the gum out. The oils in the peanut butter dissolve the chewing gum. For more ways to remove gum, see page 127.

- **Johnson's Baby Oil.** To moisturize paw pads, rub a few drops of Johnson's Baby Oil into the pads.

- **Kingsford's Corn Starch.** Soothe rough paw pads by applying Kingsford's Corn Starch as you would baby powder or moisturizer. The corn starch seals in moisture.

- **Lubriderm.** If your dog or cat suffers from dry, cracked, or callused paw pads, apply a few drops of Lubriderm and massage it into the pads. To prevent your pet from licking off the moisturizer, apply the Lubriderm right before mealtime, so your pet will be distracted by food long enough to let the moisturizer penetrate the thick pads.

- **Neosporin.** Paw pads may seem as tough as the soles of your shoes, but they can get burned if you pet stands on a hot surface. After washing the paw pads with soap and water (see Ivory Soap on page 214), apply a dab of Neosporin to each pad. Cover with a gauze bandage and secure in place with first-aid tape.

- **Neosporin and Lubriderm.** If your pet has scraped or cut paw pads, apply a dab of Neosporin so the antiseptic ointment will help prevent infection, and then rub some Lubriderm (or Fruit of the Earth Aloe Vera Gel) into the pad to moisturize it.

- **Noxzema.** Noxzema, the skin cream originally invented in 1914 by pharmacist Dr. George Bunting in the prescription room of his Baltimore drugstore as a sunburn remedy, moisturizes tender paw pads. The camphor, menthol, and eucalyptus oil will prevent your pet from licking her paws.

- **Pam Cooking Spray.** Spray tender paw pads with a very light coat of Pam Cooking Spray and rub into the skin. The oils moisturize dry skin.

- **Trojan Non-Lubricated Condoms.** To protect an injured dog or cat paw from getting wet in the rain, unroll a Trojan Non-Lubricated Condom on the dog's foot.

- **Vaseline Petroleum Jelly.** To moisturize rough paw pads, soak your pet's paws in warm water for five minutes, and, while still wet, rub in a small dab of Vaseline Petroleum Jelly. Then cover your pet's paws with small cotton socks to prevent him from licking off the petroleum jelly.

- **Wesson Vegetable Oil.** To remove a stubborn burr from your pet's paw, apply a few drops of Wesson Vegetable Oil, and then use a pair of tweezers to pull it free. Wash out any residual oil with soapy water, rinse clean, and pat dry. For more ways to free burrs, see page 275.

- **Ziploc Storage Bags.** If your pet injures a foot and your veterinarian prescribes soaking the appendage in a medicinal solution, fill a Ziploc Storage Bag with the liquid, place your pet's foot in the bag, and seal it shut as much as possible. Hold your pet still while the foot soaks for the required time.

For Dogs Only

- **Arm & Hammer Baking Soda.** To clean grime, salt, and snow-melting chemicals from your dog feet, fill a bathtub with two inches of water, dissolve one cup Arm & Hammer Baking Soda in the water, and have your pet stand in the water. Or dissolve one-half cup Arm & Baking Soda in a bucket of water and wash your pet's paws. The baking soda will soothe the burning caused by the chemicals used to melt ice and snow.

- **Pam Cooking Spray.** Before your dog romps in the snow, spray her paw pads with a light coat of Pam Cooking Spray to prevent snow from getting packed between the pads.

- **Trojan Non-Lubricated Condoms.** To protect your dog's paws from rock salt when walking in the snow, put on four Trojan Non-Lubricated Condoms.

- **Vaseline Petroleum Jelly.** To protect your dog's paws from sidewalk ice and rock salt in the winter months, rub a dab of Vaseline Petroleum Jelly into his paws before taking him for a walk or letting him outside. Be sure to wipe the remaining petroleum jelly off your dog's feet before letting him back in the house. Otherwise he may track grease stains on the floors, carpets, and furniture.

- **Ziploc Storage Bags.** To prevent your dog from getting rock salt stuck in his paws when you take him for a walk in the snow, slip your dog's paws into four Ziploc Storage Bags to create plastic boots, and fasten them in place with rubber bands. If they slip off, cover the bags with baby socks.

PET PEEVES

- Although dog and cat paw pads are thick and tough, the animals are still walking barefoot, making them susceptible to abrasions, lacerations, and burns. Avoid letting your pet run on hot pavement.

- If you notice that your pet is limping, examine his paws for any signs of injury.

- Moisturize your pet's paw pads only to soothe soreness. Too much moisturizing will make the paw pads soft, which makes them susceptible to injury.

- To prevent your long-haired pet from getting matted hair between her toes, trim back the hair with a pair of grooming scissors.

- To stop your pet from licking his paws obsessively, have your pet fit with an Elizabethan collar—a conical plastic casing that fits around the animal's neck.

- Use a soft towel to dry your pet's feet after a wet walk or run outside. Too much moisture can irritate the paw pads.

Poison

For Dogs and Cats

- **CharcoCaps Activated Charcoal.** Feed your pet one capsule of Charco-Caps Activated Charcoal (by mixing it with water or milk, if necessary). The charcoal absorbs toxins from the stomach before the stomach can absorb them into your pet's system. Then take your pet to the veterinarian for immediate attention. (Don't confuse activated charcoal with charcoal briquettes. Activated charcoal is a charcoal that has been processed with oxygen to be extremely porous and absorb odors or other substances.)

- **Heinz White Vinegar.** If your pet consumed an alkaline toxin such as drain cleaner, do not inducing vomiting (otherwise, the poison will burn a second time coming back up). Instead, fill a turkey baster or bulb syringe with three tablespoons Heinz White Vinegar and three tablespoons of water, and squirt the solution toward the back of his mouth. The acetic acid will neutralize the alkali in his stomach, reducing the burn. Then take your pet to a veterinarian for treatment.

- **Hydrogen Peroxide.** If your dog or cat swallows pills, antifreeze, or toxic substances (except for caustic substances) and you can't get professional help immediately, fill a turkey baster or bulb syringe with one tablespoon hydrogen

GET YOUR PET TO THE VET

Name your poison! If your pet has consumed poison, call your veterinarian, a veterinary hospital, or a poison control center immediately. Let your pet drink as much water as he wants. When you take your pet to the veterinarian, bring along a sample of the toxic substance and the product's container, packaging, or label.

peroxide for every ten pounds your pet weights, tip your pet's head back, and squirt the liquid toward the back of his mouth. Within five minutes, the hydrogen peroxide should make your pet vomit. If not, wait ten minutes and repeat a second time. (Don't try a third time; too much hydrogen peroxide can be dangerous.) Then take your pet to a veterinarian for treatment.

- **Morton Salt.** If your dog or cat swallowed a noncorrosive poison and you need to induce vomiting, dissolve one teaspoon Morton Salt (plain, not iodized) in warm water, fill a turkey baster or bulb syringe with the salt water, tip your pet's head back, and squirt the liquid toward the back of his mouth. Within five minutes, the salt should make your pet vomit. Then take your pet to a veterinarian for treatment.

- **Nestlé Carnation Nonfat Dry Milk.** If your dog or cat has consumed a corrosive poison (containing acids, alkalis, or petroleum distillates) and isn't showing signs of wooziness, give your pet milk to dilute the poison and relieve any irritation by coating his stomach, esophagus, and mouth. If you don't have any fresh milk, mix three ounces Nestlé Carnation Nonfat Dry Milk and eight ounces water, and get your pet to drink the solution. Then take your pet to the veterinarian for immediate attention.

- **Phillips' Milk of Magnesia.** If your dog or cat devoured an acidic substance by drinking bleach or chewing a battery, give your pet one teaspoon Phillips' Milk of Magnesia for every five pounds your pet weighs. The milk of magnesia will counteract the acid. Then take your pet to a veterinarian.

PET PEEVES
FATAL ATTRACTIONS

- Signs of poisoning for a pet include: drooling, panting, gasping, vomiting, diarrhea, burns on the mouth, lack of coordination, bleeding, convulsions, and coma.

- If you can identify what poison product your pet has consumed, read the label on the container for a possible antidote.

- Use a blanket as a stretcher for your pet. Place your dog or cat in the center of the blanket, and have two people each lift two corners of the blanket to carry the pet.

- Dogs and cats love the taste of antifreeze, which can be deadly even if your pet drinks only a small amount. Keep your pets away from any puddles under or near cars, and store antifreeze in a sturdy, tightly sealed container.

- Dogs and cats love eating the poison pellets that kill snails. Keep these out of reach.

- Never let a pet drink from a toilet that has a cleaner or freshener in the tank or bowl. The chemicals in toilet cleaners and fresheners are toxic to cats and dogs. Either stop using toilet cleaners and fresheners, or keep the seat down to prevent pets from using the toilet as a water bowl.

- Store harmful cleaning products in a safe, secure location that your pets cannot possibly reach or get into.

- **ReaLemon.** Never induce vomiting if your pet drank a caustic substance like drain cleaner. The poison will burn a second time coming back up. Instead, fill a turkey baster or bulb syringe with three tablespoons ReaLemon lemon juice and three tablespoons water, and squirt the solution toward the back of his mouth. The citric acid will neutralize the alkali in his stomach, reducing the burn. Then take your pet to a veterinarian for treatment.

- **Ziploc Storage Bag.** Before taking your poisoned pet to your veterinarian, collect a sample of your pet's vomit in a Ziploc Storage Bag, along with any item your pet may have chewed and the product's container.

Rabbits

Cage

- **Dawn Dishwashing Liquid.** Clean your rabbit's cage once or twice a week by confining your rabbit to a room or secondary cage, and then sweeping out the cage and scrubbing the floor with a bucket of warm, soapy water made with a few drops of Dawn Dishwashing Liquid. Rinse with clean water.

- **Dustbuster.** To clean a rabbit cage, use a whiskbroom to loosen any debris or hair, and then vacuum with a Dustbuster.

Cleaning

- **Huggies Baby Wipes.** To clean your rabbit's fur and get rid of any loose hairs without brushing or combing, wipe your pet with a hypoallergenic, fragrance-free Huggies Baby Wipe.

Dehydration

- **Coca-Cola.** During hot, humid weather, fill clean, empty two-liter Coca-Cola bottles with water, freeze, and place in the hutch to keep your rabbit comfortable and prevent dehydration.

Ear Mites

- **Johnson's Baby Oil.** To eradicate ear mites, put a few drops of Johnson's Baby Oil in your rabbit's ears, and then wipe out the excess oil with a cotton ball. Repeat if necessary. The mineral oil smothers the mites and dissolves the waxy debris. For more ways to eliminate ear mites, see page 90.

Feeding

- **Downy Fabric Softener.** To make a handy scoop, cut an empty, clean Downy Fabric Softener jug in half diagonally. Use the half with the handle to scoop up rabbit pellets and reach inside the hutch to refill the food bowl.

Furniture

- **Heinz Chili Sauce.** To stop your pet rabbit from nibbling on the wooden legs of furniture, rub the furniture legs with Heinz Chili Sauce, and then wipe it off. Rabbits can't stand the stuff.

Hairballs

- **Dole Pineapple Juice.** Rabbits cannot vomit, so they have no way to regurgitate impacted hairballs. Feeding a rabbit pineapple juice helps lubricate the digestive tract, allowing the animal to excrete the hairball. Consult your veterinarian to make sure the hairball doesn't develop into a more serious situation requiring surgery.

Housebreaking

- **Tidy Cats** and **USA Today.** To housebreak a new rabbit, place the bunny in an enclosed area with plenty of newspaper on the floor. When the rabbit relieves itself, place a shallow cat litter box over the spot filled with Tidy Cats cat box filler. The rabbit will return to the spot and learn to use the litter box, which you should clean daily.

Litter Box

- **_USA Today._** When your rabbit chooses to use one corner of her cage as the bathroom, put a litter box lined with _USA Today_ in that spot. Fill the box with timothy hay (or any other grass hay except alfalfa), pelleted-newspaper litter, or shredded pages of _USA Today._ Change the litter box daily.

Pooper Scooper

- **Clorox.** To make a handy pooper-scooper, cut an empty, clean Clorox Bleach jug in half diagonally. Use the half with the handle to scoop up any mess.

Toys

- **Bounty Paper Towels.** Rabbits love playing with clean, empty Bounty Paper Towel rolls.

- **Charmin Toilet Paper.** An empty Charmin Toilet Paper roll placed inside the cage creates a perfect play toy for a rabbit.

- **Kleenex Tissues.** Provide your rabbit with toys to satisfy her natural desire to dig and chew, such as a clean, empty Kleenex Tissue box.

- **Slinky.** A Slinky makes a great pet toy for rabbits. They love to pull on the spring toy and toss it around in their cage.

- **_USA Today._** Fill a cardboard box halfway with shredded pages from _USA Today_ to make a digging box for your rabbit.

PET PEEVES
THE BUNNY HOP

- Rabbits are lagomorphs, not rodents. Lagomorphs have four upper incisor teeth while rodents have only two. Lagomorphs are predominantly herbivores, while rodents are omnivores.

- Rabbits and hares are not the same thing. Rabbits are born blind and without fur, while hares, which are larger and have longer ears than rabbits, are born with vision and fur.

- The Belgian hare is actually a rabbit, and the jack rabbit is actually a hare.

- There are more than 60 breeds of domestic rabbits, ranging in size from two to thirteen pounds.

- Never lift a rabbit by its ears. A rabbit's ear muscles are easily torn. To pick up your rabbit, support his forequarters with one hand and his hindquarters with the other hand. Otherwise, you risk injuring the rabbit's spine.

- Have your rabbit spayed to prevent unwanted litters or neutered to stop spraying in males.

- Rabbits have no way to regurgitate hairballs. Prevent any potential complications by grooming your rabbit regularly and feeding your pet a high-fiber diet to keep his digestive tract well lubricated.

- Keep your rabbit in a cage indoors where he can interact with your family, not in an outdoor hutch in unnatural isolation where the approach of a predator may give him a heart attack.

- Wire-bottom cages can cut up your rabbit's feet. Buy a cage with a solid bottom, or if you already own a wire cage, cover the bottom with a sheet of plywood or corrugated cardboard. Place plenty of straw, hay, or aspen shavings in the cage so your rabbit can build a comfortable nest.

- Remove droppings and urine from your rabbit's cage every day.

- Do not house a rabbit with other rabbits unless all are spayed and neutered.

- Keep the temperature between 65 and 80 degrees Fahrenheit to keep your rabbit comfortable.

- Give your rabbit a safe exercise area with plenty of room to run and jump, either fully enclosing an outdoor spot with a fence (and keeping a close eye on your rabbit to prevent an escape attempt) or by rabbit-proofing an appropriate indoor area (and keeping all electrical wires inaccessible).

- Rabbits are delicate animals easily frightened when held, cuddled, or carried around by children. Distressed rabbits tend to scratch or bite, and rabbits dropped accidentally by children can break their legs and backs.

- An old telephone book makes an excellent chew toy for a rabbit.

- Your rabbit's diet should consist of unlimited grass hay (to keep his digestive system healthy), good-quality rabbit pellets, and fresh, leafy greens. Rabbits love beet greens, bok choy, broccoli, Brussels sprouts, carrots, celery, cucumbers, green beans, kale, mustard greens, peas, spinach, sprouts, squash, and turnips.

- Rabbits eat weeds, most notably crabgrass, dandelions, knotweed, and ragweed. Rabbits also eat poison ivy—without suffering any ill effects.

- Make clean, fresh water available at all times, either in a sturdy bowl or from a bottle that attaches to the cage.

- Never use any clay cat box litter in a rabbit's litter box. The dust can cause respiratory or gastrointestinal problems in rabbits.

- Rabbits sometimes eat their own feces to aid digestion and obtain additional nutrients.

- Groom your rabbit regularly with a soft brush to remove shedding hair and keep his coat healthy.

- Trim your rabbit's nails with a pair of dog nail trimmers. Rabbits keep their nails trimmed by digging, but domesticated rabbits rarely get that opportunity.

- In John Steinbeck's 1937 novel *Of Mice and Men,* Lennie Small repeatedly says, "Tell me about the rabbits, George."

- When rabbits sense danger or feel anxious, they thump their rear legs on the ground, just like Thumper in the 1942 animated Walt Disney movie *Bambi.*

GET YOUR PET TO THE VET

Hop to it! If your rabbit stops eating or defecating for more than twelve hours or has watery diarrhea, runny nose and eyes, dark red urine, or fur loss accompanied by red, swollen skin, take your pet to the veterinarian immediately.

Reptiles and Amphibians

Bowls

For Snakes Only

- **Clorox Bleach.** Snakes are sensitive to dishwashing liquids and soaps. Wash your snakes' water bowl with three-quarters cup Clorox Bleach to one gallon water. Rinse thoroughly.

Handling

For Frogs and Toads Only

- **Dial Soap.** If you must handle an amphibian with your bare hands, wash your hands with Dial Soap and rinse thoroughly to protect the animal from the oils and salts emitted by your skin. Frogs and toads carry and breed salmonella bacteria. After handling a frog or toad, wash your hands thoroughly with antibacterial Dial Soap to protect yourself from possible infection.

Pet Tricks
Snakebites

- **Dial Soap.** If your snake bites you and the wound is superficial, wash the wound thoroughly with Dial Soap and water. Then apply a disinfectant (see Neosporin below).

- **Neosporin.** After washing a superficial snakebite with antibacterial soap (see Dial above), apply a dab of Neosporin.

- **Playtex Living Gloves.** If you must pick up an amphibian, put on a pair of Playtex Living Gloves, dampen the gloves with running water, and then pick up your pet with your cupped hand (without squeezing the creature). When you're finished, wash the gloves with soapy water and rinse clean.

For Snakes Only

- **Purell Instant Hand Sanitizer.** Snakes commonly carry and breed salmonella bacteria. After handling a snake, always wash your hands thoroughly with Purell Instant Hand Sanitizer.

For Turtles Only

- **Purell Instant Hand Sanitizer.** Turtles commonly carry and breed salmonella bacteria. Never kiss a turtle or hold it close to your face. After handling a turtle, always wash your hands thoroughly with Purell Instant Hand Sanitizer.

Terrariums

For Snakes Only

- **Clorox Bleach.** To thoroughly clean your snake's terrarium (at least twice a month), remove all furniture (branches, vines, water bowls, and Astroturf) from the enclosure and immerse them in a bin filled with one part Clorox Bleach and nineteen parts water. Let sit for one hour, and then rinse clean and sun dry. Discard all used substrate (newspaper, gravel, etcetera). To disinfect the enclosure, fill a sixteen-ounce trigger-spray bottle with two cups water and add two tablespoons Clorox Bleach. Spray the entire enclosure, let stand for fifteen minutes, rinse thoroughly with water, and dry with a clean towel. Line the bottom of the enclosure with fresh newspaper and return the cage furniture.

- **USA Today.** Line the bottom of the snake enclosure with several sheets of *USA Today*.

For Turtles Only

- **USA Today.** Fill the bottom of the tank with a shredded copy of *USA Today* to create a substrate.

PET PEEVES

COLD-BLOODED FACTS

- Never bring a snake close to your mouth or allow it to breathe in your face.

- When washing your snake's food and water bowls, keep them separate from your own dishes and use separate sponges and scrubbers from your own.

- Remove excretions and uneaten food from your snake's terrarium daily, change the water and clean the water bowl daily, and change the flooring at least every other day.

- Do not serve live prey to your snake. A hostile rodent can harm your snake.

- After your snake eats a meal, leave him alone for several days to prevent stress from interfering with proper digestion.

- Snakes shed their skin every one to three months. Do not handle your snake while he sheds, otherwise you risk damaging the new skin. If your snake fails to shed completely, place him in a shallow water bowl for one to two hours to prompt the shedding to finish.

- If a snakebite becomes discolored or heals slowly, see a doctor to make sure you're not suffering from infection or salmonella.

- When cleaning your pet reptile or amphibian's terrarium home, confine your pet to a second terrarium to prevent any possibility of escape.

- The word *amphibious* means "double life," and these creatures live both on land and in water.

- All amphibians are best left untouched. Otherwise, the oils and salts from human hands coat the creature's skin, possibly clogging the frog, toad, or newt's fragile, mucous-coated breathing mechanism.

- Despite what you've read in fairy tales or seen in the movies, never kiss a frog or toad or hold it close to your face. Frogs and toads commonly carry and breed salmonella bacteria.

- Contrary to popular belief, turtles and tortoises are not the same thing. A turtle lives in water, swims well, has webbed feet, and is either carnivorous or omnivorous; a tortoise lives on land, cannot swim, has unwebbed feet, and is generally an herbivore. Scientifically, however, turtles and tortoises are classified as turtles.

- In captivity, turtles can live up to twenty years.

Ringworm

For Dogs and Cats

- **Betadine Skin Cleanser.** To prevent the ring-like bald patches on your dog or cat's body from getting infected, wash them daily with Betadine Skin Cleanser. This antiseptic soap will keep the minor fungal infections from developing into more severe bacterial infections.

- **Clorox Bleach.** Wash any pet bedding, sheets, or furniture covers in hot water and add one cup Clorox Bleach to the wash load. The bleach helps kill any of the contagious fungus and keeps it from spreading to people in your home.

- **Clorox Bleach.** After brushing, combing, or trimming the hair of your infected pet, soak the brush, comb, scissors, or clipper blades for five minutes in a solution made with one ounce Clorox Bleach and one quart water. Then wash the brush or comb with soap and water, and rinse clean.

- **Fruit of the Earth Aloe Vera Gel.** To combat a ringworm infection, apply Fruit of the Earth Aloe Vera Gel to the spot several times a day.

- **Heinz Apple Cider Vinegar.** Saturate a cotton ball with Heinz Apple Cider Vinegar and apply to the ringworm area three times a day. The acid in the vinegar kills the fungus.

- **Lamisil.** The fungus that causes ringworm is closely related to athlete's foot. So, any antifungal cream that eliminates the tinea that causes athlete's foot should also cure a ringworm infection. Rub a small dab of Lamisil Antifungal Cream into the affected area twice a day. Be sure to consult with your veterinarian to make sure Lamisil is a suitable antifungal cream for your pet.

- **Listerine.** To control ringworm, saturate a cotton ball with Listerine and dab the affected skin twice a day. The antiseptic kills the fungus.

- **McCormick Alum.** To treat ringworm, mix one-eighth teaspoon McCormick Alum with the white from one large egg, clean the affected area well, and apply the alum-and-egg solution to the spot, and let dry. Repeat daily until the malady vanishes.

- **Purell Instant Hand Sanitizer.** Until you've killed all the ringworm on your dog or cat, avoid petting and cuddling your pet so you don't catch the fungus. If you must touch your pet, wash your hands with Purell Instant Hand Sanitizer.

- **ReaLemon.** Saturate the affected area with ReaLemon lemon juice three times a day. The acid kills the fungus.

GET YOUR PET TO THE VET

A familiar ring? If ringworm spreads over your pet's body and the sores become red and ooze pus, take your pet to the veterinarian immediately.

PET PEEVES
A VICIOUS CIRCLE

- Despite its misleading name, ringworm is not caused by a worm infestation. Ringworm is an infection of skin, hair, and nails by several types of highly contagious fungi similar to athlete's foot and jock itch.

- Ringworm causes unsightly ring-shaped patches of flaky skin that itch and tend to go away on their own within one to three months.

- An infestation of ringworm indicates that the animal's health is weak or that he is stressed or ill. Better nutrition will help your pet fight off the disease.

- Trimming the hair around the bare spot decreases the likelihood that the ringworm will spread. Use an electric razor and carefully dispose of the trimmed hair to avoid further infection.

- Humans can catch ringworm from pets and vice versa.

- Regular grooming prevents ringworm from spreading by removing fungal spores before they can infect other areas of your pet's body.

- Vacuum up shed hair that might be infected with the fungus to avoid further contamination.

- If you have more than one pet, keep the infected pet isolated from the others. If you decide to treat your infected pet with an antifungal shampoo, treat all of your pets at the same time.

Scratching

For Dogs and Cats

- **3M Sandpaper.** If your pet scratches on the cabinet door where you store her food or treats, use masking tape to adhere a sheet of 3M Sandpaper to the trouble spot. Instead of scratching the woodwork, your pet will file her own nails.

For Cats Only

- **Con-Tact Paper.** To dissuade a cat from scratching your sofa or any other upholstered furniture, roll back a sheet of clear Con-Tact paper to stick to itself and adhere the sticky sheet to the furniture. Cats hate sticky surfaces and will stay away.

- **Country Time Lemonade.** Dissolve one-half teaspoon Country Time Lemonade drink mix and two cups rubbing (isopropyl) alcohol in a sixteen-ounce trigger-spray bottle. Spray the solution on whatever furniture the cat loves scratching. Cats despise the smell of lemon and will stay away from that piece of furniture.

- **Glad Trash Bags.** If your cat is scratching the sofa, cut open a Glad Trash Bag along the seams and cover your furniture with the plastic. Cats despise the feeling of plastic and stay away.

- **Heinz Chili Sauce.** Here's a spicy way to stop your cat from scratching furniture. Rub wooden furniture legs with Heinz Chili Sauce, and then wipe it off. Cats can't stand the smell.

- **Heinz White Vinegar** and **Heinz Apple Cider Vinegar.** Mix five ounces Heinz White Vinegar, five ounces Heinz Apple Cider Vinegar, and five ounces water in a sixteen-ounce trigger-spray bottle. Shake well. Spray the solution on whatever furniture your cat loves to scratch. Reapply every few days.

- **Lemon Pledge.** Cats hate the smell of citrus, so you can easily stop your cat from scratching wood furniture by polishing the furniture with Lemon Pledge. The lemon scent keeps the cat away.

- **McCormick Ground (Cayenne) Red Pepper** and **Scotch Tape.** Sprinkle McCormick Ground (Cayenne) Red Pepper on the sticky side of strips of Scotch Tape and hang the strips (with the pepper facing out) from the side of the furniture that your cat loves to scratch.

- **McCormick Pure Lemon Extract.** To stop your cat from scratching the furniture, saturate a cotton ball with McCormick Pure Lemon Extract and either rub it into the furniture, set it on a saucer, or hang it from an aluminum tea ball over the trouble spot. Refresh the lemon extract once a week until you're satisfied that your cat will no longer scratch that spot.

- **Old English Lemon Oil Furniture Polish.** Rubbing your wood furniture with Old English Lemon Oil not only rejuvenates the wood, giving the furniture a wonderful luster, but the strong lemon scent repels cats, preventing them from scratching the wood.

- **Old Spice Aftershave Lotion.** Mix one part Old Spice Aftershave Lotion with ten parts water in a spray bottle and spray the solution wherever cats are giving you trouble. Cats dislike the smell of Old Spice and will keep away.

- **Oust Air Sanitizer.** Cats hate the smell of oranges and lemons. Simply spray whatever item the animal loves scratching with Oust Air Sanitizer (Citrus Scent), and the cat will no longer find that item appealing in the least.

- **ReaLemon.** Mix six ounces ReaLemon lemon juice, three ounces water, and one ounce of rubbing (isopropyl) alcohol in a sixteen-ounce trigger-spray bottle. Shake well and spray whatever furniture your cat loves to scratch. Reapply as needed.

- **Reynolds Wrap.** While you're training the cat to use a scratching post, place strips of Reynolds Wrap to cover up the spots on the furniture where the pet has been scratching. Cats hate the feeling of aluminum foil.

- **Saran Wrap.** Cats also dislike scratching plastic. Adhere sheets of Saran Wrap on spots on the furniture where the pet has been scratching until you've successfully trained the cat to use a scratching post instead.

- **Scotch Double Sided Tape.** Cats despise double-sided tape. Adhere a few strips to your sofa or any furniture that you don't want the cat using as a scratching post. The cat will quickly learn to go elsewhere.

- **Tabasco Pepper Sauce.** Spray or rub Tabasco Pepper Sauce on the furniture you want your cat to stop scratching. The hot sauce wipes off easily, but test an inconspicuous spot first to make sure it doesn't stain.

- **Tang.** Dissolve one-half teaspoon Tang powdered drink mix and two cups rubbing (isopropyl) alcohol in a sixteen-ounce trigger-spray bottle. Spray the solution on whatever items the cat loves scratching. Cats despise the smell of oranges and will give up on that item.

- **USA Today.** If your cat scratches you, immediately give her a swat with a rolled-up section of *USA Today*. This mimics the way another cat would react and gets your message across quickly.

PET PEEVES

STARTING FROM SCRATCH

- Contrary to popular belief, cats do not scratch furniture to sharpen their claws. They scratch furniture to mark their territory. The pads in their feet secrete a scent undetectable by humans.

- Place a scratching post near the furniture, wall, or cabinet that the cat has been scratching. Once the cat starts scratching the post instead of the furniture, you can gradually move the post to a more appropriate spot.

- You can make a scratching post by securing a two-foot tall pine post to a eighteen-square-inch wooden base with wood screws, and then stapling a carpet remnant around the post.

- To get a cat to start using a new scratching post, rub catnip into the post.

- If your cat's scratching post gets tatty, don't throw it away. The fact that the cat is using the post means he will continue using it.

Separation Anxiety

For Dogs Only

- **Easy Cheese.** To allay your dog's separation anxiety whenever you leave the house, calm your pet before you walk out the door by spraying some aerosol Easy Cheese inside a hollow chew toy.

- **Jif Peanut Butter.** If your dog experiences separation anxiety whenever you leave the house, calm your pet before you walk out the door by giving her a hollow toy stuffed with Jif Peanut Butter. If you limit giving your pet this special treat to just before your impending departures,  your dog will learn to look forward to your absences. Distracted by the special treat, your dog will spend hours enthusiastically trying to work the peanut butter out of the toy.

- **Knorr Beef Bouillon.** Bring a cup of water to a boil, and dissolve one Knorr Beef Bouillon cube in the cup. Soak a rawhide bone or stick in the broth for five minutes, and then place it on a paper towel to dry. Before you leave the house, give your dog the beef-flavored rawhide bone, so he'll have hours of lip-smacking entertainment to distract him from your absence.

- **Pam Cooking Spray** and **McCormick Garlic Salt.** To attract your dog to his chew toys, spray his cloth toys with Pam Cooking Spray. Dogs love the taste of oil. To make the toy even more appealing, sprinkle on some McCormick Garlic Salt, which dogs find irresistible.

- **Philadelphia Cream Cheese.** You can also stuff that hollow toy with Philadelphia Cream Cheese to give your dog hours of entertainment to help forget about you while you're out of the house.

Pet Tricks
Fear of Thunder

If your dog is afraid of thunder, train your dog to relax by gradually acclimating him to the sound of thunder by simulating an artificial storm. Make your dog sit or lie down and reward him with a treat. With your dog still sitting, play a recording of thunder at a low volume and give him another treat and affectionate praise. Gradually increase the volume, and continue rewarding the dog with a treat and praise. Slowly lower the volume to off. Repeat these sessions for a few days. During a genuine thunderstorm, make the dog sit or lie down and reward him with treats and praise if he remains calm. If your dog displays anxiety, ignore him.

PET PEEVES

- If frightened when left alone, dogs attempt to cope with the anxiety by barking, chewing, digging, whining, escaping, or urinating and defecating in improper spots.

- To prevent your dog or cat from getting lonely, turn on the radio and leave it playing when you leave the house. The sounds from the radio, particularly talk radio, will keep your pet company.

- Dogs get lonely when left all alone because they are instinctively pack animals.

- To alleviate your dog's separation anxiety, acclimate him to your absence by leaving the house for one minute—without an emotional goodbye or hello. Leave the dog in a confined area with a chew toy and a bowl of water. Repeat this several times until the animal realizes that you always come back. Gradually increase the amount of time you are gone.

- Before leaving the house, take your dog out for a vigorous walk to burn off some of that anxious energy.

- When you leave the house at night, leave on some lights for your pet to reduce her anxiety.

- To stop your dog from panicking during your absences, consider crate-training your dog to give the animal peace of mind in the security of a mock den.

- If you constantly leave your dog alone for extended periods of time, consider getting a second pet to keep your dog company.

- Before you and your family leave the house on Monday morning, after a full weekend at home giving your pet abundant attention, give your pet a good walk or playtime session and a favorite chew toy.

- If your dog gets anxious whenever you take suitcases out of the closet, let your dog play in the suitcases when you're not planning a trip. This way, when you're preparing to go on a trip, your dog won't have an anxiety attack when you take out the suitcases.

Shedding

For Dogs and Cats

- **Bounty Paper Towels.** To prevent a dog or cat from shedding all over the house, dampen a sheet of Bounty Paper Towel and run it over the animal's fur. The paper towel collects the loose hair.

- **Dustbuster.** Use a Dustbuster with a brush attachment to vacuum shedding hair from your dog or cat (unless the noise from the hand-held vacuum frightens your pet). Many pets love the sensation, which doubles as a massage. To train your pet to tolerate the Dustbuster, first stroke your pet with the Dustbuster turned off, offering constant praise and reassurance. On a second occasion, turn the Dustbuster on, but do not touch your pet with it, again extolling and encouraging the animal. At a later time, once your pet has grown accustomed to the Dustbuster, vacuum the animal's coat.

- **Huggies Baby Wipes.** Wipe down your dog or cat's coat with a hypoallergenic, fragrance-free Huggies Baby Wipe to pick up shedding hair.

- **Playtex Living Gloves.** To remove shedding pet hair from your dog or cat, put on a pair of Playtex Living Gloves, fill a bucket with water, dip the gloves in the water, and run your fingers and palms along the fur to allow

Pet Tricks
Picking Up Shed Hair

- **Alberto VO5 Hair Spray.** To remove clinging pet hair from furniture, drapes, and carpet, spray a fine mist of Alberto VO5 Hair Spray on a damp towel or washcloth and wipe the upholstered furniture.

- **Bounce.** To sweep up pet hair from furniture, clothes, or bedding, simply wipe the affected area with a clean, used sheet of Bounce, which magnetically gathers all the hairs.

- **Downy Fabric Softener.** To make vacuuming up pet hair a snap, mix two table-spoons Downy Fabric Softener and one cup water in a sixteen-ounce trigger-spray bottle, shake well, and spray the carpet liberally. Let dry and vacuum. The fabric softener eliminates any static electricity, making the hair easier to vacuum.

- **Dustbuster.** If you don't have a powerful vacuum cleaner, use a Dustbuster to suck pet hair out of carpets, rugs, and upholstered furniture.

- **Endust.** To mop pet hair from floors, spray the head of a dust mop with a light coat of Endust, let stand overnight to allow the oil to spread out evenly throughout the strands, and then mop with long strokes. The Endust helps the mop magnetically attract pet hair. To clean the mop, shake it outside.

- **Huggies Baby Wipes.** To clean hair from baseboards, furniture, and upholstery, wipe with a Huggies Baby Wipe.

the rubber to collect shedding hair. Dip the hair-covered gloves in the water again. The wet rubber attracts the pet hair, and the water in the bucket rinses it off.

- **Star Olive Oil.** To slow a dog or cat from shedding, add one tablespoon Star Olive Oil to your pet's food. The oil keeps the animal's coat shiny and simultaneously reduces shedding.

- **L'eggs Sheer Energy Panty Hose.** To clean pet hair from under a bed or sofa on a wood or tile floor, cut off one leg from a clean, used pair of L'eggs Sheer Energy Panty Hose, place it over the end of a broomstick, and secure it in place with a rubber band. Slide the nylon-covered broomstick under the bed or sofa and move it back and forth.

- **Oral-B Toothbrush.** Brush up shed pet hair from crevices of furniture with a clean, used Oral-B Toothbrush.

- **Playtex Living Gloves.** To remove pet hair from clothes, furniture, and bedding, put on a pair of Playtex Living Gloves, fill a bucket halfway with water, dip the gloves in the water, wipe the area affected by the pet hair, and dip the gloves in the water again. The wet rubber attracts the pet hair, and the water in the bucket rinses it off.

- **Scotch Packaging Tape.** Wrap Scotch Packaging Tape around your hand with the sticky-side out and pat the stray pet hairs on furniture or your clothes with the tape. The pet hairs will stick to the tape.

- **Silly Putty.** Roll Silly Putty into a ball, flatten it into a pancake, and use it to pat hair-covered furniture. The hairs stick to the Silly Putty.

- **Static Guard.** To remove pet hair from clothes and furniture, spray Static Guard directly on the item, and then use a lint brush to sweep away the hair.

- **Velcro.** To decrease shedding in the house, adhere strips of Velcro around the rim of your pet's flexible door. When your dog or cat brushes against the strips, the Velcro will grab loose hair.

PET PEEVES
SPLITTING HAIRS

- Most dogs and cats shed most profusely in the spring.

- Brushing your pet helps collect shedding hair before it clings to the furniture and carpets. After using a brush, switch to a comb to lift up even more hair. For more ways to groom your pet, see page 123.

- To loosen hair before brushing or combing, give your pet a warm bath. For more ways to bathe your pet, see page 13.

- Warm temperatures trigger pets to shed. If your dog or cats starts shedding heavily during the winter months, turn down the heat in your home.

- To vacuum pet hair from floors more effectively, sweep the area with a dampened broom first.

- For a simple way to remove pet hair from furniture, clothes, and carpets, rub the affected spot with a damp sponge.

- To reduce shedding from a thick-haired dog, consider giving your pet a trim.

For Dogs Only

- **Lubriderm.** To control shedding, massage Lubriderm into your dog's coat once every two weeks.

- **Star Olive Oil.** Another way to manage shedding is to massage a few drops of Star Olive Oil in your dog's skin once every two weeks.

Sinus Problems

For Dogs and Cats

- **Huggies Baby Wipes.** If your dog or cat suffers from congestion or a runny nose, gently wipe the nose with Huggies Baby Wipes. The moistened towelettes gently remove accumulated mucus from your pet's sore nose, and the lanolin and aloe vera help soothe any irritation.

- **Little Noses Decongestant Nose Drops.** To thin coagulated mucus and help clear your dog or cat's sinuses, give your pet a few drops of Little Noses Decongestant Nose Drops. Simply tip your pet's head back with one hand. Holding the dropper in the other hand, place one or two drops of the saline solution in each nostril. Keep the animal's head tipped back for a minute or two to give the nose drops sufficient time to work. Repeat twice a day.

- **Vicks VapoRub.** Add a dab of Vicks VapoRub to the front tray of a hot water vaporizer. The moisture and the menthol help soothe your pet's troubled nose and open his sinuses.

For Cats Only

- **Chicken of the Sea Tuna.** To assure that your congested cat is getting sufficient nutrition to keep her immune system strong to fight off the sniffles, feed your cat Chicken of the Sea Tuna, whose strong aroma is sure to give your cat a healthy appetite.

GET YOUR PET TO THE VET

Keep your nose clean! If your dog or cat experiences a fever, discharges thick, discolored mucus, and seems lethargic, take your pet to the veterinarian immediately to check for a bacterial infection.

PET PEEVES

BREATHING EASY

- A congested cat might refuse to eat because he cannot adequately smell his food. Gently heat up the cat food to a lukewarm temperature or add warm water to his kibble, enhancing the smell to better lure the cat. The hot meal also helps unblock clogged sinuses.

- When you take a hot bath or shower, bring your congested dog or cat into the bathroom to let the steam provide natural relief.

- A dog's sense of smell may be more than 100 times more developed than a human's sense of smell. Dogs can detect odors millions of times too faint for people to perceive.

- Dogs and cats use their highly developed sense of smell to discover new terrain, recognize people and other animals, and sense activity in the world.

- A gland inside the dog's nose provides fluid to keep the animal's nose moist—enabling the dog to detect odors. Dogs also keep their nose moist by licking it.

- A cat's sense of smell is more powerful than a human's sense of smell, but weaker than a dog's sense of smell.

- Aside from their noses, cats also smell using a vomeronasal organ located in the roof of their mouth.

- Cats use their acute sense of smell to hunt prey, determine the freshness of food, and to identify their own territories, which they mark with their own scent.

Skunks

For Dogs and Cats

- **Arm & Hammer Baking Soda.** To deodorize skunk odor from a dog or cat, make a thick paste from Arm & Hammer Baking Soda and warm water, apply the paste to the animal's fur, and let dry. The sodium bicarbonate absorbs the skunk smell.

- **Arm & Hammer Baking Soda, Hydrogen Peroxide,** and **Dawn Dishwashing Liquid.** While working as a chemist at Molex, Inc., Paul Krebaum of Lisle, Illinois, concocted a solution to subdue the horrible reek of hydrogen sulfide gas. He modified the formula so a colleague could use the solution as a skunk remedy. *Chemical & Engineering News* reported the recipe in 1993. In a bucket, mix one-quarter cup Arm & Hammer Baking Soda, one quart hydrogen peroxide, and one teaspoon Dawn Dishwashing Liquid. Use a scrub brush to work this solution into your skunked pet's fur, and then rinse well.

- **Bausch & Lomb Eye Wash.** Dogs generally approach a skunk face first and get sprayed in the eyes. To relieve the stinging from the skunk oil, flush your dog's eyes with Bausch & Lomb Eye Wash, following the directions on the box. If your dog scratches its eyes or squints for more than an hour, take him to your veterinarian.

- **Budweiser** and **McCormick Pure Vanilla Extract.** Mix three cans (twelve fluid ounces each) Budweiser beer and two tablespoons McCormick Vanilla Extract, saturate your pet's fur with the solution, rub it in well, and let sit for five minutes, making sure the animal does not lick off any of the alcoholic beverage. Rinse clean with warm water.

- **Campbell's Tomato Juice.** To eliminate skunk odor on your dog or cat, wear rubber gloves to avoid getting the skunk odor all over yourself (see Playtex Living Gloves on page 253), wash your dog outside in a tub or plastic wading pool with his regular shampoo (or one of the shampoo treatments listed here), rinse clean, and dry with a towel. Pour Campbell's Tomato Juice (several large cans may be necessary) over your pet, and rub the tomato juice into his coat, making sure to saturate his coat. Sponge the tomato juice over the pet's face. Let stand for ten to twenty minutes, however long your pet will bear. Rinse well and shampoo again. Repeat the tomato juice treatment again if necessary. The acids from the tomatoes neutralize the skunk smell. (Please note that tomato juice will dye a pet with white fur a peculiar shade of pink or orange for some time.)

- **Canada Dry Club Soda.** For a simple way to de-skunk your dog or cat, saturate your pet with warm Canada Dry Club Soda and work it into the animal's coat. Let it sit for ten minutes, allowing the effervescent action of the club soda to do its magic, and then shampoo the pet. Rinse clean with water.

- **Coca-Cola.** Fill a watering can with Coca-Cola, saturate your dog or cat with the Real Thing, and let it soak in for five minutes. Then rinse clean with warm water. The acids in the Coca-Cola eradicate the heinous smell of skunk spray.

- **Colgate Regular Flavor Toothpaste.** Scrub your skunked dog or cat with Colgate Regular Flavor Toothpaste and rinse thoroughly with warm water. The mildly abrasive toothpaste removes the skunk odor and leaves your pet smelling minty fresh.

- **Dawn Dishwashing Liquid.** Environmentalists use Dawn Dishwashing Liquid to clean crude oil from endangered species after oil spills. Since skunk spray is oil, lathering up your pet with Dawn Dishwashing Liquid breaks down the skunk oil, which washes away when you rinse with warm water. Repeat if necessary.

- **Heinz Ketchup.** Rub Heinz Ketchup into your pet's coat, wait until the ketchup begins to darken, and then wash the condiment off thoroughly.

Pet Tricks
Say Sayonara to Skunks

- **Bounce.** To keep skunks away from your house and pet, hang fresh sheets of Bounce from your fence posts, shrubs, or trees. The oleander fragrance naturally repels skunks. When the Bounce sheets dry out, mist them with water to revitalize the scent.

- **Ex-Lax.** To chase skunks from your yard without a one-on-one confrontation, place a few pieces of Ex-Lax Chocolate Laxative in spots where the skunks will find them. The skunks eat the Ex-Lax, experience uncontrollable bowel movements, and flee the area. To avoid predators, skunks stay away from any area where they leave their droppings.

- **Gold Medal Flour.** To make sure skunks have left their den beneath your home (before blocking off the entrance), sprinkle a light, even coat of Gold Medal Flour in front of the entry. Soon after dark, examine the flour for paw prints indicating that the skunks have gone out for the evening.

- **McCormick Ground (Cayenne) Red Pepper** and **Ivory Dishwashing Liquid.** Mix three teaspoons McCormick Ground (Cayenne) Red Pepper, one-half teaspoon Ivory Dishwashing Liquid, and two cups water in a sixteen-ounce trigger-spray bottle. Shake well and spray the spicy solution around the perimeter of the yard to repel skunks. The dishwashing liquid works like glue to make the cayenne pepper stick to fences, trees, and bushes.

Repeat if necessary. Note that Heinz Ketchup will dye a pet with white fur an interesting shade of pink or orange for some time. Hopefully, you'll prefer a pink pet to a odiferous one.

- **Heinz White Vinegar.** To deodorize skunk smell from a dog or cat, mix equal parts Heinz White Vinegar and water, saturate the pet's fur with the solution, let sit for ten minutes, and rinse clean with water. Repeat if necessary.

- **Old Spice Aftershave Lotion** and **L'eggs Sheer Energy Panty Hose.** Skunks hate the smell of perfume. To chase a skunk out from under your house, from a storage shed, or even your garage, simply sprinkle Old Spice Aftershave Lotion (or even Channel #5) around the area. Or cut off the foot from a clean, used pair of L'eggs Sheer Energy Panty Hose, saturate some cotton balls with Old Spice Aftershave Lotion, place them inside the sachet, tie and knot, and hang it anywhere you wish to fend off skunks.

- **Parsons' Ammonia.** To chase skunks away, soak old rags in a mixture of equal parts Parsons' Ammonia and water and place the pungent rags wherever the animals enter your yard or laze. The skunks, mistaking the ammonia for the urine of other animals, will find another place to play.

- **Speed Stick.** Unscrew the green translucent deodorant stick from the dispenser, use a knife to slice the deodorant stick into chunks, and place them in whatever space you wish the skunks to leave. Fragrance repels skunks.

- **Tabasco Pepper Sauce, McCormick Garlic Powder,** and **Wesson Corn Oil.** Mix two tablespoons Tabasco Pepper Sauce, two tablespoons McCormick Garlic Powder, one-quarter teaspoon Wesson Corn Oil, and two cups water in a sixteen-ounce trigger-spray bottle. Shake well and spray the solution around the perimeter of your yard to repel skunks.

PET PEEVES

THE SKUNK DEBUNKED

- A skunk can spray its foul-smelling musk accurately to a distance of up to twelve feet. The pungent odor lingers for several days.

- Before spraying an enemy, the striped skunk stamps its front feet and hisses or growls.

- Skunks are nocturnal—active during the night, asleep during the day.

- To prevent skunks from building a den in your yard or moving in under your house or deck, clear away brush and wood piles, cut back overgrown shrubbery, seal off any potential entrances to under your house or deck, don't leave pet food outside overnight, and keep outdoor garbage cans sealed securely.

- Skunks are nocturnal, so if skunks have taken up residence under your house, wait until dark (when the skunks leave to prowl the neighborhood) to seal up any entrance holes. If you suspect the adult skunks have left their young behind, call in a pest control specialist or wait until fall or winter for the babies to grow older and go out at night.

- No matter how many times a dog gets sprayed by skunks, he will confront a skunk whenever the opportunity arises.

- **Hunt's Tomatoes.** For a more powerful skunk treatment than tomato juice, use diced Hunt's Tomatoes. Rub the diced tomatoes and the accompanying juice into your pet's coat, let dry on the fur, and rinse the animal clean thoroughly with a hose. Of course, the diced tomatoes will dye a pet with white fur a funky shade of pink or orange for a short time, but it's better for your pet to look unusual than to smell unusual.

- **Johnson & Johnson Cotton Balls.** To protect your pet's ears from any de-skunking solution you use, place a Johnson & Johnson Cotton Ball in each ear before bathing.

- **Lava Soap.** To dissolve skunk spray oil on your dog or cat, wash your pet with Lava Soap (bar or liquid), using a brush to scrub deeply into the coat.

Rinse well and wash the animal again with her regular shampoo. (The natural pumice in Lava Soap may irritate your pet's skin.)

- **Listerine.** To deodorize the smell of skunk spray on a dog or cat, apply Listerine antiseptic mouthwash full strength to the affected areas (avoiding the pet's eyes and ears). The antiseptic neutralizes the stench of skunk oil. Then shampoo and rinse the animal clean. Cool Mint makes the pet smell better than the original mediciney flavor.

- **Massengill Medicated Disposable Douche.** The ingredients in Massengill Medicated Disposable Douche neutralize skunk odor. Mix two packets of Massengill powder, following the directions on the package. Simply wash your sprayed animal with this feminine hygiene product, let stand for fifteen minutes, and then shampoo and rinse well.

- **McCormick Pure Vanilla Extract.** To mask the smell of skunk odor until it dissipates naturally, saturate a soft, clean cloth with McCormick Pure Vanilla Extract and wipe down your pet. Or mix twelve ounces McCormick Pure Vanilla Extract in one gallon water, let your pet soak in the solution for ten minutes, wash him with his regular shampoo, and rinse clean.

- **Nestlé Carnation Evaporated Milk.** To deodorize skunk from a dog or cat, saturate your pet's fur with Nestlé Carnation Evaporated Milk, let dry thoroughly, and then shampoo your pet. Rinse clean with water.

- **Paul Mitchell Tea Tree Special Shampoo.** Lather up your skunked pet with Paul Mitchell Tea Tree Special Shampoo to neutralize the scent, let sit for five minutes, and then rinse clean with warm water. The tea tree oil in the shampoo eradicates the skunk smell.

- **Playtex Living Gloves.** When washing the skunk spray from your pet, wear Playtex Living Gloves to avoid getting the skunk smell all over you.

- **ReaLemon.** Wash down your pet with several bottles of ReaLemon lemon juice (avoiding the animal's eyes), let soak in for ten minutes, wash with soap and water, and rinse clean. The acids in lemon juice eliminate skunk odor.

- **Star Olive Oil.** Before bathing your pet to treat skunk odor, apply a drop of Star Olive Oil to your dog or cat's eyes to prevent irritation from the treatment.

Pet Tricks
Quelling Skunk Odors Indoors

- **Arm & Hammer Baking Soda, Hydrogen Peroxide,** and **Dawn Dishwashing Liquid.** The same solution that works on pets also neutralizes skunk odor from furniture, carpets, and walls. In a bucket, mix one-quarter cup Arm & Hammer Baking Soda, one quart hydrogen peroxide, and one teaspoon Dawn Dishwashing Liquid. Apply this solution to items contaminated by skunk odor, wait for the smell to dissipate, and rinse clean.

- **Heinz White Vinegar.** To deodorize the stench of skunk spray in the house, wash anything that came into contact with your pet, and then place bowls of Heinz White Vinegar around the house. The vinegar absorbs the odor.

- **Kingsford Charcoal Briquets.** After washing anything contaminated with skunk spray, fill several clean, used coffee cans with untreated Kingsford Charcoal Briquets. Place the containers on various shelves throughout the house to absorb the skunk odors.

- **Maxwell House Coffee.** Fill a bowl with one-half cup fresh Maxwell House Coffee grounds and set the bowl on a shelf in whatever room reeks of skunk odor. The coffee grounds absorb the stench.

- **McCormick Pure Peppermint Extract.** To freshen the air around your house, mix two teaspoons McCormick Pure Peppermint Extract and two cups of water in a sixteen-ounce trigger-spray bottle. Spray the air in your home. Or saturate a cotton ball with the peppermint extract and place it on saucer.

- **McCormick Pure Vanilla Extract.** To deodorize the smell of skunk from inside a car, saturate a rag with McCormick Pure Vanilla Extract and place it inside an open container on the floor of the backseat.

- **Simple Green.** To clean skunk spray from concrete walls or floors, open all windows and doors to the room (if indoors) and set up fans to ventilate. In a bucket, mix one cup Simple Green All-Purpose Cleaner to ten cups hot water and scrub the concrete surfaces with the soapy solution. After scrubbing, mop away as much moisture as possible. Run the fans with the windows and doors open until everything air dries.

Spraying

For Cats Only

- **Con-Tact Paper.** If the sight of other cats outside prompts your cat to spray, obscure the view by adhering frosted Con-Tact Paper over the glass to give your cat privacy.

- **Country Time Lemonade.** After cleaning the sprayed area thoroughly, dissolve one-half teaspoon Country Time Lemonade drink mix and two cups rubbing (isopropyl) alcohol in a sixteen-ounce trigger-spray bottle. Spray the solution on whatever furniture or walls the cat sprays. The smell of lemon repels cats.

- **Heinz Chili Sauce.** To stop your cat from spraying wooden furniture, clean the sprayed spot well. Rub the furniture with Heinz Chili Sauce and wipe it off. Cats can't stand the smell.

- **Heinz White Vinegar** and **Heinz Apple Cider Vinegar.** Mix five ounces Heinz White Vinegar, five ounces Heinz Apple Cider Vinegar, and five ounces water in a sixteen-ounce trigger-spray bottle. Shake well. After cleaning the sprayed area thoroughly, spray the vinegar solution on the spot. Reapply every few days.

Cat Got Your Tongue?
SOLVE-IT-YOURSELF CAT SPRAY MYSTERY

If you can't tell where your cat sprayed in your home, make the room pitch dark, and then turn on an ultra-violet blacklight. Cat spray glows an iridescent yellow color under blacklight.

- **Lemon Pledge.** Cats hate the smell of citrus, so you can easily stop your cat from spraying wood furniture by polishing the furniture with Lemon Pledge. The lemon scent keeps the cat away.

- **McCormick Black Pepper.** To prevent a cat from continually spraying the same spot, clean the sprayed area thoroughly, and then sprinkle McCormick Black Pepper on the spot. Pepper repels cats.

- **McCormick Pure Lemon Extract.** To stop your cat from spraying furniture or walls, clean the affected area thoroughly, saturate a cotton ball with McCormick Pure Lemon Extract, and either set it on a saucer or hang it from an aluminum tea ball over the trouble spot. Refresh the lemon extract once a week until you're satisfied that your cat will no longer spray that spot.

- **Old English Lemon Oil Furniture Polish.** Rubbing your wood furniture with Old English Lemon Oil rejuvenates the wood and gives the furniture a wonderful luster, and the strong lemon scent also repels cats, preventing them from spraying the wood.

- **Old Spice Aftershave Lotion.** Mix one part Old Spice Aftershave Lotion with ten parts water in a trigger-spray bottle. After cleaning the sprayed area thoroughly, spray the solution on the spot. Cats dislike the smell of Old Spice and will keep away.

- **Oust Air Sanitizer.** Cats hate the smell of oranges and lemons. After cleaning the sprayed spot completely, spritz Oust Air Sanitizer (Citrus Scent) in the area. The cat will no longer find that object tempting.

- **ReaLemon.** Mix six ounces ReaLemon lemon juice, three ounces water, and one ounce rubbing (isopropyl) alcohol in a sixteen-ounce trigger-spray bottle. Shake well and mist whatever furniture or surface your cat loves to spray. Reapply as needed.

- **Reynolds Wrap.** Another way to dissuade a cat from marking a familiar spot is to place strips of Reynolds Wrap aluminum foil around the spot. Cats detest aluminum foil and steer clear.

- **Scotch Double Sided Tape.** Cats loathe double-sided tape. Adhere a few strips of Scotch Double Sided Tape around the spot the cat loves to mark. The cat will stay away.

- **Scotchgard.** If your cat tends to spray your furniture or walls, use Scotchgard to give the upholstery or walls a protective coating to prevent the fabric or drywall from absorbing the odor.

- **Tabasco Pepper Sauce.** Spray or rub Tabasco Pepper Sauce on any wood furniture you want your cat to stop spraying. The hot sauce wipes off easily, but test an inconspicuous spot first to make sure it doesn't stain.

- **USA Today.** Placing crinkled pages from *USA Today* on the spot where the cat typically sprays can also ward off the animal.

GET YOUR PET TO THE VET

Get relief! If your cat starts spraying unexpectedly, strains to urinate, or urinates more frequently, take your pet to the veterinarian to check if he has diabetes, a blocked urethra, or a urinary tract infection.

PET PEEVES

HITTING THE MARK

- Sexually mature male cats mark their territory with urine laced with a pheromone that people consider vile.

- The best way to stop your cat from spraying is to have the cat neutered, which lowers his production of male hormones. Ninety percent of neutered cats cease spraying if the procedure is done before the cat attains sexual maturity at six months.

- Neutering your cat keeps the pet population under control and extends the feline's life span by two to three years.

- Have your cat neutered before he starts spraying, otherwise his marking habits may become a firmly entrenched part of his behavior.

- For cats, urine on vertical surfaces indicates spraying. Urine on flat surfaces typically indicates an elimination problem.

- Cats typically spray doors, furniture, and walls.

- Cats tend to spray in the same spot repeatedly, but they never soil the area where they eat or sleep. To stop your pet from spraying the same spot, move his food or water dish or his bedding to that area.

- Spraying might also be triggered by stress factors, such as a major change in routine, a move to a new house, or a new person or pet moving into the house. To calm your pet, stick to the same routine and feeding schedule, and keep your pet's bowls, bedding, and litter box in the same place.

- For cats, spraying is a completely natural, innate act, and no amount of punishment will stop the behavior.

- If your cat is spraying to compete against another pet in your home, either keep the animals separated (in different rooms or floors of the house) or teach the animals to get along (by playing with all your animals at the same time).

Stains

Feces

Carpets

- **Arm & Hammer Baking Soda** and **Heinz White Vinegar.** After discarding the solid feces, pour Arm & Hammer Baking Soda over the remaining stain followed by enough Heinz White Vinegar to make the baking soda bubble and fizz. Let sit for ten minutes, and then wipe up. The stain comes right out of the carpet, and the baking soda and vinegar deodorize the spot.

- **Aunt Jemima Corn Meal.** To deodorize a pet accident, sprinkle the spot with Aunt Jemima Corn Meal and let sit for several hours. Brush up the corn meal and vacuum. The corn meal will absorb the odor.

- **Bounty Paper Towels.** To clean up watery excrement, blot with Bounty Paper Towels. The quick-picker-upper lives up to its name when it comes to getting a distasteful job done quickly.

- **Canada Dry Club Soda** and **Arm & Hammer Baking Soda.** After disposing of the solid feces, pour a small amount of Canada Dry Club Soda onto the soil stain and blot up with paper towel. Cover with a layer of Arm & Hammer Baking Soda, let it sit for several hours to let the baking soda neutralize the odor, and then vacuum clean.

- **Gillette Foamy.** To scrub away a obstinate feces stain from carpeting, spray a dab of Gillette Foamy over the spot, scrub gently with a wet scrub brush, and blot with a clean, wet cloth.

- **Huggies Baby Wipes.** To clean a feces stain from the carpet, rub the stain with a Huggies Baby Wipe.

- **Listerine.** After cleaning feces from the carpet, disinfect and deodorize the spot by using a spray bottle to apply a light mist of full-strength Listerine antiseptic mouthwash. Let air-dry. The antiseptic kills germs and bacteria.

- **Maxwell House Coffee.** To deodorize the stench of excrement from carpet, cover the affected spot with Maxwell House Coffee grounds. Let sit overnight, and then brush and vacuum up the coffee.

- **McCormick Pure Vanilla Extract.** To deodorize a feces stain, mix two tablespoons McCormick Pure Vanilla Extract and one tablespoon water, dampen a sponge with the solution, and use it to pat the affected spot on the carpet.

- **Murphy Oil Soap.** To clean feces stains from carpet, mix one-quarter cup Murphy Oil Soap to one gallon water. Using a clean sponge, dampen the spot with the solution, and then blot with a clean cloth.

- **Playtex Living Gloves.** Before picking up excrement or scrubbing related stains, put on a pair of Playtex Living Gloves to avoid touching the feces or contracting any possible bacterial infection.

- **Purell Instant Hand Sanitizer.** After removing the solid feces from the carpet, squeeze a drop of Purell Instant Hand Sanitizer on the subsequent stains and blot with a cloth to clean and disinfect the spot.

- **Shout.** If the feces leave a stain on the carpet, wipe up debris with a damp cloth, spray Shout Stain Remover on the spot, let sit for five minutes, and then blot with a damp cloth until the stain disappears.

- **Simple Green.** After disposing of the solid feces, mix one ounce Simple Green All-Purpose Cleaner and one cup water in a trigger-spray bottle and spray the remaining carpet stain with the soapy solution. Blot up the soapy water with a damp cloth and air-dry.

- **Smirnoff Vodka.** Saturate a soft, clean cloth with Smirnoff Vodka and gently dab the remaining feces stain, until it comes clean. Blot with a second cloth dampened with cool water and air-dry.

- **Spot Shot.** You spray it on, and it lifts the stain in seconds after you dab it with a towel. Does not work on my couch though, which is white cotton.

- **Spray 'n Wash.** Spritz any remaining feces stains on the carpet with Spray 'n Wash, let sit for five minutes, and then blot clean with a clean, wet cloth. This prewash laundry stain remover cleans the stain and freshens the carpet with fragrance.

- **Tide.** To clean a feces stain from carpet, mix one teaspoon liquid Tide and one cup water and gently scrub the stain with this color-safe solution. Rinse with cool water, blot, and let dry.

- **20 Mule Team Borax.** After discarding the solid feces, saturate a cloth with water and blot the carpet to remove as much of the remaining stain as possible. Sprinkle 20 Mule Team Borax to cover the affected area. Let dry and vacuum. (Before treating, test an inconspicuous spot on the carpeting with a paste made from 20 Mule Team Borax and water to make sure the borax does not remove any color from the carpet.)

- **Windex.** To clean feces stains from carpet, blot up as much of the stain as possible, spray the affected area with Windex, and then wipe clean with a soft cloth.

- **Ziploc Storage Bags.** To scoop up poop hygienically, turn a Ziploc Storage Bag inside out, put your hand inside the bag like a glove, pick up the mess, pull the bag right-side out again, seal shut, and discard.

Floors

- **Bounty Paper Towels.** To clean up watery excrement, blot with Bounty Paper Towels. The quick-picker-upper lives up to its name when it comes to getting a distasteful job done quickly.

- **Huggies Baby Wipes.** After discarding the feces, clean any residue from the floor with a Huggies Baby Wipe.

- **Purell Instant Hand Sanitizer.** To disinfect the floor after cleaning up pet feces, squirt some Purell Instant Hand Sanitizer on the spot, let it sit for fifteen seconds, and then wipe up with a sponge.

- **Vicks VapoRub.** To trick your sense of smell so you can withstand a foul odor emanating from your pet's feces, put a dab of Vicks VapoRub under your nostrils.

- **Ziploc Storage Bags.** To scoop up poop hygienically, turn a Ziploc Storage Bag inside out, put your hand inside the bag like a glove, pick up the mess, pull the bag right-side out again, seal shut, and discard.

Urine

Carpets

- **Aunt Jemima Corn Meal.** To deodorize a pet urine stain, blot up as much urine as you can, sprinkle the spot with Aunt Jemima Corn Meal, and let sit for several hours. Brush up the corn meal and vacuum. The corn meal absorbs the odor.

- **Canada Dry Club Soda** and **Arm & Hammer Baking Soda.** After using cloth or paper towels to blot up as much urine as possible from the carpet, pour a small amount of Canada Dry Club Soda onto the stain, rub gently with a sponge, and then blot up with paper towel. Let dry thoroughly, sprinkle on Arm & Hammer Baking Soda, let it sit forty-eight hours, and then vacuum up. The baking soda neutralizes the odor, preventing your pet from detecting the odor of urine and using that spot again.

See the Light

SOLVE-IT-YOURSELF PET URINE MYSTERY

If you can't tell where your dog or cat urinated in your home, make the room pitch dark, and then turn on an ultraviolet blacklight. Both dog and cat urine glow an iridescent yellow color under blacklight.

- **Clorox Bleach.** If the urine stain has saturated the carpet padding and permeated the wood subfloor, before re-carpeting the room, mix three-quarters cup Clorox Bleach and one gallon of water, mop the subfloor thoroughly, and let air-dry.

- **Glad Trash Bags.** If you use an enzyme product such as Nature's Miracle to deodorize a urine or feces stain, use a pair of scissors to slice open a Glad Trash Bag along the seams, saturate the stain with the enzyme product, and cover the area with the plastic bag. Weight down the plastic with books for forty-eitht hours to prevent the enzyme product from drying out before it digests the protein in the stain.

- **Heinz White Vinegar.** To clean and deodorize dog or cat urine stains from carpet, blot up as much urine as possible with cloth or paper towels, flush several times with lukewarm water, and blot again. Then apply a mixture of equal parts Heinz White Vinegar and cool water. Blot, rinse, and let air-dry. The lingering scent of vinegar (undetectable to humans) will also prevent your pet from staining that same spot again.

- **Huggies Baby Wipes.** To blot and clean a pet urine stain from carpeting, use Huggies Baby Wipes.

- **Hydrogen Peroxide, Arm & Hammer Baking Soda,** and **Ivory Dishwashing Liquid.** To overpower a stubborn urine odor embedded in carpeting, mix one cup hydrogen peroxide, one tablespoon Arm & Hammer Baking Soda, and one-half teaspoon Ivory Dishwashing Liquid. Apply the solution to the stain with a damp sponge. Let dry and vacuum clean.

- **Listerine.** To remove the odor of urine from carpet, mix one-half cup Listerine antiseptic mouthwash and one cup water in a sixteen-ounce trigger-spray bottle, shake well, and spritz the urine stain. Let sit for two hours, and then blot with a paper towel.

- **Lysol.** After blotting up as much urine as possible, mix one-half cup Lysol All Purpose Cleaner and one quart water in a bucket. Use a sponge dampened in the solution to clean the affected area of the carpeting. Blot, rinse with water, blot again, and let air-dry. The Lysol disinfects and deodorizes the stain.

- **Massengill Medicated Disposable Douche.** To get rid of the smell of urine, blot up as much of the urine as possible, apply Massengill Medicated Disposable Douche to the spot, and let dry. Repeat if necessary.

- **McCormick Pure Almond Extract.** To deodorize the stench of pet urine stain from carpet, saturate a cotton ball with McCormick Pure Almond Extract and rub it on the affected area (or, if you're feeling bold, pour a few drops directly on the carpet).

- **Morton Salt.** Cover a damp urine stain on carpet with a mountain of Morton Salt. If the urine stain has dried on the carpet, make a paste of salt and water and apply it to the stain. Let sit for twenty-four hours, sweep up the excess salt, and then vacuum clean. Salt is highly absorbent and will suck the urine out from the carpet.

- **Oxi Clean.** To clean a urine stain from carpet, mix one tablespoon (one-half scoop) Oxi Clean and two cups hot water and wet the trouble spot with the solution. Let sit for one minute, blot with a clean, dry cloth, and air-dry. Repeat if necessary. (Before treating, test an inconspicuous spot on the carpeting with a paste made from Oxi Clean and water to make sure the solution does not remove any color from the carpet.)

- **Pampers.** To blot up a pet urine stain from carpeting, place a Pampers disposable diaper over the urine stain, sit several heavy books on top of the diaper to keep it pressed flat against the stain, and let sit for one hour. The super-absorbent polymer flakes in the diaper will suck up the urine.

- **Parsons' Ammonia.** If the urine bleaches the carpet, sponge the affected area with Parsons' Ammonia, which sometimes brings back the original color. Then flush the ammonia from the carpet with soapy water and blot dry so the smell of ammonia doesn't lure your pet to soil the spot again.

- **ReaLemon.** To clean and deodorize dog or cat urine stains from carpet, blot up as much urine as possible with cloth or paper towels, flush several times with lukewarm water, and blot again. Then apply a mixture of equal parts ReaLemon lemon juice and cool water. Blot, rinse, and let air-dry.

- **Smirnoff Vodka.** After blotting up as much urine as possible, saturate the area with Smirnoff Vodka and let air-dry. Repeat if necessary. The alcohol in the vodka kills the smell of the urine.

- **Stayfree Maxi Pads.** To blot up a urine stain, use a Stayfree Maxi Pad. The highly absorbent maxi pad sucks up most of the urine from the carpet. After using any liquid listed here to saturate the stain, blot again with a fresh Stayfree Maxi Pad.

- **Thompson's WaterSeal.** If pet urine soaks through the carpet padding and into the subfloor, rip up the carpet and padding, and seal the subfloor with Thompson's WaterSeal. Replace the carpet and padding.

- **Tidy Cats.** To blot a pet urine stain from the carpet, cover the stain with one cup Tidy Cats and step on the mound to press the absorbent clay into the puddle. Let stand for two hours, sweep up the mess, and vacuum.

- **20 Mule Team Borax.** To neutralize the smell of pet urine stains in carpeting, blot up as much of the urine as possible, dampen the spot with water, rub in 20 Mule Team Borax, let dry, and then vacuum or brush clean. (Before treating, test an inconspicuous spot on the carpeting with a paste made from 20 Mule Team Borax and water to make sure the borax does not remove any color from the carpet.)

- **Woolite.** After blotting up the urine, flush the spot with water and blot well. Pour a few drops of Woolite on a wet sponge and apply to the stain by patting (not rubbing). Flush with water, blot thoroughly, and air-dry.

Clothing and Fabrics

- **Clorox 2.** To wash pet urine from clothing or other fabrics, rinse the garment or item well with cool water, soak the item in Clorox 2 (a non-chlorine bleach) for thirty minutes, and launder as usual in your regular wash load.

PET PEEVES

WASTE IS A TERRIBLE THING TO MIND

- Do not clean up pet urine or feces stains with ammonia or an ammonia-based cleanser. Urine contains ammonia, so by cleaning the stain with ammonia, you might inadvertently attract your dog or cat back to that same spot to urinate again.

- Completely deodorize dog or cat urine and feces stains, otherwise your pet will relocate the scent and soil the spot continuously.

- Household hints maven Mary Ellen Pinkham wrote, "I think the phrase 'man's best friend' was obviously created before wall-to-wall carpet was invented."

- Urine stains left to dry in carpeting and padding can reek for what seems like an eternity and perpetually attract your pet to return to urinate on the same spot again and again. Urine stains also provide the perfect breeding ground for bacteria, which produce their own disagreeable odors.

- Urine stains in carpet can reappear over time. If the urine spreads wide underneath the carpet and padding, as the stain dries, the urine wicks back up to the surface.

- Pet urine can affect the color of dyes in the carpet or furniture, depending on the content of the urine and how quickly and efficiently you clean it up.

- Once pet urine is absorbed into the backing of the carpet, complete success from the use of an odor remover is unlikely.

- **Dawn Dishwashing Liquid** and **Parsons' Ammonia.** To remove urine stains from clothing and fabrics, mix equal parts Dawn Dishwashing Liquid, Parsons' Ammonia, and water. Apply the mixture to the spot. Let sit for five minutes, rinse thoroughly with water, and then launder as usual. (Do not use ammonia on acrylic, silk, spandex, or wool.)

- **Heinz White Vinegar.** To deodorize clothes and fabrics stained with pet urine, add one cup Heinz White Vinegar to your washing machine as it fills with water.

- **Morton Salt.** Dissolve one-half cup Morton Salt in a bucket of water, soak the urine-stained clothing or fabric in the salt water for one hour, and then launder as usual. Salt water breaks down the urine.

- **Spot Shot.** Saturate the urine stain on clothing or other fabrics with Spot Shot Instant Carpet Stain Remover, let sit for one minute, and launder as usual. (Do not use Spot Shot on dry-clean-only fabrics, non-colorfast garments, or silk.)

Floors

- **Arm & Hammer Baking Soda.** To clean a urine stain from a waxed floor, blot up as much urine as possible, and then sprinkle Arm & Hammer Baking Soda to cover the stain. Let sit for ten minutes, brush up, and wipe clean.

- **Arm & Hammer Baking Soda** and **Hydrogen Peroxide.** To clean pet urine from a hardwood floor, fill a spray bottle with hydrogen peroxide, spray the affected area, let sit for ten minutes, and then cover the spot with a thick layer of Arm & Hammer Baking Soda. Let sit another ten minutes, and then gently scrape up the caked baking soda. The baking soda absorbs the moisture and stain and simultaneously eliminates the odor. The hydrogen peroxide disinfects the area. Repeat several times.

- **Bounty Paper Towels, Hydrogen Peroxide, Glad Trash Bags,** and **Kingsford Corn Starch.** To clean dry black urine stains from hardwood floors, cover the stains with Bounty Paper Towels, and then saturate the towels with hydrogen peroxide. Cover the wet paper towels with Glad Trash Bags garbage bags to seal in the liquid and let sit for one hour. Repeat if necessary. Wipe dry with more paper towels, cover the affected area with Kingsford Corn Starch, and let sit overnight to absorb the remaining moisture. In the morning, sweep up the cornstarch and let air-dry.

- **Heinz White Vinegar.** To deodorize a pet urine stain on the floor and dissuade your dog or cat from urinating on the same spot again, mist that area with Heinz White Vinegar. The pungent scent will fend off the animal.

- **Parsons' Ammonia** and **Murphy Oil Soap.** To clean pet urine from a vinyl floor, blot up the urine and, with the room well ventilated, mop the floor with Parsons' Ammonia to strip off the old wax. Then mop the floor with a bucket of soapy water made with a few drops of Murphy Oil Soap. Rinse clean, let air-dry, and apply a new coat of wax to the floor.

- **Simple Green.** To clean dog or cat urine from a concrete floor, open all windows and doors to the room (if indoors), and set up fans to ventilate. In a bucket, mix one cup Simple Green All-Purpose Cleaner to ten cups hot water and scrub the concrete floor with the solution. After scrubbing, mop up as much moisture as possible. Run the fans with the windows and doors open until everything dries.

- **Tidy Cats.** To clean pet urine from a hardwood floor, blot up the urine, and then cover the stain with Tidy Cats cat box filler. Let sit overnight. The clay absorbs the urine from the wood. Repeat if necessary.

- **Tidy Cats** and **Tide.** To absorb pet urine from a concrete floor, blot up as much urine as possible and cover the remaining stain with Tidy Cats cat box filler. Place a sheet of cardboard on top of the litter, and then step on the cardboard to grind the litter into the concrete floor. Let sit overnight, and in the morning, sweep up the litter and mop the floor with a few drops of liquid Tide in a bucket of water.

Mattresses

- **Arm & Hammer Baking Soda.** To absorb and deodorize pet urine from a mattress, sprinkle Arm & Hammer Baking Soda on the mattress, let sit for several hours, and then vacuum clean.

- **Canada Dry Club Soda** and **Arm & Hammer Baking Soda.** To clean urine from a mattress, blot up as much liquid as possible, pour a small amount of Canada Dry Club Soda over the stained area, and immediately blot again. The effervescent action of the club soda causes the urine to bubble to the surface. Let the spot dry completely, and then cover with Arm & Hammer Baking Soda (see above).

- **Heinz White Vinegar.** To clean urine from a mattress, blot up the urine and flush the affected area several times with lukewarm water, blotting thoroughly each time. Then apply a mixture of equal parts Heinz White Vinegar and cool water. Blot, rinse, and let air-dry. The vinegar neutralizes the stench of urine.

- **Hydrogen Peroxide, Arm & Hammer Baking Soda, and Ivory Dishwashing Liquid.** Mix sixteen ounces hydrogen peroxide, one-quarter cup Arm & Hammer Baking Soda, and three drops Ivory Dishwashing Liquid in a spray bottle. Spray the solution on the affected area on the mattress, saturating the spot. Let air-dry, but after eight hours place a fan nearby to speed up the process and prevent mildew.

- **Listerine.** To eliminate the smell of pet urine from a mattress, use a spray bottle to apply full-strength Listerine antiseptic mouthwash to the spot and let air-dry. The antiseptic breaks down the urine and kills the stench.

- **Massengill Medicated Disposable Douche.** To eliminate the smell of urine from a mattress, blot up as much of the urine as possible, apply Massengill Medicated Disposable Douche to the spot, and let air-dry. Repeat if necessary.

- **Oxi Clean.** After blotting up the urine, mix one tablespoon (one-half scoop) Oxi Clean and two cups hot water. Wet the affected area on the mattress with the solution. Let sit for one minute, blot with a clean, dry cloth, and air-dry. Repeat if necessary.

- **Pampers.** To blot up urine, place a Pampers disposable diaper over the stain, sit several heavy books on top of the diaper to keep it pressed flat against the stain, and let sit for one hour. The super-absorbent polymer flakes in the diaper will soak up the urine.

- **Spot Shot.** After blotting up as much urine from the mattress as possible, stand the mattress on its side against a wall (to prevent the urine from soaking deeper into the mattress), and spray the stain with Spot Shot Instant Carpet Remover. Let stand for a few minutes, blot with a clean cloth, and then wipe with a damp cloth to remove any residue.

- **20 Mule Team Borax.** To neutralize pet urine odors on a mattress, dampen the affected spot with water, rub in 20 Mule Team Borax, let dry, and then vacuum or brush clean.

- **Tidy Cats.** To absorb and deodorize a pet urine stain from a mattress, cover the stain with Tidy Cats, let sit for twenty-four hours, brush clean, and then vacuum up any remaining dust.

Upholstery

- **Aunt Jemima Corn Meal.** To deodorize a pet urine stain, blot up as much urine as you can, sprinkle the spot with Aunt Jemima Corn Meal, and let sit for several hours. Brush up the corn meal and vacuum. The corn meal absorbs the odor.

- **Canada Dry Club Soda** and **Arm & Hammer Baking Soda.** To clean pet urine from upholstered furniture, blot up as much urine as possible using cloth or paper towels. Pour a small amount of Canada Dry Club Soda onto the stain, and then blot up quickly. Cover the spot with Arm & Hammer Baking Soda, let it dry, and then vacuum up. The baking soda absorbs the stain and simultaneously neutralizes the odor, preventing your pet from detecting the odor of urine and using that spot again.

- **Heinz White Vinegar.** To clean and deodorize dog or cat urine stains from upholstery, blot up as much urine as possible with cloth or paper towels, flush several times with lukewarm water, and blot again. Then apply a mixture of equal parts Heinz White Vinegar and cool water. Blot, rinse, and let air-dry. The residual scent of vinegar will also dissuade your pet from wetting the same spot again.

- **Hydrogen Peroxide.** To clean pet urine from upholstered furniture, blot up as much urine as possible and apply hydrogen peroxide to the stain. When the bubbling subsides, blot, flush with water, and blot again. Let air-dry.

- **Listerine.** After blotting up urine from the upholstery, use a trigger-spray bottle to spritz Listerine antiseptic mouthwash on the spot and let air-dry. The antiseptic breaks down the urine and kills the stench.

- **Massengill Medicated Disposable Douche.** After blotting up the urine from your upholstered furniture, fill a trigger-spray bottle with Massengill Medicated Disposable Douche and let dry.

- **20 Mule Team Borax.** To neutralize pet urine odors on upholstery, blot up the urine, dampen the affected area with water, and rub in 20 Mule Team Borax. Let air-dry, and then vacuum or brush clean.

- **USA Today.** To remove the smell of dried urine from upholstered furniture, open a copy of USA Today and spread several sheets of the newspaper over the couch or chair. Place an old blanket on top of the newspaper (to hold the sheets in place) and let sit for several days. When you remove the blanket and newspapers, the smell will be gone. Newsprint absorbs odors.

Vomit

- **Arm & Hammer Baking Soda.** To clean pet vomit from carpet, scrape up all the chunks and blot up as much of the excess liquid as possible, and then cover the stain with Arm & Hammer Baking Soda. Let sit overnight, and then brush up the baking soda and vacuum the spot. The baking soda neutralizes the gastric acid, absorbs the liquid, and deodorizes the stench.

Pet Tricks
Preventing Accidents

For Dogs and Cats

- **Glad Trash Bags.** To keep your dog or cat off any area of the carpet or floor where they have previously left a mess, cut open a Glad Trash Bag along the seams and cover the spot with the plastic. Dogs and cats despise the feeling of plastic and stay away.

- **Heinz White Vinegar.** Fill a trigger-spray bottle with equal parts Heinz White Vinegar and water. Shake well. After cleaning the mess completely, spray the vinegar solution on the spot. Reapply every few days. The vinegar neutralizes the odor and repels pets.

- **McCormick Ground (Cayenne) Red Pepper.** To dissuade your dog or cat from urinating or defecating in any particular place in your house, sprinkle McCormick Ground (Cayenne) Red Pepper on the spot. The sharp aroma will chase away your pet.

- **Tabasco Pepper Sauce.** Rub Tabasco Pepper Sauce on any wood furniture you want your cat to stop spraying. The hot sauce wipes off easily, but test an inconspicuous spot first to make sure it doesn't stain.

For Cats Only

- **Country Time Lemonade.** After cleaning the pet stain thoroughly, dissolve one-half teaspoon Country Time Lemonade drink mix and two cups rubbing (isopropyl) alcohol in a sixteen-ounce trigger-spray bottle. Mist the spot with the solution to repels cats.

- **McCormick Pure Lemon Extract.** To discourage your cat from urinating in the same spot in your house, saturate a cotton ball with McCormick Pure Lemon Extract and set it on a saucer or hang it from an aluminum tea ball over the trouble spot. Refresh the lemon extract once a week until you're satisfied that your cat will no longer use that spot.

- **Old Spice Aftershave Lotion.** To stop your cat from leaving deposits on the same spot on your carpet or floor, mix one part Old Spice Aftershave Lotion with ten parts water in a trigger-spray bottle. After cleaning the affected area thoroughly, spray the solution on the spot. Old Spice repels cats.

- **Oust Air Sanitizer.** Cats hate the smell of oranges and lemons. After cleaning the stained spot completely, spritz Oust Air Sanitizer (Citrus Scent) in the area to discourage your cat from going there.

- **Reynolds Wrap.** To dissuade your cat from soiling or wetting a familiar spot, place strips of Reynolds Wrap aluminum foil over the spot in question. Cats will not step onto aluminum foil.

- **Scotch Double Sided Tape.** Since cats loathe the feeling of double-sided tape on their paw pads, adhere a few strips of Scotch Double Sided Tape around the spot on your carpeting or floor that the cat has previously used as a litter box. The cat will steer clear of the sticky tape.

- **Canada Dry Club Soda.** Clean up as much vomit as possible, pour Canada Dry Club Soda on the remaining stain, and blot with towels. Repeat until the offending color vanishes. The carbonation in the club soda lifts the stain from the carpet.

- **Huggies Baby Wipes.** To clean pet vomit from the carpet, rub the stain with a Huggies Baby Wipe.

- **Hydrogen Peroxide.** If, after you clean the vomit from the carpet, the spot looks discolored, apply hydrogen peroxide to the affected area, let soak for fifteen minutes, and blot. Repeat if necessary.

- **Listerine.** To deodorize the smell of pet vomit from the carpet, mix equal parts Listerine antiseptic mouthwash and water in a spray bottle, shake well, and then spray over the affected area.

- **ReaLemon** and **McCormick Cream of Tartar.** If the gastric acid in the vomit leave the carpet discolored after cleaning, apply ReaLemon lemon juice to the affected area, let soak for fifteen minutes, and blot. Repeat if necessary. If the stain remains, mix ReaLemon lemon juice and McCormick Cream of Tartar into a paste, apply to the spot, and let dry. Then brush or vacuum up.

- **Tidy Cats.** If your pet vomits on the carpet, cover the spill with Tidy Cats, let sit overnight, and then brush up and vacuum. The clay granules absorb the liquid and deodorize the muss.

- **20 Mule Team Borax.** After scraping up as much vomit as you can, sponge and blot the area with water, and then sprinkle with dry 20 Mule Team Borax powder to cover the entire spot. Let sit for two hours and vacuum clean. (Be sure to test for color fasting using a paste of borax and water in an inconspicuous spot first.)

- **Vicks VapoRub.** To trick your sense of smell so you can withstand the foul stench of vomit, put a dab of Vicks VapoRub under your nostrils.

Stickers and Burrs

For Dogs and Cats

- **Crisco All-Vegetable Shortening.** To remove burrs from a dog or cat's fur, wear work gloves (to avoid getting pricked by the burs), work a dab of Crisco All-Vegetable Shortening into the affected areas, and pry the burrs loose. Shampoo the animal to remove the vegetable shortening.

- **Johnson's Baby Oil.** If you don't have any vegetable shortening, work Johnson's Baby Oil into the hair surrounding the burrs, and then pry each burr loose. Shampoo your pet to wash out the mineral oil, rinse clean, and towel dry.

- **Johnson's Baby Shampoo.** Apply a dab of Johnson's Baby Shampoo to the burr, wait a few minutes, and then comb out the burr.

- **Kingsford's Corn Starch.** For a less messy way to remove burrs from an animal's coat, put on a pair of work gloves, rub Kingsford's Corn Starch into your dog or cat's coat, and pluck the burrs free. Then brush out the corn-starch, which doubles as a dry shampoo.

- **Lubriderm.** Apply a few drops of Lubriderm moisturizing lotion to the burr, wait a little while for the lanolin to penetrate and soften the prickly husk, and then comb out the thing.

- **Pam Cooking Spray.** Spray the sticker or burr with Pam Cooking Spray, and then brush. The vegetable oil helps ease the cocklebur from fur.

- **Star Olive Oil.** If your long-eared dog gets a foxtail stuck in his ear and you can't take him to the veterinarian immediately, put a few drops of warm Star Olive Oil in your pet's ear to soften the foxtail and relieve some of the irritation until you can get proper medical attention.

- **Vaseline Petroleum Jelly.** Coat the stubborn sticker or burr with Vaseline Petroleum Jelly, and then use a comb or brush to pry the prickly invader loose. Shampoo the spot to wash out the petroleum jelly.

- **WD-40 and Dawn Dishwashing Liquid.** In an emergency, a spritz of WD-40 helps remove burrs from any animal's hair. Use a few drops of Dawn Dishwashing Liquid and water to wash out the WD-40, rinse thoroughly, and towel dry.

- **Wesson Corn Oil.** To remove burrs from a dog or cat's hair, saturate the area with Wesson Corn Oil, and then comb or brush out the burr. Wash with pet shampoo, rinse immediately, and towel dry.

GET YOUR PET TO THE VET

Stick around! If your dog or cat gets a foxtail embedded in his ears, nose, or eyes, take your pet to the vet immediately to remove the prickly invader before it causes serious complications.

PET PEEVES

STICKY SITUATIONS

- Crushing the burrs with a pair of pliers (without pinching your pet's skin) makes the burrs easier to comb out.

- If you can't remove a burr with any of the brand-name products listed here, use a pair of round-nosed safety scissors to carefully clip it out of your pet's hair.

- Certain plants produce burrs or stickers, prickly seedcases with stiff bristles or hooks that attach themselves to passersby, for widespread distribution.

- When attached to pets, burrs can irritate skin and cause serious infection.

- Check your pet to make sure burrs have not lodged between toes, in the armpits, or in crevices around the private parts.

- Remove burrs before your pet starts licking the affected area, causing the surrounding hair to shrink and tighten.

- Remove foxtails and any slivers from your pet's fur immediately. Foxtails swiftly puncture skin and travel through a pet's body, harming tissues and possibly even organs, or they lodge in the nose or ears, potentially producing a painful abscess.

- In the early 1940s, Swiss inventor George de Mestral went on a walk with his dog. When he returned home, he noticed that cockleburs covered his pants and his dog's coat. Examining the cockleburs under a microscope, de Mestral discovered that each one consisted of hundreds of natural hook-like shapes, and he decided to use this as the basis for developing a two-sided fastener. He made one side with stiff hooks resembling the burrs and the other side with soft loops like the fabric of his pants. He named his invention Velcro, combining *vel* (from velvet) with *cro* (from the French *crochet,* which means hook).

Sunburn

For Dogs and Cats

- **Coppertone Water Babies Sunscreen Lotion.** If your dog or cat spends time outside, prevent sunburn on your pet's nose, ears, and other vulnerable areas by applying a light coat of Coppertone sunscreen (with an SFP of 15 or higher). Feed your pet immediately after applying the sunscreen to distract your pet from immediately licking off the lotion. If your pet licks off the sunscreen, you can apply more. (Make sure the sunscreen you use on your pet doesn't contain any PABA, zinc, or zinc oxide, which can be dangerous if licked.)

- **Dickinson's Witch Hazel.** To relieve the pain from sunburn, use a cotton ball to apply Dickinson's Witch Hazel to the burned skin three or four times a day. Witch hazel evaporates almost instantly, cooling burned skin and providing quick relief.

- **Fruit of the Earth Aloe Vera Gel.** Rub Fruit of the Earth Aloe Vera Gel into your pet's face and ears to soothe and moisturize the skin.

- **Lubriderm.** Rubbing a few drops of Lubriderm moisturizing lotion into your dog or cat's sunburned skin moistures and soothes the irritation.

- **Nestea.** Mix up two cups unsweetened Nestea Ice Tea according to the directions on the jar, pour the solution into a sixteen-ounce trigger-spray bottle, and spray your pet's skin with the solution. The tannic acid in the tea relieves sunburn pain.

- **Quaker Oats** and **L'eggs Sheer Energy Panty Hose.** To relieve your dog or cat from sunburn pain, use a blender to grind one cup Quaker Oats into a fine powder. Cut off the foot from a clean, used pair of L'eggs Sheer Energy Panty Hose, fill with the powdered oats, and tie a knot in the nylon. Tie the oatmeal sachet to the spigot, letting it dangle in the flow of water as the tub fills with cool water. Bathe your pet for five to ten minutes in this inexpensive and soothing oatmeal bath.

- **Solarcaine.** It may be made for humans, but Solarcaine works just as well on cats and dogs to soothe sunburn pain. Simply spray Solarcaine on your pet's sunburn. The local anesthetic relieves the burning sensation almost instantly. For cats, use Solarcaine sparingly. When your cat licks herself, the anesthetic could numb her tongue.

- **Vaseline Petroleum Jelly.** To rehydrate sunburned skin on your dog or cat, rub a thin layer of Vaseline Petroleum Jelly on the affected area two or three times a day.

GET YOUR PET TO THE VET

A bright idea! If sunburn results in raw, blistered, and infected skin, take your pet to a veterinarian.

PET PEEVES

HERE COMES THE SUN

- Dogs and cats lazing in sunshine often get sunburn on the bridges of their noses, the tips of the ears, and the skin of their bellies.

- Pets with white fur and those that live at high altitudes are more likely to experience sunburn.

- As with humans, sunburn and excessive exposure to the sun's rays can cause a dog or cat to develop skin cancer.

- To avoid sunburn, keep your pet out of the sun during the peak hours of the day between 9 a.m. and 3 p.m.

- If your pet is prone to sunburn, buy a cap specially designed to shade your pet's ears and nose. Put your dog in a T-shirt to protect his belly from sunburn, and if your pet sits inside by a sunny window, draw the blinds or curtains.

- If your pet spends a lot of time outdoors, make sure you provide sufficient shaded areas.

- For a simple way to soothe sunburn pain, use a trigger-spray bottle to mist the affected area on your pet with cool water. Or apply a washcloth dampened with cool water to the spot.

Tails

For Dogs and Cats

- **Betadine Solution.** If your dog or cat's tail seems irritated and is missing fur in several places, wash the affected areas with Betadine Solution several times a week. The antibacterial cleanser will kill any infection, soothe the soreness, and expedite healing.

- **Coca-Cola.** Put a few pennies in a clean, empty Coca-Cola can and tape the opening shut. To stop your dog or cat from nibbling her own tail, simply shake the can a few times. Dogs and cats find the sound of coins jangling in a can disconcerting and will likely stop chewing their tails.

- **Cortaid.** If your dog or cat constantly chews his tail, clogged glands may be causing inflamed pimples and other skin irritations. Apply a thin coat of Cortaid to soothe the skin. The hydrocortisone cream fights inflammation.

- **Dawn Dishwashing Liquid.** If your dog or cat's tail looks ragged or filthy, set the animal by the side of the sink, let her tail hang into the sink, and use Dawn Dishwashing Liquid and water to shampoo her tail. Rinse well and repeat.

- **Kingsford's Corn Starch.** If the glands at the base of your dog or cat's tail discharge excessive fluid, resulting in greasy, tender, and irritated skin, sprinkle a light coat of Kingsford's Corn Starch on the affected area. Corn-starch absorbs excess moisture, keeping the skin dry so it can heal. Wait five minutes, and then comb or brush out the powder. Repeat once or twice a week until the secretions cease or the symptom disappears.

- **Orville Redenbacher Gourmet Popping Corn.** To make a shaker, place a dozen unpopped kernels of Orville Redenbacher Gourmet Popping Corn in a clean, empty plastic water bottle and seal the cap on tightly. Whenever your dog starts chewing his own tail, rattle the homemade maraca. The jar-ring noise will prompt your dog to stop nibbling.

- **Oxy Sensitive Spot Treatment.** If your dog or cat has blackheads or other acne pimples on her tail, apply Oxy Sensitive Spot Treatment. The benzoyl peroxide in the ointment will unclog the glands causing the prob-lem. (Do not use any ointment with more than 5 percent benzoyl peroxide.)

- **USA Today.** To prevent your dog or cat from being mesmerized by his own tail, chasing it around in circles and chewing the skin, roll up a copy of *USA Today* and smack it against a chair or the floor to surprise your pet and divert his attention.

GET YOUR PET TO THE VET

Is the tail wagging the dog? If your pet compulsively nibbles or constantly chases and catches his tail, or if your pet breaks his tail, consult your veterinarian.

PET PEEVES
WORKING YOUR TAIL OFF

- If your dog or cat won't stop nibbling her tail, she may have fleas. See page 107 for a variety of ways to detect and combat fleas.

- Dogs and cats commonly and occasionally become spellbound by their own tails and start spinning around to catch them.

- Beware any dangerous household items that might harm your pet's tail, such as a whirling fan, a rocking chair, a reclining chair, or a pull-out bed.

- To get your dog or cat to stop chasing her tail, say "No!" and squirt water from a squirt gun or spray bottle at her body (not face).

- Your pet's tail is an extension of the spine, and if your pet breaks or fractures his tail, the damaged end hangs flaccid.

For Dogs Only

- **Frisbee.** A dog tends to chew her tail to cope with anxiety. To relieve that stress, toss a Frisbee for your dog to chase after. Exercise relieves stress and diverts your dog's attention away from her tail.

- **Wilson Tennis Balls.** To prevent your dog for chasing and chewing his own tail, distract your pet by tossing a Wilson Tennis Ball for him to chase after. Exercise and playtime will likely abate the anxiety that results in tail chewing.

Teeth

For Dogs and Cats

- **Arm & Hammer Baking Soda.** To brush and whiten your pet's teeth, dip a wet toothbrush in a box of Arm & Hammer Baking Soda and brush the pet's teeth. The abrasive powder will stick to the wet bristles of the toothbrush, clean the teeth, and freshen the animal's breath.

- **Arm & Hammer Baking Soda, Morton Salt, Glycerin, and McCormick Pure Peppermint Extract.** To make homemade pet toothpaste, in an airtight container, mix six teaspoons Arm & Hammer Baking Soda, one-third teaspoon Morton Salt, four teaspoons glycerin, and two teaspoons McCormick Pure Peppermint Extract. Mix until you attain the texture of regular toothpaste. Store in the refrigerator.

- **Campbell's Beef Broth.** If your pet refuses to let you put a toothbrush in her mouth, open up a can of Campbell's Beef Broth and dip the bristles in the broth. While beef broth will never be more effective than quality pet toothpaste, brushing your dog or cat's teeth with broth is better than not brushing your pet's teeth at all. And once your pet feels comfortable having you brush her teeth with broth, she might be more willing to accept toothpaste.

- **Chicken of the Sea Tuna.** For another foolproof way to induce your pet (particularly cats) to let you brush her teeth, drain the water from a can of water-packed Chicken of the Sea Tuna into a cup and dip the bristles of the toothbrush in the tuna-flavored water. The tuna water certainly won't give your pet minty-fresh breath, but at least you'll be removing harmful plaque from her teeth. Store the tuna-flavored water in an airtight container in the refrigerator for future use.

- **Easy Cheese.** To familiarize your dog or cat with a toothbrush to make brushing enjoyable for both of you, squeeze a dollop of Easy Cheese aerosol cheese on a soft toothbrush, and let your dog or cat lick it off. Repeat this every day for a week. Then slowly introduce your pet to the concept of moving the toothbrush back and forth, little by little advancing to some brushing.

- **Gold Medal Whole Wheat Flour, Bisquick Baking Mix, Blue Bonnet Margarine,** and **Karo Corn Syrup.** Having your pet chew abrasive biscuits helps scrub the bacteria-laden film of plaque from his teeth. For homemade teeth-cleaning biscuits, combine one-and-a-half cups Gold Medal Whole Wheat Flour, one-and-half cups Bisquick Baking Mix, one-half cup fresh mint leaves (loosely packed), one-quarter cup milk, four tablespoons Blue Bonnet Margarine, one egg, and one-and-a-half tablespoons Karo Light Corn Syrup in a food processor until the mint is chopped and a large ball of dough forms. Press or roll on a floured board to a thickness of one-quarter to one-half inch. Cut into 1- x 2-inch strips (or use a bone-shaped cookie cutter) and place the strips on a nonstick cookie pan. Bake at 375 degrees Fahrenheit for twenty minutes or until lightly brown. Cool and store in airtight container. Makes approximately thirty biscuits.

- **Johnson & Johnson Cotton Balls.** Clean your cat or dog's teeth once a week with a Johnson & Johnson Cotton Ball dipped in warm water.

- **Knorr Beef Bouillon.** If your dog or cat refuses to let you brush his teeth with pet toothpaste, bring a cup of water to a boil, dissolve one Knorr Beef Bouillon cube in the cup, and let cool. Dip the bristles of the toothbrush in the bouillon. Your pet will eagerly let you brush her teeth with the bouillon-flavored toothbrush, and the simple act of brushing helps remove plaque from teeth, regardless if you're using toothpaste. Once your pet grows accustomed to having you brush her teeth, try switching to toothpaste.

- **L'eggs Sheer Energy Panty Hose.** To get your pet used to having your fingers inside his mouth to prepare for eventually brushing his teeth with a toothbrush, wrap a piece of a clean, used pair of L'eggs Sheer Energy Panty Hose around your forefinger and rub the outsides of his upper and lower teeth. Do this for less than a minute and when you're finished, reward your pet with a treat. Repeat once a day for a week, and then graduate to using a toothbrush.

- **McCormick Garlic Powder.** If your dog or cat dislikes the toothpastes formulated especially for pets, mix one teaspoon McCormick Garlic Powder and one cup lukewarm water. Moisten the brush with the garlic solution, and then brush your pet's teeth. Dogs and cats love garlic, and although you're not brushing with any toothpaste, you're still brushing your pet's teeth.

PET PEEVES

SINKING YOUR TEETH INTO IT

- Dogs and cats rarely get cavities.

- Dogs and cats do get plaque, which causes periodontal disease. This infection leads to erosion of gum tissue and the bones that support the teeth. You'll need a veterinarian to treat periodontal disease.

- More than 80 percent of dogs and cat over three years of age have some degree of periodontal disease.

- Brushing your pet's teeth can prevent periodontal disease by removing plaque.

- Never brush your pet's teeth with a toothpaste made for people. Human toothpastes typically contain detergents that can cause stomach upset in animals. People spit out the toothpaste after brushing. Dogs and cats swallow the toothpaste, so they need a safe, edible toothpaste.

- Brush your teeth in front of your pet to familiarize your pet with the concept and demonstrate how harmless it is. This awareness will help make your pet less resistant to having his teeth brushed.

- Pet stores sell toothpastes concocted especially for cats and dogs, including toothpastes flavored with beef and chicken.

- If your cat resists having her teeth brushed, wrap your pet in a towel so you can restrain her without getting scratched.

- If your pet refuses to let you brush her teeth with a toothbrush, consider buying a finger toothbrush—a rubber finger glove with bristles on the tip.

Teething

For Dogs and Cats

- **Campbell's Beef Broth.** To get your teething puppy or kitty to chew on a toy rather than your personal items or furniture, cook up a can of Campbell's Beef Broth according to the directions on the label. Soak a rawhide bone or any other toy in the broth for five minutes, and let dry. The alluring scent makes the toy virtually impossible for your pet to ignore.

- **Con-Tact Paper.** To prevent your puppy or kitten from chewing through electrical cords and getting electrocuted, save the cardboard tubes from your wrapping paper (or buy thin cardboard mailing tubes), cover the unsightly cardboard with attractively designed Con-Tact paper, and run your electrical cords through the tubes.

- **Fels-Naptha Soap.** To prevent puppies or kittens from chewing electrical cords and risking shocks or electrocution, rub the cords with Fels-Naptha Soap.

- **Jif Peanut Butter.** To make sure your pet teethes on his chew toys, make them more enticing by coating them with Jif Peanut Butter. A hollow toy stuffed with peanut butter will keep your pet entertained for hours.

- **Scotch Packaging Tape.** To prevent a teething puppy or kitten from chewing through electrical wiring and getting a deadly shock, use Scotch Packaging Tape to secure electrical cords to the floor.

For Dogs Only

- **Wilson Tennis Balls.** To tire out your dog so he won't have the energy to chew your personal belongings, toss a Wilson Tennis Ball for your dog to chase after repeatedly. Exercise and plenty of attention will make your dog content.

PET PEEVES

MOUTHING OFF

- Cover electrical outlets with safety plugs to prevent puppies and kittens from licking them.

- To soothe your dog's gums made sore from teething, saturate a clean, old washcloth with water, freeze it, and then give it to your dog to chew on.

- Puppies teethe between three and six months of age, when baby teeth make way for adult teeth. Kittens teethe between two and four months of age.

- Give your puppy or kitten a few chewing toys to divert her attention away from your personal items. Rubbing your hands over the toy gives it your scent, which will attract your pet.

- If you discover your puppy or kitten teething on a forbidden item, give a sharp "No!" and give your pet an acceptable chewing toy. When the animal starts chewing the toy, bestow him with warm praise.

- Do not scold your pet for teething on a taboo object unless you catch your pet in the act. Dogs and cats have short memories, and the belated reprimand will merely confuse the animal.

- To soothe your pet's sore gums, hold the animal's chin in one hand and massage the outside of her mouth with your free index finger.

- Giving a pet plenty of playtime and exercise tires her out and reduces the need for chewing.

- Feed your teething pet an ice cube, either by hand or by placing it in her food bowl. The ice helps relieve teething pain.

Ticks

For Dogs and Cats

- **Betadine Solution.** After removing an embedded tick, dab the area with Betadine Solution. The antiseptic solution provides extra protection against infection and tick-borne diseases.

- **Jif Peanut Butter.** To remove a feeding tick from a dog or cat, wear a pair of gloves and cover the tick with a thick glob of Jif Peanut Butter. The peanut butter suffocates the parasite, causing it to back out of the skin.

- **Johnson's Baby Oil.** Put a drop of Johnson's Baby Oil on an attached tick to loosen the tick from the skin. Then, wearing a pair of gloves, extract the tick with tweezers, grasping the tick at the skin line as close to the head as possible and pulling gently but steadily. Loosening the tick with mineral oil helps remove the tick intact.

- **Krazy Glue.** Put a drop of Krazy Glue on a broom straw, apply to the embedded tick, let dry, and then gently but steadily pull the tick from the skin.

- **Liquid Paper.** Painting the body of an attached tick with this typewriter correction fluid seals off the openings through which it breathes, causing the parasite to suffocate and release its grip.

- **Listerine.** Place a few drops of Listerine antiseptic mouthwash on the feeding tick's head and wait approximately ten minutes. The antiseptic will cause the tick to let go.

- **Maybelline Clear Nail Polish.** Painting the embedded tick with a few drops of Maybelline Clear Nail Polish suffocates the pesky insect, prompting it to release its grip.

- **Neosporin.** After removing an engorged tick, dab the area with Neosporin. The antibiotic ointment provides extra protection against infection and tick-borne diseases.

- **Playtex Living Gloves.** Before removing a feeding tick from your pet's body, put on a pair of Playtex Living Gloves to avoid contact with your skin. Ticks can also transmit diseases to humans.

- **Skin So Soft.** Repel ticks by moisturizing your pet's coat with Skin So Soft Body Lotion. The oh-so-soft moisturizer repulses ticks.

- **Smirnoff Vodka.** Place a few drops of Smirnoff Vodka on the attached tick's head and wait approximately ten minutes. The alcohol will prompt the tick to let go.

- **Vaseline Petroleum Jelly.** Wearing a pair of gloves, cover the embedded tick with a dab of Vaseline Petroleum Jelly. This suffocates the parasite, causing it to back out of the skin.

GET YOUR PET TO THE VET

Get ticked off! Ticks spread Lyme disease, Rocky Mountain spotted fever, and ehrlichiosis. If your pet stops eating, has achy joints, sores, fever, diarrhea, or partial paralysis, take your pet to the veterinarian immediately.

PET PEEVES

WHAT MAKES THEM TICK?

- Ticks—parasites related to mites and spiders—require blood to complete their life cycles and feed on warm-blooded animals. Ticks' teeth are bent backward, which helps the parasites cling to their hosts.

- When gorging on a host's blood, ticks balloon up to fifty times their normal size.

- Ticks spread Lyme disease and Rocky Mountain spotted fever.

- Lyme disease often reveals itself first as a small rash that looks like a bull's-eye target, flu-like symptoms, and Bell's palsy (paralysis in one side of the face). If left untreated, the disease can escalate to arthritis, meningitis, and neurological damage. If caught early, Lyme disease can be treated with antibiotics.

- Ticks have eight legs, making them arachnids, not insects.

- Female ticks lay up to five thousand eggs at one time.

- Ticks live several feet off the ground on tall grass and weeds, lingering until a potential host passes by. Keeping your lawn cut minimizes this scenario.

- Young ticks usually attach themselves to small rodents and then move on to larger animals. Banishing rodents from your yard helps keep ticks away.

- When hiking with your dog in tick-infested areas, stick to well blazed trails, avoiding tall grass and weeds.

- When you and your pet return home from a romp through tick country, carefully examine your pet for ticks, particularly around his ears and under his legs. If you discover ticks on your pet that have yet to embed themselves and start feeding, spray your pet with a tick insecticide and comb them out.

- If you spot a feeding tick on your pet, when removing it, avoid squeezing the tick's body, which can inject the tick's blood into your pet, causing infection. Remove a tick by using tweezers to grasp the tick at the skin line or as close to the tick's head as possible and gently pull it out (making sure not to leave the tick's head embedded in the pet's skin). Place the tick in a small container filled with rubbing (isopropyl) alcohol. Mark the date on the container. The alcohol kills and preserves the tick so your veterinarian can identify it and test it for diseases, should your pet start showing symptoms of a tick-borne disease.

- **Wesson Vegetable Oil.** Place a drop of Wesson Vegetable Oil on the feeding tick. Then, using a pair of tweezers, grasp the tick at the skin line as close to the head as possible and pull gently but steadily. The vegetable oil loosens the tick from the skin so you can remove the bloated pest intact.

- **Ziploc Storage Bags.** After removing an engorged tick, place it in a jar of alcohol to kill it, put the dead tick in a tightly sealed Ziploc Storage Bag, and write the date on the bag. Take the tick to a veterinarian to have it analyzed at a lab for Lyme disease or any other tick-borne diseases.

Toys

For Dogs and Cats

- **Wilson Tennis Balls** and **L'eggs Sheer Energy Panty Hose.** To make a highly entertaining toy for your dog or cat, cut off both legs from a clean, used pair of L'eggs Sheer Energy Panty Hose, insert a Wilson Tennis Ball into the toe of the first leg, put the first leg inside the second leg (to double the strength of the nylon), and tie a knot three inches above the tennis ball and more knots at three-inch intervals (or use an old sock and sew up the open end of the sock). The stocking (or sock) gives your pet more to grip and also prevents the ball from rolling under the furniture.

- **Ziploc Storage Bags.** When traveling, carry your pet's toys in Ziploc Storage Bags for easy access.

For Dogs Only

- **Easy Cheese.** To enhance your dog's chew toy, spray some aerosol Easy Cheese inside it.

- **Jif Peanut Butter.** Stuff a hollow dog toy with peanut butter, to create a special treat for your dog.

- **Knorr Beef Bouillon.** To make a rawhide bone more engaging for your dog, bring one cup water to a boil and dissolve one Knorr Beef Bouillon cube in the cup. Soak a rawhide bone or stick in the broth for five minutes, and then place it on a paper towel to dry. Your dog will spend hours enjoying the beef-flavored rawhide bone.

- **Pam Cooking Spray** and **McCormick Garlic Salt.** To attract your dog to his chew toys, spray his cloth toys with Pam Cooking Spray and sprinkle on some McCormick Garlic Salt. Dogs love the taste of vegetable oil and find garlic irresistible.

- **Philadelphia Cream Cheese.** You can also stuff that hollow toy with Philadelphia Cream Cheese to give your dog hours of entertainment to help forget about you while you're out of the house.

For Cats Only

- **Charmin Toilet Paper.** The empty cardboard tube from a roll of Charmin Toilet Paper makes an excellent play toy for cats.

- **Dawn Ultra Dishwashing Liquid, Karo Corn Syrup,** and **Glad Drinking Straws.** Entertain your cat with bubbles. Mix one-quarter cup Dawn Ultra Dishwashing Liquid, one tablespoon Karo Light Corn Syrup, and thirty ounces distilled or soft water (not hard water) in a shallow bowl or a pie tin. Diagonally cut the end of a Glad Drinking Straw, dip into bubble soap, and blow.

- **Glad Flexible Straws.** A few Glad Flexible Straws make a favorite plaything for cats.

- **Kleenex Tissues.** Wad up a few Kleenex Tissues and toss them around the house. Cats love to retrieve them. (To prevent an aggressive cat from pulling tissues out of the box, simply set the box upside-down.)

- **L'eggs Sheer Energy Panty Hose.** To make a catnip ball, cut off the foot from a clean, used pair of L'eggs Sheer Energy Panty Hose, stuff the toe with catnip, and knot it.

Pet Tricks
Toilet Paper Antics

- **Charmin Toilet Paper.** To prevent a cat from unrolling toilet paper, take the cardboard tube from a used roll of Charmin Toilet Paper, use a pair of scissors to slice it open lengthwise, and fit it over the full roll of toilet paper.

- **Coca-Cola.** Put a few pennies in a clean, empty Coca-Cola can and tape the opening shut. To train your cat to stop unrolling the toilet paper, balance the homemade shaker on top of the toilet paper roll. When the cat tries to unroll the toilet paper, the resulting crash of an aluminum can filled with jangling coins will frighten her away.

- **Dixie Cups.** Here's a mischievous way to teach your cat to stop unrolling the toilet paper. Fill a Dixie Cup halfway with water and balance it on the top of the roll. When your cat attempts to unroll the toilet paper, she'll be frightened away by a splash of water.

- **Saran Wrap.** Tape a sheet of Saran Wrap to the wall so it hangs over the toilet paper roll. Cats veer away from plastic.

- **Oral-B Dental Floss.** Hang up a crystal in the window. The sunlight will cast ever-changing rainbow patterns on the walls, floor, and furniture, keeping your cat fascinated and engrossed.

- **Oral-B Dental Floss.** Use a one-foot length of Oral-B Dental Floss to hang a crumpled-up ball of paper from a two-foot-long stick. Dangle the paper ball in front of your cat and watch your cat have fun batting it around.

- **Reynolds Wrap.** A crumpled-up ball of Reynolds Wrap can keep your cat entertained for hours. Cats find the shiny aluminum foil irresistible.

- **Scotch Double Sided Tape.** To keep your cat from playing in trouble spots, like the space behind the refrigerator or entertainment unit, put Scotch Double Sided Tape across the entrance. Cats avoid walking across sticky surfaces.

- **Scotch Tape.** When you've used up a roll of Scotch Tape, take off the empty plastic roll. Cats love playing with them.

- **Uncle Ben's Converted Brand Rice.** To make a great toy for your cat, fill an empty pill bottle with uncooked Uncle Ben's Converted Brand Rice and seal the childproof cap securely.

- **Ziploc Freezer Bags.** Seal a Ziploc Freezer Bag closed except for the last inch of the zip-top, inflate the bag like a balloon, and seal the rest of the zip-top shut. Let your cat play with the durable, makeshift balloon.

Pet Projects
CATNIP: WHAT THE HECK IS IT?

Catnip causes most cats to go a little crazy—rubbing the catnip, rolling over it, purring, and frantically leaping about. Then, after a few minutes, the cat will suddenly lose all interest—having acclimated to the catnip. An hour or two later, after being separated from the catnip, the catnip will once again trigger the same manic reaction.

Catnip is the common name for *Nepeta cataria*, a genus of about 250 species of flowering plants. The leaves and stems of Nepeta contain the chemical nepetalactone, which stimulates most cats' pheromonic receptors, triggering a temporary euphoria. Catnip does not affect all cats. Large cats like tigers can also be sensitive to catnip, but young kittens and older cats are less likely to experience a reaction. Catnip is both harmless and nonaddictive, and no plant is known to have the same effect on humans.

At the turn of the twentieth century, Dr. A.C. Daniels—a shop owner in Boston, Massachusetts, selling his patent medicines to people, along with products for horses, dogs, sheep, and cows—became the first person to market catnip and catnip toys to cat owners. He introduced a gray flannel mouse that could be filled with Summit Brand Catnip as a play toy for cats. In 1907, he patented the world's first catnip ball—a hollow wooden ball that could be filled and refilled with catnip. Dr. A.C. Daniels used his face and signature on all of his products and advertising.

In 1914, Charles C. Rogers and Nellie Kidder purchased and incorporated the A.C. Daniels Company. In 1954, Henry Van Baay purchased the business, and five years later, Dr. Donald W. Hey purchased the product line and moved the business to Webster, Massachusetts, where it remains to this day. Over the years, as Americans adopted more household pets, the company's line of feline toys expanded, and products for cows, sheep, and poultry slowly diminished.

PET PEEVES
LETTING THE CAT OUT OF THE BAG

- Never give your pet any of your old shoes as a toy. Otherwise, all the shoes in your house become fair game.

- Cats and dogs find open toilet bowls irresistible. To prevent your pet from drinking from the toilet (a great way to pick up a disease), swimming in the toilet, or drowning in the toilet, keep the lid shut.

- Make sure all dog toys are sturdy and suitable for chewing without breaking off into sharp or spongy pieces that can be swallowed. Appropriate dog toys include hard rubber balls, rawhide chew toys, and Frisbees.

- Great toys for cats include paper bags, Ping-Pong balls, empty thread spools, and empty cardboard boxes.

- Do not let a cat play with yarn, thread, ribbon, string, twine, or rubber bands. All pose a serious choking danger if swallowed. Cats have barbed tongues that make spitting things out extremely difficult. Once cats start swallowing something, they usually cannot stop.

- Keep the strings on your blinds out of your cat's reach by wrapping up the cords and securing them with rubber bands.

- Keep all wastebaskets out of reach of cats and kittens to prevent your pet from eating something harmful.

- To keep your cat or dog amused, set up a birdfeeder outside a window to attract some winged entertainers.

- To prevent your cat from unrolling rolls of toilet paper, hang the roll so the paper unwinds from underneath. To prevent your cat from shredding the entire roll of toilet paper, purchase a plastic shield that fits over the roll from a pet-supply store. Or simply keep the bathroom door closed.

Training

For Dogs and Cats

- **BenGay.** To train your dog or cat to stop chewing on a specific object, coat the object with a dab of BenGay. The smell will repel the animal. For more ways to train a pet to stop chewing, see page 60.

- **Glad Trash Bags.** If your dog or cat refuses to stay off the sofa, cut open a Glad Trash Bag along the seams and cover your furniture with the plastic. Pets despise the feeling of plastic and stay away. For more ways to train your pet to stay off the furniture, see page 114.

- **McCormick Black Pepper.** To keep dogs or cats out of your flowerbed or vegetable garden, sprinkle the garden beds with McCormick Black Pepper. Dogs and cats have a keen sense of smell, and the scent of pepper repels them. For more ways to keep your pet out of your garden, see page 313.

- **ReaLemon.** If your dog or cat starts begging while you're trying to enjoy a meal, fill a spray bottle with water, add one teaspoon ReaLemon lemon juice, and shake well. Whenever your pet leaps into action, spray him with a blast of the lemony water. He'll go running for cover and quickly learn to steer clear of your meals. For more ways to train a pet to stop begging, see page 27.

- **Revlon Clear Nail Enamel.** To prevent metal identification tags from jangling like sleigh bells, coat the tags with Revlon Clear Nail Enamel, which deadens the sound.

For Dogs Only

- **Coca-Cola.** To stop your dog from digging up your backyard, put a few pennies in a clean, empty Coca-Cola can and tape the opening shut. When you catch your dog digging, exclaim "No" in a firm voice, and shake the can vigorously. The disturbing sound of coins jangling in a can will stop a dog in his tracks. For more ways to train your dog to stop digging, see page 86.

- **L'eggs Sheer Energy Panty Hose.** If you can't find your dog's leash, pull one leg of a clean, used pair of L'eggs Sheer Energy Panty Hose through your dog's collar and tie the two feet together with a square knot. The panty hose doubles as a leash.

- **Listerine.** To train a dog to cease bad behavior, fill a spray bottle with equal parts Listerine antiseptic mouthwash and water. When the dog misbehaves, spray the solution in the dog's mouth (avoiding the dog's eyes) and say "No!" The side benefit? The solution eliminates doggy breath.

- **ReaLemon.** To train a dog to stop barking, when your dog starts barking, squirt some ReaLemon lemon juice in the dog's mouth (not eyes) and say "Quiet!" The lemon juice is nontoxic and harmless, providing simple and effective behavior modification. For more ways to deal with a barking, see page 11.

For Cats Only

- **Heinz Chili Sauce.** To stop your cat from scratching furniture, rub the wooden furniture legs with Heinz Chili Sauce, and then wipe it off. Cats can't stand the odor. For more ways to train your pets to stop scratching furniture, see page 234.

- **Heinz White Vinegar.** To train your cat to stay away from a particular area or off a countertop or specific piece of furniture, any time the cat approaches that forbidden area, gently dab a cotton ball dampened with Heinz White Vinegar on your cat's lips. Place the wet cotton ball on a saucer on the spot as added discouragement. For more ways to keep a cat off furniture, see page 114.

- **Maxwell House Coffee.** To prevent a cat from having a love affair with your houseplants, add used Maxwell House Coffee grounds to the top of the potting soil. Kitty will be turned off by that nasty scent. The coffee grounds, filled with nutrients, also fertilize the plants. For more ways to train a cat to stay away from houseplants, see page 175.

PET PEEVES
TEACHING AN OLD DOG NEW TRICKS

- Keep your dog or cat properly tagged with your pet's name, address, and telephone number in case your pet gets lost.

- Declawing your cat so he won't scratch you or your furniture is cruel and inhumane. This painful operation is like surgically amputating all your fingertips at the first joint. Declawing also lessens a cat's ability to defend against dogs and other animals.

- To train your cat to stay off tabletops, countertops, and furniture, fill a spray bottle or squirt gun with water and spritz your cat anytime she ventures onto forbidden territory. The cat will quickly learn to steer clear of those spots.

- Never pick up a cat by the nape of his neck.

- Other substitutes for a leash: a rope, clothesline, or long leather belt.

- You can make a dog collar from an old leather belt. Simply punch holes in the belt where needed to make the collar the proper size and cut off the excess.

- Adhere reflective automotive tape or small, red bicycle reflectors to your pet's collar, so motorists can spot your pet at night.

- Always check your clothes dryer to make sure the cat isn't curled up inside the warm, cozy drum before loading wet clothes and shutting the door to run the machine.

Pet Tricks
Training Tips

- Only one person in your family should train your puppy, starting when the animal reaches seven weeks of age. Whoever trains the animal should have a great deal of patience and plenty of time to devote to the animal.

- Whenever you command your dog or cat, make eye contact first. Eye contact shows the pet that you're serious.

- Use simple, clear, one-word commands. Dogs do not understand complex sentences.

- If your dog does something wrong, discipline the dog immediately. Dog's have short memories, and if you delay for even a minute, the dog won't understand why she's being punished.

- When disciplining your dog or cat, never call your pet's name and then scold him. Reserve use of his name for praise and reward.

- Never beckon a dog to scold him. The dog will think you're punishing him for coming to you. Instead, walk over to your pet to reprimand him.

- Never chastise a dog for more than a few seconds. Otherwise, the dog will forget why he's being scolded and will no longer connect the punishment with the behavior.

- Give positive reinforcement for good behavior immediately by praising your dog overzealously.

Traveling

Bowls

For Dogs and Cats

- **Cool Whip.** A clean, empty Cool Whip tub makes a perfect water or food bowl when traveling with your pet. You can even pre-measure one serving and keep it stored in the Cool Whip tub. Or place some ice cubes in the tub before hoping in the car. As the ice melts, your pet will have clean, fresh, cold water.

- **Frisbee.** When camping or hiking, turn a Frisbee upside down to improvise a convenient (and portable) food or water dish for your dog or cat.

- **Ziploc Freezer Bags.** In a pinch, fill a Ziploc Freezer Bag with water and hold it open with both hands to create an instant water bowl.

Car Sickness

For Dogs and Cats

- **Dramamine.** To fend off car sickness, an hour before traveling, split a fifty-milligram tablet of Dramamine into quarters and give one quarter (12.5 milligrams) to your cat or small dog at least one hour before traveling. For medium to large dogs, give twenty-five to fifty milligrams before traveling. (Dramamine is more effective at preventing car sickness before it occurs than stopping car sickness once it arises.) According to veterinarians, Dramamine is safe for most healthy dogs and cats. Do not give Dramamine to any pet with bladder problems or glaucoma without first consulting your veterinarian.

Carriers

For Dogs and Cats

- **USA Today.** Before putting your dog or cat in a carrier, place a section of USA Today on the floor of the carrier to absorb any unforeseen accidents.

Food

For Dogs and Cats

- **Glad Trash Bags.** When you're on the road, store that bag of dry pet food inside a Glad Trash Bag to prevent it from spilling over and to protect the contents from insects and other pests.

Poop

For Dogs Only

- **Ziploc Storage Bags.** If you're traveling with your dog, take along a box of Ziploc Storage Bags to clean up after him at rest stops. Turn the bag inside-out, put your hand inside the bag, and grab the poop. Pull the bag right-side out, seal it shut, and discard it in an outdoor trash can.

For Cats Only

- **Rubbermaid, Ziploc Storage Bags,** and **Arm & Hammer Baking Soda.** When traveling with a cat, carry along a re-sealable, airtight Rubbermaid container filled with cat box filler to create a traveling litter box. Carry along Ziploc Storage Bags to scoop up the poop, and occasionally sprinkle the litter with Arm & Hammer Baking Soda to keep it smelling fresh.

Treats

For Dogs and Cats

- **Ziploc Storage Bags.** Keep treats in Ziploc Storage Bags when training or traveling to keep them handy, fresh, and protected from insects.

Water

For Dogs and Cats

- **McCormick Pure Peppermint Extract.** To encourage your dog or cat to drink any unfamiliar-smelling water on your journey, a few days before your departure, start adding a few drops of McCormick Pure Peppermint Extract to the water every time you refill his drinking bowl. Take the bottle of peppermint extract along on your trip, and add a few drops to your pet's drinking water during your travels to make the smell of any water familiar to your animal.

PET PEEVES

- To improvise a pet carrier, use a laundry basket (or two laundry baskets, one of them placed upside down on top of the other, laced together).

- When making a long-distance car ride with your dog or cat, take along a plastic cooler with ice for your pet. The melting ice provides a fresh supply of cold, refreshing water for your pet.

- To prevent your pet from getting diarrhea from the mineral content of water in a new location, carry water from home, if possible, or purchase distilled or spring water along your route.

- If your dog or cat becomes overly anxious when traveling, consult your veterinarian to check whether she suggests prescribing an appropriate and safe tranquilizer for your pet. Do not give human medications to your pet without speaking with your veterinarian. Most human medications can be harmful or fatal to pets.

- When traveling with your pet, make certain the animal is wearing an identification collar.

- Several days before traveling with your dog or cat, open the pet carrier and place it on the floor for your pet to explore it and grow accustomed to it.

- To avoid carsickness, refrain from feeding your pet for six hours before starting the car trip.

- When traveling, make sure to leash your dog before opening the car door at a rest stop or your destination. Otherwise, your dog might leap out of the car and get hit by another vehicle or run away and get lost.

- When traveling with a cat, keep the cat inside the carrier until you get indoors at your destination. Otherwise, the cat might leap out of the car and run away, never to be found.

Vomiting

For Dogs and Cats

- **Campbell's Beef Broth.** After your dog or cat stops vomiting, feed your pet a small amount of Campbell's Beef Broth every few hours to prevent dehydration.

- **Gatorade.** Vomiting quickly depletes vital liquids from a dog or cat's body. Eliminate all solid food and milk from your pet's diet. Fill her water bowl with fruit punch–flavored Gatorade, which pets seem to love. Gatorade quickly replaces the lost minerals—sodium, potassium, and chloride—and prevents dehydration. (If your pet refuses to drink Gatorade, switch back to water.)

- **Gerber Baby Food.** Once you've weaned your pet back to eating solid food (see Uncle Ben's Converted Brand Rice on page 308), you can help revive your pet's strength by introducing Gerber Beef and Beef Gravy.

- **Kaopectate.** Once your dog or cat stops vomiting, use a turkey baster or bulb syringe to give your pet one teaspoon of Kaopectate for every ten pounds your pet weighs. Kaopectate will help soothe your pet's upset stomach. Hold your pet's head back, squirt the medicine toward the back of his throat, hold his mouth closed, and stroke his throat until he swallows. Be sure to consult your veterinarian for the precise dosage for your pet.

- **Pedialyte.** After your dog or cat experiences a bout of vomiting, pour Pedialyte into your pet's water bowl to quickly replace her electrolytes. Drinking water will replace most electrolytes, but drinking an electrolyte solution such as Pedialyte, formulated for babies, quickly replaces crucial minerals like potassium and sodium. (Not all pets will drink Pedialyte, so keep another bowl of water available.)

- **Uncle Ben's Converted Brand Rice.** To get your dog or cat's digestive system back to normal after a vomiting jag, refrain from feeding your pet any solid food for twenty-four hours. Break your pet's fast by serving small portions of two parts cooked Uncle Ben's Converted Brand Rice and one part cottage cheese every four hours. The bland food will help ease your pet back to a normal diet, which you can start feeding after another twenty-four hours.

For Dogs Only

- **Pepto-Bismol.** Use a turkey baster or an oral syringe to give your dog one-half teaspoon Pepto-Bismol for every ten pounds of weight every four to six hours for up to two days. (Never give Pepto-Bismol to a cat without first consulting a veterinarian. Cats have difficulty metabolizing some of the ingredients, which can nauseate them.)

GET YOUR PET TO THE VET

Bring it up! Vomiting can be a sign of serious illness, such as poisoning from eating houseplants, kidney failure (in dogs), or feline distemper (in cats). If you suspect your pet consumed something poisonous or if vomiting persists for more than twenty-four hours, get your pet to a veterinarian immediately.

For Cats Only

● **Vaseline Petroleum Jelly.** To prevent your cat from getting hairballs, place a dab of Vaseline Petroleum Jelly on one of the cat's paws. The cat will lick off the petroleum jelly, which lubricates her digestive track, allowing hairs to travel naturally out the proper end. Apply the petroleum jelly once a day for four days. For more ways to prevent hairballs, see page 133.

PET PEEVES
EVERYTHING'S COMING UP ROSES

● If your dog or cat is vomiting without any other signs of illness or poisoning, stop feeding your pet all food until the vomiting ceases. Make sure your pet drinks plenty of water during the fast to avoid dehydration.

● If your sick pet resists drinking water, place one fresh ice cube in her bowl every fifteen minutes, allowing her to lick up the water slowly.

● Keep the toilet lid closed to stop your pet from drinking excessively and to prevent bacterial contamination from complicating matters.

● Dogs and cats tend to vomit from eating rancid garbage or dead rodents or birds.

● All dogs and cats sometimes eat grass, causing them to vomit. No one knows for certain whether animals eat grass to intentionally purge a disagreeable substance from their system or because they simply find grass appetizing.

● Since the gastric acid in vomit can permanently bleach the color of carpet or fabric, act quickly to clean up the mess. Sponge the spot on carpet and upholstery with water to dilute the acids and blot well. On clothing, flush the spot with cool water.

● To help your veterinarian access the situation, report the frequency and appearance of your pet's vomit, most notably its color and texture and whether it contained blood or stool.

Wounds

For Dogs and Cats

- **Betadine Solution.** To prevent a wound from getting infected, apply Betadine Solution, and then flush the wound clean with lukewarm running water. Pat dry with a towel.

- **Hibiclens.** After flushing the wound for at least five minutes with lukewarm running water, wash the affected area with Hibiclens antibacterial soap. Then apply Neosporin (see page 311) and bandage with gauze.

- **K-Y Jelly.** After getting the bleeding under control, smear a thin coat of water-soluble K-Y Jelly around the wound and use a pair of scissors to trim the hair from around the bite wound. The jelly traps the cut hairs and prevents them from falling into the wound. Then wash away the jelly. Trimming the hair from around the wound helps keep the wound clean.

- **L'eggs Sheer Energy Panty Hose.** An injured animal tends to become defensive and might snap at you if you attempt to provide help. Before treating a wounded dog or cat, protect yourself from serious bites by muzzling your pet's mouth closed. Improvise a muzzle by cutting off a leg from a clean, used pair of L'eggs Sheer Energy Panty Hose, wrapping it several times around your pet's mouth, and tying the ends back behind the animal's ears. Do not cover the animal's nostrils. Remove the impromptu muzzle if the pet experiences difficulty breathing, starts vomiting, or bleeds from the mouth.

- **Neosporin.** After washing and drying the wound (see Hibiclens on page 310), apply Neosporin ointment to the wound to prevent infection by killing any bacteria. Then bandage the area with gauze, secured in place with first-aid tape.

- **Stayfree Maxi Pads** and **L'eggs Sheer Energy Panty Hose.** Use a Stayfree Maxi Pad as a compress to stop the bleeding from a wound by applying firm pressure for a few minutes. In an emergency, you can hold the maxi pad in place by tying it with L'eggs Sheer Energy Panty Hose.

- **Tampax Tampons** and **L'eggs Sheer Energy Panty Hose.** Use a Tampax Tampon as a compress for wounds to control heavy bleeding. Apply firm pressure for several minutes until the bleeding stops. In an emergency, you can hold the tampon in place by tying it with L'eggs Sheer Energy Panty Hose.

- **Wesson Vegetable Oil.** If you're unable to bandage a wound on your dog or cat, dab some Wesson Vegetable Oil liberally on the wound. Vegetable oil can stop the bleeding.

GET YOUR PET TO THE VET

Deep trouble! If your pet gets a deep laceration, abrasion, puncture wound, or bite mark; if a wound bleeds heavily or won't stop bleeding; or if a wound develops an infection, take your pet to the veterinarian.

PET PEEVES

LICKING YOUR WOUNDS

- If your dog or cat gets severely wounded or injured, use a blanket as a stretcher. Place your pet in the center of the blanket and have two people each lift two corners of the blanket to carry the animal.

- If you can't muzzle the animal before administering treatment, loosely wrap your pet's head in a pillowcase or hand towel to avoid the possibility of being bitten.

- Stop any bleeding by applying firm pressure with your hand, a cloth, or gauze. Once you get the bleeding under control, clean the wound.

- Do not use hydrogen peroxide or isopropyl alcohol to clean a deep wound. These antiseptics might aggravate damaged tissue.

- Rather than bandaging a minor wound on your dog or cat, use electric clippers to trim the hair around the wound to allow air-drying. Hair retains bacteria, dirt, secretions, and debris, hindering the healing process.

- While some wounds require bandages, most do not. Bandages tend to slow healing.

- If your dog or cat starts instinctively licking the wound, let him do so. Licking cleans the wound and might speed healing.

- If your dog won't stop disturbing the wound, have your pet fit with an Elizabethan collar— a conical plastic casing that fits around the animal's neck.

- A deep wound might require stitches (and possibly anesthesia) or antibiotics.

Yards

For Dogs and Cats

- **McCormick Ground (Cayenne) Red Pepper, Colman's Mustard Powder,** and **Gold Medal Flour.** To prevent pets from destroying flower beds and vegetable gardens, mix two ounces McCormick Ground (Cayenne) Red Pepper, three ounces Colman's Mustard Powder, and five ounces Gold Medal Flour. Sprinkle the mixture around the forbidden areas.

- **Reynolds Wrap.** If you keep your pet's bedding outdoors in cold weather, line the inside of the bedding box with Reynolds Wrap, and then add the bedding. The aluminum foil will reflect your pet's body heat and help keep her a tad warmer.

- **Tabasco Pepper Sauce, McCormick Chili Powder,** and **Ivory Dishwashing Liquid.** To prevent your dog or cat from destroying your flower beds and vegetable garden, mix two tablespoons Tabasco Pepper Sauce, one teaspoon McCormick Chili Powder, one-half teaspoon Ivory Dishwashing Liquid, and two cups water in a sixteen-ounce trigger-spray bottle. Shake well and spray the solution around the perimeter of your flower beds and vegetable gardens to repel cats and dogs. (The dishwashing liquid helps the spicy solution stick to the plants.)

For Dogs Only

- **Arm & Hammer Baking Soda.** If dogs urinate on your lawn and cause yellow burn spots, dissolve one cup Arm & Hammer Baking Soda in one gallon water in a watering can. Saturate the existing yellow burn spots every three days. The baking soda deodorizes the dry urine (preventing the offending dog from recognizing and reusing the spot) and neutralizes the acidity (allowing the grass to recuperate its color).

- **Coca-Cola.** During hot, humid weather, fill clean, empty two-liter Coca-Cola bottles with water, freeze, and place them in the doghouse to keep your dog comfortable.

- **Lipton Chamomile Tea.** To stop fleas from infesting your dog, place a few Lipton Chamomile Tea bags in the doghouse. Chamomile repels fleas.

- **McCormick Ground (Cayenne) Red Pepper.** To stop neighborhood dogs from using your lawn as a bathroom, sprinkle McCormick Ground (Cayenne) Red Pepper on the lawn. Dogs have a keen sense of smell, and one whiff of cayenne pepper sends them seeking another place to do their business. Repeat after a rainstorm or after the sprinklers water the lawn.

- **Morton Salt.** To repel fleas from a doghouse, sprinkle Morton Salt into the cracks and crevices inside the doghouse. Or dissolve two tablespoons Morton Salt in two cups water in a sixteen-ounce trigger-spray bottle, and spray the inside of the doghouse with the salt water. Salt dehydrates fleas.

- **Pine-Sol.** To clean and deodorize a doghouse, mix one-half cup Pine-Sol in a bucket of water and wash the house thoroughly.

- **Tabasco Pepper Sauce and McCormick Ground (Cayenne) Red Pepper.** To train your dog to stop digging up your compost pile, mix four tablespoons Tabasco Pepper Sauce and four tablespoons McCormick Ground (Cayenne) Red Pepper in one quart water. After you've turned your compost, shake the spicy solution well and sprinkle it over the pile. Repeat every day for two weeks until your dog gets the message.

For Cats Only

- **Bounce.** To keep neighborhood cats out of your yard, hang fresh sheets of Bounce on your fence posts, shrubs, or trees. The fragrance of oleander in the Bounce is a natural cat repellent. When the Bounce sheets dry out and lose their scent, mist them with water from a spray bottle to revive the bouquet.

- **Heinz White Vinegar.** To keep your cats out of your flower or vegetable garden, fill a trigger-spray bottle with Heinz White Vinegar and spray around the border of the garden (or the perimeter of your yard). Or soak a cloth or sponge with vinegar and place it in the garden. The pungent aroma of vinegar repels cats.

- **Maxwell House Coffee.** To keep cats out of your flower or vegetable garden and prevent them from digging up the soil, work used Maxwell House Coffee grounds into the soil around the plants. The coffee grounds repel cats while simultaneously providing nutrients for the plants.

PET PEEVES
RIGHT IN YOUR OWN BACKYARD

- An indoor cat can live for fifteen to twenty years, while an outdoor cat is more likely to fall prey to a moving car, dog, coyote, poison, disease, or malicious human being.

- If your cat gets stuck up in a tree, leave it alone. If your cat can climb up a tree, your cat will eventually climb back down.

- If your pet spends a lot of time outdoors, make sure you provide plenty of fresh water—perhaps even two water bowls, with one placed under a faucet turned on to drip slowly.

- When buying or building a doghouse, make sure it is waterproof and well insulated, sits high off the ground, and fits your dog snugly, providing just enough room for your dog to enter, turn around, and lie down. Line the floor with straw or wood shavings to keep your dog cozy and warm, hang a plastic wind flap over the door, and make sure the roof extends over the door to create a shady porch.

Acknowledgments

At Rodale, I am grateful to my editor, Karen Bolesta, for suggesting that I write this book and making it her pet project. Her unleashed enthusiasm and passion made working on this book a delight.

No amount of thanks can properly express my appreciation to my agent and dear friend, Stephanie Tade, for her veracity, tenacity, and wonderful sense of humor.

I am also deeply indebted to ace researcher Debbie Green, expert copy editor Jennifer Bright Reich, talented designer Chris Rhoads, and gifted illustrator Glen Mullaly. My heartfelt thanks to my superb veterinary consultant Dr. Alan Chrisman of Jefferson Animal Hospital in Port Jefferson, New York. I am especially grateful to my colleague and friend Vicki Lansky for bequeathing her extensive library to me. Thanks also to animal lover Mardi Minogue and thoroughbred racing expert Stephen Wolfson for sharing their wealth of horse sense.

A very special thanks to my manager Barb North and the hundreds of people who have visited my website and taken the time to send me e-mails sharing their ingenious tips for the brand-name products we all know and love.

Above all, all my love to Debbie, Ashley, and Julia.

The Fine Print

All-New Hints from Heloise by Heloise (New York: Perigee, 1989)

Amazing Apple Cider Vinegar by Earl L. Mindell with Larry M. Johns (Lincolnwood, Illinois: Keats, 1999)

"Animal Doctor: A Safe Way To Get Fleas to Take a Powder" by Dr. Michael W. Fox, *Washington Post,* November 23, 2008

Another Use For by Vicki Lansky (Deephaven, Minnesota: Book Peddlers, 1991)

The ASPCA Complete Guide to Pet Care by David L. Carroll (New York: Plume, 2001)

The Bag Book: Over 500 Greats Uses—and Reuses—for Paper, Plastic, and Other Bags to Organize & Enhance Your Life by Vicki Lansky (Minnetonka, Minnesota: Book Peddlers, 2000)

Baking Soda Bonanza by Peter A. Ciullo (New York: HarperPerrenial, 1995)

Betty-Anne's Helpful Household Hints by Betty-Anne Hastings with Mary-Beth Connors (New York: Ventura Books, 1983)

Birds for Dummies by Gina Spadafori and Brian L. Speer (New York: Wiley, 1999)

Cats for Dummies by Gina Spadafori and Paul D. Pion (Foster City, California: ID Books Worldwide, 1997)

Clean & Green: The Complete Guide to Nontoxic and Environmentally Safe Housekeeping by Annie Berthold-Bond (Woodstock, New York: Ceres Press, 1990)

The Complete Home Veterinary Guide, Third Edition by Chris C. Pinney (New York: McGraw Hill, 2004)

Consumer Guide Handbook of Helpful Hints (New York: Beekman House, 1980)

Dear Anne and Nan by Anne B. Adams and Nancy Nash-Cummings (New York: Bantam, 1992)

The Doctor's Book of Home Remedies by the Editors of *Prevention* Magazine Health Books (Emmaus, Pennsylvania: Rodale, 1990)

The Doctor's Book of Home Remedies for Dogs and Cats by the Editors of *Prevention* Magazine Health Books (Emmaus, Pennsylvania: Rodale, 1996)

Dog Owner's Home Veterinary Handbook by Debra M. Eldredge, Liisa D. Carlson, Delbert G. Carlson, and James M. Giffin (Hoboken, New Jersey: Howell Book House, 2007)

Dr. Pitcairn's Complete Guide to Natural Health for Dogs & Cats by Richard H. Pitcairn and Susan Hubble Pitcairn (Emmaus, Pennsylvania: Rodale, 1995)

Earl Proulx's Yankee Home Hints by Earl Proulx (Dublin, New Hampshire: Yankee, 1993)

Favorite Helpful Household Hints by the Editors of Consumer Guide (Skokie, Illinois: Publications International, 1986)

Great Gardening Formulas edited by Joan Benjamin and Deborah L. Martin (Emmaus, Pennsylvania: Rodale, 1998)

The Guinness Book of World Records (New York: Bantam, 1998)

Haley's Hints by Graham Haley and Rosemary Haley (New York: New American Library, 1995)

"Hartz Content: The Good Life of Leonard Stern" by Gigi Mahon, *New York Magazine,* May 5, 1986, pages 42–48

Heloise Conquers Stinks and Stains (New York: Perigee, 2002)

Heloise from A to Z by Heloise (New York: Perigee, 1992)

Heloise Household Hints for Singles by Heloise (New York: Perigee, 1993)

Help! from Heloise by Heloise (New York: Avon, 1981)

Hints from Heloise by Heloise (New York: Arbor House, 1980)

Household Hints, Fall 1987, Volume 5, Number 3 (New York: Harris Publications, 1987)

Household Hints & Formulas by Erik Bruun (New York: Black Dog and Leventhal, 1994)

Household Hints & Handy Tips by Reader's Digest (Pleasantville, New York: Reader's Digest Association, 1988)

Household Hints Almanac, Spring 1987, Volume 2, Number 1 (New York: Harris Publications, 1987)

Household Hints Almanac, Winter 1990, Volume 5, Number 1 (New York: Harris Publications, 1990)

Household Hints for Upstairs, Downstairs, and All Around the House by Carol Rees (New York: Henry Holt and Company, 1982)

How to Do Just About Anything by the Editors of *Reader's Digest* (Pleasantville, New York: Reader's Digest, 1988)

How to Do Just About Everything by Courtney Rosen and the eHow Editors (New York: Simon & Schuster, 2000)

K.I.S.S. Guide to Cat Care by Steve Duno (New York: DK Publishing, 2001)

K.I.S.S. Guide to Living with a Dog by Bruce Fogle (New York: DK Publishing, 2000)

A Kid's Herb Book For Children of All Ages by Lesley Tierra (Brandon, Oregon: Roberd D. Reed, 2000)

Lemon Magic: 200 Beauty and Household Uses for Lemons and Lemon Juice by Patty Moosbrugger (New York: Three Rivers Press, 1999)

The Life, History, and Magic of the Dog by Fernand Mery (New York: Grosset & Dunlap, 1968)

Mary Ellen's Complete Home Reference Book by Mary Ellen Pinkham (New York: Three Rivers Press, 1994)

Mary Ellen's Greatest Hints by Mary Ellen Pinkham (New York: Fawcett Crest, 1990)

Mary Ellen's Wow!: Ideas That Really Work! by Mary Ellen Pinkham with Dale Ronda Burg (Minneapolis, Minnesota: Mary Ellen Books, 1992)

Natural Healing for Dogs and Cats by the editors of *Prevention* Health Books (Emmaus, Pennsylvania: Rodale, 2001)

"Newscripts" by K.M. Reese, *Chemical & Engineering News,* October 18, 1993

101 Essential Tips: Aquarium Fish by Dick Mills (New York: DK Publishing, 1996)

1001 Hints & Tips for Your Garden by the editors of *Reader's Digest* (Pleasantville, New York: Reader's Digest, 1996)

1001 Ingenious Gardening Ideas edited by Deborah L. Martin (Emmaus, Pennsylvania: Rodale, 1998)

1,628 Country Shortcuts From 1,628 Country People by the editors of *Country* and *Country Woman* magazines (Greendale, Wisconsin; Reiman Publications, 1996)

Pet Clean-Up Made Easy by Don Aslett (Cincinnati, Ohio: Writer's Digest Books, 1988)

The Pet Lover's Guide to Cat & Dog Skin Diseases by Karen L. Campbell (St. Louis, Missouri: Elsevier Saunders, 2006)

Practical Problem Solver by *Reader's Digest* (Pleasantville, New York: Reader's Digest, 1991)

Reader's Digest Book of Facts (Pleasantville, New York: Reader's Digest, 1987)

The Resourceful Gardener's Guide edited by Christine Bucks and Fern Marshall Bradley (Emmaus, Pennsylvania: Rodale Press, 2001)

Rodale's Book of Hints, Tips & Everyday Wisdom by Carol Hupping, Cheryl Winters Tetreau, and Roger B. Yepsen, Jr. (Emmaus, Pennsylvania: Rodale Press, 1985)

Shoes in the Freezer, Beer in the Flower Bed: And Other Down-Home Tips for House and Garden by Joan Wilen and Lydia Wilen (New York: Fireside, 1997)

Strange Stories, Amazing Facts (Pleasantville, New York: Reader's Digest, 1976)

Talking Dirty with the Queen of Clean by Linda Cobb (New York: Pocket Books, 1999)

Vet on Call: The Best Home Remedies for Keeping Your Dog Healthy by Pets Part of the Family (Emmaus, Pennsylvania: Rodale, 1999)

The Veterinarian's Guide to Natural Remedies for Dogs: Safe and Effective Alternative Treatments and Healing Techniques from the Nations Top Holistic Veterinarians by Martin Zucker (New York: Three Rivers Press, 2000)

Vinegar: Over 400 Various, Versatile & Very Good Uses You've Probably Never Thought Of by Vicki Lansky (Minnetonka, Minnesota: Book Peddlers, 2004)

Vinegar, Duct Tape, Milk Jugs & More by Earl Proulx and the Editors of *Yankee* Magazine (Emmaus, Pennsylvania: Rodale, 1999)

The World Book Encyclopedia (Chicago: World Book, 1985)

Yankee Magazine's Practical Problem Solver: 1,001 Ingenious Solutions to Everyday Dilemmas by Earl Proulx (Dublin, New Hampshire: Yankee, 1998)

Your Happy Healthy Pet: Hamster, 2nd Edition by Betsy Sikora Siino (New York: Wiley, 2007)

Your Happy Healthy Pet: Parakeet, 2nd Edition by Julie Rash Mancini (New York: Wiley, 2006)

Trademark Information

"Accent" is a registered trademark of B&G Foods, Inc.

"Adolph's" is a registered trademark of Unilever.

"Alberto VO5" is a registered trademark of Alberto-Culver USA, Inc.

"Arm & Hammer" and "Clean Shower" are registered trademarks of Church & Dwight Co, Inc.

"Aunt Jemima" is a registered trademark of the Quaker Oats Company.

"Bayer" is a registered trademark of Bayer Corporation.

"Bag Balm" is a registered trademark of Diary Association Co, Inc.

"Bausch & Lomb" is a registered trademark of Bausch & Lomb Incorporated.

"Ben Gay" is a registered trademark of Pfizer Inc.

"Benadryl" is a registered trademark of McNeil-PPC, Inc.

"Betadine" is a registered trademark of Perdue Phara L.P.

"Betty Crocker" is a registered trademark of General Mills, Inc.

"Bisquick" is a registered trademark of General Mills, Inc.

"Blue Bonnet" is a registered trademark of ConAgra Foods.

"Bon Ami" is a registered trademark of Bon Ami Company.

"Bounce" is a registered trademark of Procter & Gamble.

"Bounty" is a registered trademark of Procter & Gamble.

"Budweiser" is a registered trademark of Anheuser-Busch, Inc.

"Bufferin" is a registered trademark of Novartis Consumer Health Inc.

"Calgon" is a registered trademark of Reckitt Benckiser Inc.

"Campbell" is a registered trademark of Campbell Soup Company.

"Canada Dry" is a registered trademark of Cadbury Beverages Inc.

"Carnation" and "Nestlé" are registered trademarks of Société des Produits Nestlé S.A., Vevey, Switzerland.

"Cascade" is a registered trademark of Procter & Gamble.

"ChapStick" is a registered trademark of A. H. Robbins Company.

"CharcoCaps" is a registered trademark of W.F. Young, Inc.

"Charmin" is a registered trademark of Procter & Gamble.

"Cheerios" is a registered trademark of General Mills, Inc.

"Chicken of the Sea" is a registered trademark of Chicken of the Sea International.

"Clorox" is a registered trademark of the Clorox Company.

"Coca-Cola" and "Coke" are registered trademarks of the Coca-Cola Company.

"Colman's" is a registered trademark of World Finer Foods, Inc.

"Colgate" is a registered trademark of Colgate-Palmolive.

"Concern" is a registered trademark of Woodstream Corporation.

"Con-Tact" is a registered trademark of Rubbermaid, Incorporated.

"Conair" is a registered trademark of Conair Corporation.

"Cool Whip" is a registered trademark of Kraft Foods.

"Coppertone" and "Water Babies" are registered trademarks of Schering-Plough HealthCare Products, Inc.

"Cortaid" is a registered trademark of Johnson & Johnson.

"Country Time" and "Country Time Lemonade" are registered trademarks of Kraft Foods.

"Crisco" is a registered trademark of the J. M. Smucker Co.

"Dannon" is a registered trademark of the Dannon Company.

"Dawn" is a registered trademark of Procter & Gamble.

"De-Solv-It" is a registered trademark of the Orange-Sol Group of Companies, Ltd.

"Dial" is a registered trademark of Dial Corp.

"Dickinson's" is a registered trademark of Dickinson's Brands, Inc.

"Dixie" is a registered trademark of James River Corporation.

"Dole" is a registered trademark of Dole Food Company, Inc.

"Domino" is a registered trademark of Domino Foods, Inc.

"Dove" and "White Beauty" are registered trademarks of Unilever.

"Downy" is a registered trademark of Procter & Gamble.

"Dr. Bronner's" is a registered trademark of All-One-God-Faith, Inc.

"Dramamine" is a registered trademark of McNeil-PPC, Inc.

"Dustbuster" is a registered trademark of Black & Decker.

"Easy Cheese" is a registered trademark of Kraft Foods.

"Efferdent" is a registered trademark of Warner-Lambert.

"Elmer's Glue-All" and Elmer the Bull are registered trademarks of Borden.

"Endust" is a registered trademark of Sara Lee Corporation.

"Ex-Lax" is a registered trademark of Novartis Consumer Health, Inc.

"Fels-Natptha" is a registered trademark of the Dial Corp.

"Forster" is a registered trademark of Diamond Brands, Inc.

"Frisbee" is a registered trademark of Mattel, Inc.

"Fritos" is a registered trademark of Frito Lay North America, Inc.

"Fruit of the Earth" is a registered trademark of Fruit of the Earth, Inc.

"Gatorade" is a registered trademark of the Gatorade Company.

"Gerber" is a registered trademark of Gerber Products Company.

"Geritol" is a registered trademark of GlaxoSmithKline.

"Gillette" is a registered trademark of Procter & Gamble.

"Glad" is a registered trademark of First Brands Corporation.

"Gold Medal" is a registered trademark of General Mills, Inc.

"Grandma's" is a registered trademark of B&G Foods, Inc.

"Green Giant" is a registered trademark of General Mills, Inc.

"Hain" is a registered trademark of the Hain Celestial Group.

"Hartz" and "2 in 1" are registered trademarks of Hartz Mountain Company.

"Heinz" is a registered trademark of H.J. Heinz Company.

"Hibiclens" is a registered trademark of Mölnlycke Health Care.

"Huggies" is a registered trademark of Kimberly-Clark Corporation.

"Hunt's" is a registered trademark of Hunt-Wesson, Inc.

"Ivory" is a registered trademark of Procter & Gamble.

"Jell-O" is a registered trademark of Kraft Foods.

"Jet-Puffed" is a registered trademark of Kraft Foods.

"Jif" is a registered trademark of the J. M. Smucker Co.

"Johnson's," "Johnson & Johnson," and "No More Tangles" are registered trademarks of Johnson & Johnson.

"Joy" is a registered trademark of Procter & Gamble.

"K-Y" is a registered trademark of McNeil-PPC, Inc.

"Kaopectate" is a registered trademark of Chattem, Inc.

"Karo" is a registered trademark of CPC International Inc.

"Kellogg's" is a registered trademark of the Kellogg Co.

"Kingsford" is a registered trademark of Kingsford Products Company.

"Kingsford's" is a registered trademark of ACH Food Companies.

"Kleenex" is a registered trademark of Kimberly-Clark Corporation.

"Knorr" is a registered trademark of Unilever.

"Kraft" is a registered trademark of Kraft Foods.

"Krazy" is a registered trademark of Borden, Inc.

"Kretschmer" is a registered trademark of the Quaker Oats Company.

"Lamisil" is a registered trademark of Novartis Consumer Health Inc.

"Land O Lakes" is a registered trademark of Land O Lakes, Inc.

"Lava" is a registered trademark of WD-40 Company.

"L'eggs" and "Sheer Energy" are registered trademarks of Sara Lee Corporation.

"Lewis Lab's" is a registered trademark of Lewis Laboratories International, Ltd.

"Libby's" is a registered trademark of Seneca Foods Corporation.

"Lipton," "The 'Brisk' Tea," and "Flo-Thru" are registered trademarks of Unilever.

"Liquid Paper" is a registered trademark of Sanford.

"Listerine" is a registered trademark of Warner-Lambert.

"Little Noses" is a registered trademark of Prestige Brands, Inc.

"Lubriderm" is a registered trademark of Warner-Lambert.

"Lysol" is a registered trademark of Reckitt Benckiser Inc.

"Massengill" is a registered trademark of SmithKlein Beecham.

"MasterCard" is a registered trademark of MasterCard International Incorporated.

"Maxwell House" and "Good to the Last Drop" are registered trademarks of Maxwell House Coffee Company.

"Maybelline" is a registered trademark of L'Oréal USA, Inc.

"McCormick" is a registered trademark of McCormick & Company, Incorporated.

"Metamucil" is a registered trademark of Procter & Gamble.

"Milk-Bone" is a registered trademark of Del Monte Foods.

"Miracle Whip" is a registered trademark of Kraft Foods.

"Morton" is a registered trademark of Morton International, Inc.

"Mr. Clean" is a registered trademark of Procter & Gamble.

"Mr. Coffee" is a registered trademark of Mr. Coffee, Inc.

"Mrs. Stewart's" is a registered trademark of Luther & Ford, Company.

"Murphy" is a registered trademark of Colgate-Palmolive Company.

"Neosporin" is a registered trademark of Johnson & Johnson.

"Nestea" and "Nestlé" are registered trademarks of Société des Produits Nestlé S.A., Vevey, Switzerland.

"Noxzema" is a registered trademark of Procter & Gamble.

"Ocean Spray" is a registered trademark of Ocean Spray Cranberries Inc.

"OCuSOFT" is a registered trademark of OCuSOFT, Inc.

"Old English" is a registered trademark of Reckitt Benckiser, Inc.

"Old Spice" is a registered trademark of Procter & Gamble.

"Orajel" is a registered trademark of Church & Dwight Co., Inc.

"Oral-B" is a registered trademark of Oral-B Laboratories.

"Orville Redenbacher" and "Gourmet" are registered trademarks of ConAgra Foods.

"Oust" is a registered trademark of S.C. Johnson & Sons, Inc.

"Oxi Clean" is a registered trademark of Church & Dwight Co., Inc.

"Oxy" is a registered trademark of the Mentholatum Company.

"Palmolive" is a registered trademark of Colgate-Palmolive.

"Pam" is a registered trademark of American Home Foods.

"Pampers" is a registered trademark of Procter & Gamble.

"Parsons'" is a registered trademark of Church & Dwight Co., Inc.

"Paul Mitchell" is a registered trademark of John Paul Mitchell Systems.

"Pedialyte" is a registered trademark of Abbott Laboratories.

"Pepto-Bismol" is a registered trademark of Procter & Gamble.

"Philadelphia" is a registered trademark of Kraft Foods.

"Phillips'" is a registered trademark of Bayer HealthCare LLC.

"Pine-Sol" is a registered trademark of the Clorox Company.

"Playtex" and "Living" are registered trademarks of Playtex Products, Inc.

"Pledge" is a registered trademark of S.C. Johnson & Sons, Inc.

"Post" is a registered trademark of Post Foods, LLC.

"Preparation H" is a registered trademark of Whitehall-Robbins.

"Purell" is a registered trademark of Johnson & Johnson Consumer Companies, Inc.

"Q-tips" is a registered trademark of Chesebrough-Pond's USA Co.

"Quaker Oats" is a registered trademark of the Quaker Oats Company.

"ReaLemon" is a registered trademark of Borden.

"Reddi-wip" is a registered trademark of ConAgra Foods.

"Revlon" is a registered trademark of Revlon Consumer Products Corporation.

"Reynolds," "Reynolds Wrap," and "Cut-Rite" are registered trademarks of Reynolds Metals.

"Robitussin" is a registered trademark of Wyeth.

"Rubbermaid" is a registered trademark of Newell Rubbermaid Inc.

"S.O.S" is a registered trademark of the Clorox Company.

"Saran" and "Saran Wrap" are registered trademarks of S.C. Johnson & Sons, Inc.

"Scope" is a registered trademark of Procter & Gamble.

"Scotch" and "Scotchgard" are registered trademarks of 3M.

"Shout" is a registered trademark of S.C. Johnson & Sons, Inc.

"Silly Putty" is a registered trademark of Binney & Smith Inc.

"Simple Green" is a registered trademark of Sunshine Makers, Inc.

"Skin So Soft" is a registered trademark of Avon Products.

"Slinky" is a registered trademark of James Industries.

"Smirnoff" is a registered trademark of United Vintners & Distributors.

"Solarcaine" is a registered trademark of Schering-Plough HealthCare Products, Inc.

"Speed Stick" is a registered trademark of the Colgate-Palmolive Company.

"Spot Shot" is a registered trademark of the WD Company.

"Spray 'n Wash" is a registered trademark of Reckitt Benckiser Inc.

"Star" is a registered trademark of Star Fine Foods.

"Static Guard" is a registered trademark of Alberto-Culver Company.

"Stayfree" is a registered trademark of McNeil-PPC, Inc.

"SueBee is a registered trademark of Sioux Honey Association.

"Sun-Maid" is a registered trademark of Sun-Maid Growers of California.

"Tabasco" is a registered trademark of McIlhenny Company.

"Tampax" is a registered trademark of Tambrands, Inc.

"Tang" is a registered trademark of Kraft Foods.

"Thompson's" is a registered trademark of the Thompson's Company.

"3M" is a registered trademark of 3M.

"Tide" is a registered trademark of Procter & Gamble.

Index

Underscored page references indicate sidebars.

W

Y

Z

About the Author

Joey Green—author of *Joey Green's Cleaning Magic, Joey Green's Fix-It Magic,* and *Joey Green's Gardening Magic*—got Barbara Walters to put a wet Pampers diaper on her head on *The View,* made Jay Leno shave with Jif Peanut Butter on *The Tonight Show,* conditioned Meredith Vieira's hair with Cool Whip, got Katie Couric to clean her diamond ring with Efferdent, and showed Diane Sawyer how to polish furniture with SPAM. A walking encyclopedia of quirky yet ingenious household hints, he has been profiled by the *New York Times, USA Today,* and *People.*

Green, a former contributing editor to *National Lampoon* and a former advertising copywriter at J. Walter Thompson, is the author of more than 45 books, including *Marx & Lennon: The Parallel Sayings, Contrary to Popular Belief,* and *The Zen of Oz: Ten Spiritual Lessons from Over the Rainbow.* A native of Miami, Florida, and a graduate of Cornell University, he wrote television commercials for Burger King and Walt Disney World and won a Clio Award for a print ad he created for Eastman Kodak. He backpacked around the world for two years on his honeymoon and lives in Los Angeles with his wife, Debbie, their two daughters, Ashley and Julia, a tabby cat named Einstein, and a backyard filled with hummingbirds and rabbits.

For more off-beat uses for brand-name products,
visit Joey Green on the Internet at:
www.wackyuses.com.